# THE IDES

Also by Stephen Dando-Collins

*Caesar's Legion: The Epic Saga of Julius Caesar's
Elite Tenth Legion and the Armies of Rome*

*Nero's Killing Machine: The True Story of
Rome's Remarkable Fourteenth Legion*

*Cleopatra's Kidnappers: How Caesar's Sixth Legion
Gave Egypt to Rome and Rome to Caesar*

*Mark Antony's Heroes: How the Third Gallica
Legion Saved an Apostle and Created an Emperor*

*Blood of the Caesars: How the Murder of
Germanicus Led to the Fall of Rome*

# THE IDES

## CAESAR'S MURDER AND THE WAR FOR ROME

STEPHEN DANDO-COLLINS

John Wiley & Sons, Inc.

Published by John Wiley & Sons, Inc., Hoboken, New Jersey
Published simultaneously in Canada

For general information about our other products and services, please contact our Customer
Care Department within the United States at (800) 762-2974, outside the United States at
(317) 572-3993 or fax (317) 572-4002.

Wiley also publishes its books in a variety of electronic formats. Some content that appears
in print may not be available in electronic books. For more information about Wiley products, visit our web site at www.wiley.com.

*Library of Congress Cataloging-in-Publication Data:*
Dando-Collins, Stephen, date.
    The ides : Caesar's murder and the war for Rome / Stephen Dando-Collins.
        p.   cm.
    Includes bibliographical references and index.
    ISBN 978-0-470-42523-7 (cloth : acid-free paper)
        1. Caesar, Julius—Assassination.   2. Rome—Politics and government—
265–30 B.C.   3. Rome—History—53–44 B.C.   I. Title.
    DG267.D26 2010
    937'.05092—dc22

Printed in the United States of America
10  9  8  7  6  5  4  3  2  1

Be sure to remember, not how long was Caesar's life, but how short his reign.

> —*Brutus and Cassius, Caesar's chief assassins, in a 44* B.C. *letter to Mark Antony*

# CONTENTS

# ATLAS

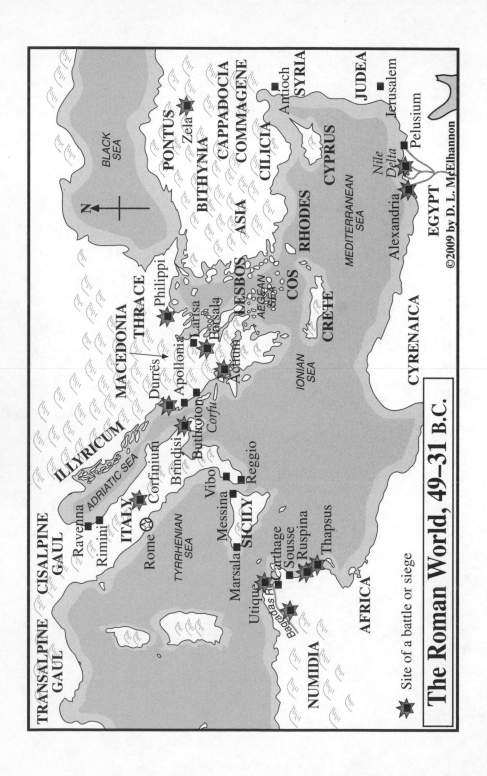

The Roman World, 49–31 B.C.

★ Site of a battle or siege

©2009 by D. L. McElhannon

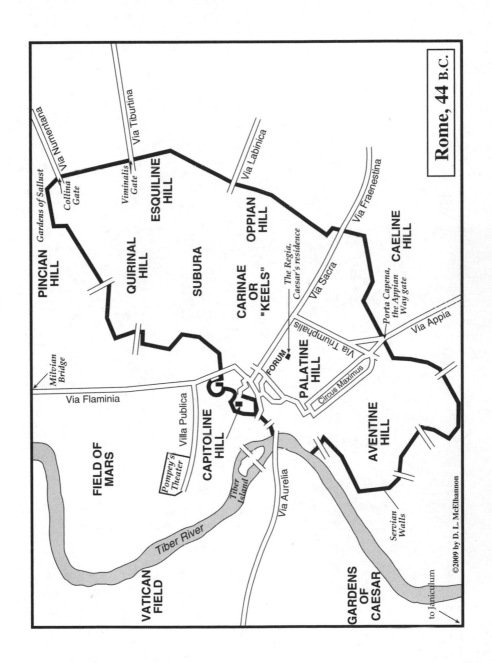

Rome, 44 B.C.

Via Numentana

Gardens of Sallust

Via Tiburtina

Collina Gate

Viminalis Gate

Via Labinica

PINCIAN HILL

ESQUILINE HILL

QUIRINAL HILL

OPPIAN HILL

Via Fraenestina

SUBURA

CAELINE HILL

Milvian Bridge

CARINAE OR "KEELS"

The Regia, Caesar's residence

Via Sacra

Porta Capena, the Appian Way gate

Via Flaminia

Via Triumphalis

FORUM

PALATINE HILL

Via Appia

Villa Publica

Pompey's Theater

CAPITOLINE HILL

Circus Maximus

FIELD OF MARS

Tiber Island

AVENTINE HILL

Via Aurelia

Tiber River

Servian Walls

VATICAN FIELD

GARDENS OF CAESAR

to Janiculum

©2009 by D. L. McElhannon

# AUTHOR'S NOTE

Millions of words have been written about Julius Caesar, but few, if any, modern accounts have delivered the "violent and complex reality" of his murder.[1]

With this book, I have striven to weed out the myths and the misinformation and lay bare the story of Caesar's murder, as it happened, beginning, as the conspiracy began, just weeks before Caesar's death, detailing the crime and attempting to make sense of the chaotic aftermath, and ending with the death of the last of the murderers.

I have long been surprised by how few historians have realized the part played by the religious festivals and customs of the day. With those events acting as both catalysts to the assassination plot and signposts of the turning points in Julius Caesar's last days, I have set out to show the influence those festivals and customs had on attitudes, timings, and events relating to the assassination.

And, finally, I have attempted to pass judgment on the victim, the assassins, and the assassination.

My sources throughout are primarily classical texts, including the ultrainformative letters written and collected by Cicero. I would stress that all the conversations in this book are taken from dialogue or narrative in those texts; I have invented nothing.

My special thanks go to my editor, Stephen S. Power, who commissioned this work; my New York literary agent, Richard Curtis, for guiding its birth; and my wife, Louise, who, as always, has been my fellow detective as the historical pieces have come together; she is my raison d'être.

# INTRODUCTION

**M**uch that has been written about Julius Caesar in modern times is twaddle. Not even his name has come down to us correctly. His full name was Gaius Iulius Caesar, and he was referred to as Gaius by Romans, who, it is believed, pronounced his last name as Kaiser, not Caesar. But if I were to talk about Gaius Iulius Kaiser no one would know to whom I was referring. So for the purposes of this work, Julius Caesar he must remain, just as Marcus Antonius must remain Mark Antony.

There are many myths about Caesar. One was that all legions associated with him bore the bull emblem. Far from true; no legion numbered above 10 is attested to having carried the bull emblem, and Caesar raised some forty legions. Another was that he was the "good guy" fighting a lone battle against the "bad guys," a black-and-white misrepresentation. For example, in 1961, a young U.S. Army officer named Norman Schwarzkopf wrote an essay while attending an advanced training course at Fort Benning, Georgia, that won him an award. That paper told of a general entering his tent after a battle and tossing his battered helmet on a cot in the corner. Later Schwarzkopf revealed to his readers that the general was Julius Caesar and that the battle just ended was the Battle of Pharsalus, in which Caesar had defeated the army led by that other Roman colossus, Gnaeus Pompeius Magnus, or Pompey the Great.

Schwarzkopf, who, thirty years later, was the U.S. general commanding Coalition forces in the Gulf War's Operation Desert Storm, used his essay to show that for an army commander, nothing much had changed in two thousand years; the same physical and mental factors still applied to a leader of men in battle. But in his essay Schwarzkopf described Pompey as "the rebel" general in the conflict. In fact, after Julius Caesar crossed the Rubicon with his troops on January 11, 49 B.C., to invade his own country and seize power in a military coup and was declared an "enemy of the state" by the Roman Senate, it was Caesar who was the rebel.

In the same vein, modern historians with socialist inclinations have put forward the view that Caesar was a sort of Robin Hood who robbed power from the Roman rich and gave it to the poor. Caesar was characterized as the champion of one side of Roman politics, the *populares*, or "popularists," against the rich nobles of the *optimates*, or "best ones." There are several things wrong with this argument.

First, both groups were made up of the wealthy members of the Senatorial Order; the populares were not some revolutionary party from the middle or lower classes opposed to the ruling aristocrats. Second, while Roman politics did divide between Sulla, leading the optimates, and Marius, leading the populares, following Sulla's Civil War victory in 82 B.C., two decades before Julius Caesar's first taste of power as a consul, the populares ceased to exist. A trawl through classical texts finds barely a mention of the optimates at the height of Caesar's career, and no mention of the populares. Caesar himself never used the terms in his writings. Neither Caesar nor classical commentators saw his bid for power as a struggle between the populares and the optimates. But the concept made for good modern storytelling.

The idea of Caesar being the representative of the mob stemmed in part from Seneca, the philosopher and chief secretary of Nero a century after Caesar's death, who wrote, "If you try to picture the period to yourself you will see on the one side the populace, the mob all agog for revolution, on the other the time-honored elect of Rome, the aristocracy and members of the Equestrian Order, and two forlorn figures, Cato and republicanism, between them."[1] But what Seneca also said was that Caesar and Pompey were in the same corner at the time, the corner of the "time-honored elect."

Ultimately, Cato the Younger decided that these "time-honored elect" were at least intent on preserving the Republic, whereas Caesar was bent on destroying it, and took a military command of republican forces under Pompey. Whether Caesar came out of the Civil War as victor or Pompey did, Cato was pessimistic, saying, "If Caesar wins, I kill myself. If Pompey, I go into exile."[2]

Caesar did not fit into any category. Caesar was a loner. His own cousin Lucius Caesar declined to support him, preferring to stay neutral, while Lucius's son fought on the republican side against Caesar. And Caesar's loyal and capable deputy in the Gallic War for nine years, Titus Labienus, not only deserted him and went over to the republicans as the Civil War broke out, he also took most of Caesar's cavalry with him.

Facing criminal charges for financial misdealing when consul in 59 B.C., charges he must have felt would stick if he came to trial, Caesar took one of only two courses of action open to him, that of facing trial or of seizing power. It was a cast of unsavory characters and loyal dependents who supported him. Of the three tribunes of the plebeians who sided with him, one was his relative Mark Antony. Another was Gaius Curio, Antony's drinking companion in their shared youth, who had been against Caesar in the Senate until Caesar bribed him by paying off his huge debts. The other was slimy Quintus Cassius, who, once he had been made governor of Farther Spain by Caesar, proceeded to rob the locals of their gold and then perish while fleeing with his loot.

The naive and simplistic socialist view of Caesar as champion of the underclass was taken up most recently in a 2003 book that credited Caesar with a "reform agenda" once he had seized power by force, reform that apparently had no place for democracy. That author's lack of familiarity with ancient Rome included describing Marcus Lepidus as Caesar's "loyal cavalry commander."[3] Lepidus was Caesar's Master of Equestrians. This title has been misconstrued by several modern authors, who have thought it meant Lepidus was master of horse, or cavalry commander, as the title came to mean in the late empire. In the Roman Republic, the Master of Equestrians was the deputy of the Dictator and had nothing to do with cavalry or their command, his title having originally meant that he was master of members of the Equestrian Order, just as his superior, the Dictator, was considered master of the commons.[4]

The 2003 author also repeated an error originally made by Suetonius, who claimed that the assassins had considered murdering Caesar at the time of the upcoming consular elections. But no consular elections were scheduled for five years. In the same text, Suetonius himself pointed out that Caesar let "only tribunes and aediles of the people be elected."[5] Appian was not confused on this point; he reported Brutus saying to the Roman people in a speech following Caesar's murder, "Caesar on the eve of his departure for another long campaign has taken the elections from you for five years ahead."[6]

Caesar was a brilliant general, a clever engineer, an administrator of genius, and a leader who demanded and commanded loyalty. He also was a corrupt politician. This was an era full of corrupt politicians, but Caesar went farther than any of his contemporaries; when he could no longer bribe his way to power, he waged war on his fellow Romans. Caesar was nonetheless a fascinating figure who stood head and shoulders above all contemporaries, apart, perhaps, from Pompey the Great, and we do Caesar no favors by painting him as a false egalitarian hero. Instead we should be asking questions about Caesar, to learn more about the man and what motivated him, and ultimately about what killed him. Was his downfall the result of the jealousy or ambition of others, or did he bring it on himself?

First and foremost, how is it that less than a year after terminating the Civil War and becoming sole ruler of the Roman Empire, and just five months after returning to Rome, the brilliant Julius Caesar was murdered by more than sixty senators, many of whom had fought on his side during the Civil War and had received significant rewards from him? What did Caesar do that turned so many against him so quickly? Had Caesar in fact gone a little mad?

Other questions also beg answers. Was Mark Antony aware of the assassination plot and let it go forward? And did the conspirators really think that with Caesar dead the Roman Republic would somehow rise anew of its own accord? Or did they have their own eyes on power?

In a bid for some answers, this dissection of the murder of Julius Caesar, based on evidence from classical sources, including key players in the drama, begins just forty-nine days before his death.

PART ONE

# THE CONSPIRACY

# I

# JANUARY 26, 44 B.C.

## SEVEN WEEKS BEFORE THE ASSASSINATION

I t started with a parade. On a fine winter's day, passing the tombs of wealthy deceased Romans that lined the stone-paved road, a vast cavalcade came up the Appian Way from the direction of the Alban Hills. At the head of that cavalcade rode Gaius Julius Caesar, Dictator of Rome.

Caesar was fifty-four years of age. Tall, well built, with a small chin, sensuous mouth, and large, dark brown eyes, his fair hair now gray, he was a good-looking man, if not handsome.[1] Yet he was vain; because he was balding, "a disfigurement which his enemies harped upon," according to his biographer Suetonius, Caesar brushed his hair forward to cover a large bald spot. To further hide his baldness, on public occasions he wore the laurel crown to which he was entitled as the winner of a Triumph. According to Suetonius, Caesar's vanity extended to having his body hair removed with tweezers.[2]

Riding through the city outskirts toward the gate in the ancient walls built around the old heart of Rome three hundred years earlier, Caesar was wearing a white tunic bordered with the broad purple stripe of the Senatorial Order, to which he had added long, fringed sleeves, contrary to Roman custom—tunics were usually short-sleeved.[3] Like all Romans, Caesar rode without stirrups, on an unshod horse and astride a saddle with four horns. Caesar frequently drove a chariot. Occasionally, traveling over long distances with baggage, he used a carriage.

Less often, he was carried in a litter. To ride at the head of the procession returning from the Latin Festival was a privilege bestowed on Caesar by a vote of the Senate.

In the all-male cavalcade behind the Dictator came hundreds of senators and other leading men of Roman society. Chief among them was Marcus Antonius—Mark Antony, as Shakespeare dubbed him. Thirty-seven-year-old Antony was related to Caesar on his mother's side. Serving under Caesar during the latter stages of the Gallic War and during the Civil War, Antony now held one of the two consulships for the year; Caesar held the other. During the Republic, which Caesar had overthrown, the two consuls had been Rome's most senior elected officials. But Caesar held the post of Dictator, officially conferred on him by a compliant Senate, which ranked him above the consuls.

Curly-headed Antony was a powerfully built man. With bulging muscles and a thick neck, he looked like a wrestler. A tough, fearless, no-nonsense soldier who personally led his troops into battle, Antony was Caesar's muscle. But Antony had let himself go over the past few years, eating and drinking to excess, so that his once "wonderful" body had become, in the words of Cassius Dio, "plump and detestable."[4]

Not far behind Caesar in the procession came thin, gangly Marcus Lepidus, who outranked Antony. Lepidus had loyally and efficiently served Caesar during the Civil War. Caesar had made Lepidus a consul for the year 46 B.C., then gave him the governorship of the Roman provinces of Nearer Spain, which took in eastern and northern Spain and Narbon Gaul in southern France. Just a year ago now, Caesar had appointed Lepidus to the post of his Master of Equestrians, in Antony's stead. The man holding this position, which then had nothing to do with horses, was deputy to a dictator.

Down through the 450-year history of the Roman Republic, a dictator had been appointed by the Senate in times of crisis, to act as sole ruler of Rome. Until Sulla made himself dictator for an extended period, it had been a temporary appointment, for a maximum of six months. In 46 B.C., inspired by Sulla's example and in contravention of the intent of the founders of the Republic, a Senate appointed by Caesar had in turn appointed him dictator for ten years. It was the Master of Equestrians' job to take charge at Rome when the dictator was away from the capital. Lepidus, while Master of Equestrians, was permitted by Caesar to continue to administer Nearer Spain and Narbon Gaul from Rome.

Caesar, the members of his Senate, and the magistrates appointed by him had been attending the four-day Latin Festival at the Alban Mount. Near present-day Castel Gondolfo, twelve miles southeast of Rome, the Alban Mount, today's Albano, was the location of the ancient city of Alba Longa. According to legend, Ascanius, son of the Trojan hero Aeneas, had established Alba Longa, which became the founding city of the Latin League. In about 600 B.C., Rome had conquered the city, an event commemorated by the annual Latin Festival.

Caesar would have especially savored the festival this year. Not only was it the first time he presided over it as Rome's indisputable sole ruler and victor in the Civil War, he also would have stayed at the Alba Longa villa previously owned by Pompey the Great, his chief opponent in Rome's bloody, recently terminated civil conflict, which came into his possession following Pompey's death. Pompey had been staying at this villa in January 49 B.C., recovering from a serious illness, when he learned that Caesar had led troops across the Rubicon River in northeastern Italy. The Rubicon was then the boundary between Cisalpine Gaul and Italy, and in crossing the river Caesar had broken Sulla's law that banned provincial governors from leading their troops across provincial boundaries and had consequently been declared an enemy of the state by the Senate. Now, having defeated the old Senate in the Civil War, and with Pompey having been murdered in Egypt, Caesar had taken possession of Pompey's Alban villa.

It being a public holiday, a vast crowd of Roman residents had flooded out of the city to line the Appian Way to watch the famous and the feted pass by on their return from Alba. As Caesar, leading the concourse, approached the Porta Capena, the Appian Way gate in the city's Servian Walls, not far from the Circus Maximus, people in the crowd cheered, waved, and called out to him.

"Long live the king!" several men yelled together.[5]

But people all around them showed their disapproval of Caesar being called king. Hundreds of years ago, before the Republic, Rome had been ruled for 240 years by seven kings, the last few of whom had been thorough despots. The very thought of Rome again being ruled by a king was abhorrent to many Romans. There was more to this than just a title. Not only was a king a sole ruler, he also ruled for life, and his descendants could rule after him. If Caesar were to become king of the Romans, then the Romans could be saddled with Caesar and his family for generations to come.

Caesar heard the men call out. He also saw the unimpressed reaction of those around them, and heard their immediate boos.[6] He called back, "My name is Caesar, not king." As the Dictator rode into the city, looking both displeased and discomforted, the crowd fell strangely silent.[7]

Later that day, once he was back at his residence on the Sacred Way in the heart of Rome, it was reported to Caesar that laurel wreaths had been placed on the heads of two statues of him that had recently been installed on the Rostra, in the Forum. The wreaths were bound with white ribbon. White was traditionally a color associated with Roman royalty, in the same way that purple had become exclusively the senatorial color. These wreaths had the appearance of royal crowns.

It also was reported to Caesar that two of the ten tribunes of the plebeians, Gaius Epidius Marullus and Lucius Caesetius Flavus, had ordered the immediate removal of these "royal diadems" and the arrest and imprisonment of the men who had hailed Caesar king earlier that day. This action won much public acclaim for the two tribunes, who were followed home by the people "with shouts and applause."[8] Caesar, however, was made "violently angry" by this.[9] He ordered the two tribunes to present themselves before him.

When they soon after appeared, the pair stood before the Dictator in probable expectation of praise and reward from Caesar—for when they had ordered the crowns removed they had "praised him before the populace as not wanting anything of the sort."[10] To the tribunes' surprise, "he accused Marullus and his friends of laying an elaborate plot to misrepresent him as aiming at despotism, and concluded that they deserved death." But Caesar spared the quaking pair from the executioner's blade, instead stripping them of their posts as tribunes.[11]

On the motion of another tribune, Helvius Cinna, the Senate subsequently erased the pair's names from the senatorial rolls, and they were banned from ever setting foot inside the Senate House again.[12] Caesar subsequently had the pair exiled from Italy.[13]

Suetonius described Caesar's reaction to this affair as an "example of his arrogance."[14] On the other hand, Velleius Paterculus, a sycophantic supporter of the imperial house, wrote seventy-three years after the event that the tribunes had brought Caesar's wrath down on their own heads through an "intemperate and untimely display of independence."[15] Caesar himself later excused his own action by saying that the two tribunes had acted in haste, and in doing so had prevented him from rejecting the royal wreaths and title of king and subsequently receiving public credit for doing so. Suetonius was to suggest that in reality Caesar was peeved "because the suggestion that he should be crowned king had been so rudely rejected."[16]

Whatever the cause of Caesar's swift punishment of Marullus and Flavus, the summary removal of the pair from an office to which they had been elected to protect the interests of the common people of Rome—tribunes of the plebs had the power of veto over acts of the Senate—was not well received by many Romans, of all classes. "The office of tribune was sacred and inviolate by ancient law and oath," wrote Appian. To Appian's mind, Caesar had made a major blunder, for "this episode particularly blackened him, as people thought he wanted the title, was responsible for the attempts to get it, and had become totally despotic."[17] With Caesar's "affront to the tribunes," said Plutarch, "he gave a fresh occasion for resentment."[18]

A ripple of anti-Caesar feeling ran through the city. But for the moment, few dared voice discontent publicly. Marcus Tullius Cicero, highly respected senator, orator, author, defense advocate, and former consul, was considered "the man of greatest influence in Rome" at this time.[19] He was one of the few to speak out, although he did it by making a jest of his criticism, poking fun at Caesar's autocratic rule by decree.

Caesar soon realized he had erred. "He noticed this himself and regretted what he had done," said Appian. Caesar said to friends, "This was the first occasion in time of peace, when I was not commanding in the field, that I have taken severe and unpalatable action."[20] Caesar seemed to be excusing the severity of his reaction by suggesting that, like many a general who becomes a civil ruler, autocratic habits died hard.

But the damage had been done. Caesar had scratched an ancient Roman wound. "From that day forward," said Suetonius, "he lay under the odious suspicion of having revived the title of king."[21] Yet, without further incitement, these events might have soon passed from memory. Unfortunately for Caesar, there would more reason for complaint before long, and again it would stem from the Dictator's own actions.

# II

# FEBRUARY 15, 44 B.C.

## THE LUPERCALIA

It was another important day on the Roman calendar of religious holidays. That calendar was not broken up into weekdays and weekends as we know them, but "vacated" days, when business was conducted, and public holidays—days when religious festivals were celebrated and during which no official business could be conducted, temples were closed, and marriages were forbidden. This is where the term *holiday* comes from; it was literally a holy day. This particular holy day, February 15, was reserved for the Lupercalia Festival.

The Lupercalia celebrated the brothers Romulus and Remus, legendary founders of Rome. According to legend, the two boys were the sons of the war god Mars and Rhea Silva, daughter of Numitor, king of Alba Longa. Numitor was deposed by his younger brother Amulius, who, to remove any threats to his long enjoyment of the throne, ordered his niece's baby sons drowned in the Tiber River. The trough in which the two boys were placed floated down the river and came to rest at the foot of the Palatine Hill, the future site of Rome. There, the babies were suckled by a wolf—*lupis* in Latin—and fed by a woodpecker before being found by a shepherd and raised as his own children. On reaching maturity, the boys defeated Amulius and restored their grandfather Numitor to his throne before establishing the settlement that became Rome, where Romulus killed Remus.

The legend had it that the she-wolf had cared for the boys in a cave, called the Lupercal, at the base of the Palatine Hill, and by Julius Caesar's time this cave had become a shrine to Romulus and Remus. Modern historians doubted the existence of such a cave until 2007, when it was accidentally discovered by archaeologists fifty feet beneath the ruins of the Palatium, or palace, of Augustus. The richly decorated cave shrine, twenty-five feet high and twenty-two feet across, has a domed ceiling, and was partly filled with rubble that would have been used to seal the cave entrance following the decree by Pope Gelasius I that banned the Lupercalia in A.D. 496. By that time the Lupercalia was the last of the ancient Roman religious festivals permitted by the Christian Church. Gelasius would replace the Lupercalia by declaring February 14 the feast day of St. Valentine.

Julius Caesar had been Rome's Pontifex Maximus, or high priest, since being elected to the part-time, lifetime post in 62 B.C., and as such was required to preside over religious festivals such as the Lupercalia. This particular festival had much more poignancy this year, for, only recently, Caesar's fawning Senate had voted in favor of declaring him a living god. Caesar's family claimed descent from the goddess Venus, but even so the declaration that a mortal Roman was a god was without precedent. Whether this was Caesar's own idea is unclear, but he did not oppose his own deification. "Few in fact," wrote Suetonius 150 years later, "were the honors that he was not happy to accept or assume."[1]

Among the trappings of "the Divine Julius," as Caesar came to be called, would be temples dedicated to him; images of him as a god that the people could worship in temples and their own homes; a senior priest dedicated to his cult; and a new college of priests, called the Julian College. It became the task of the Julian order to oversee the Lupercalia Festival in Caesar's name and "to celebrate his divinity." This year, and every year for more than five hundred years to come, the Lupercalia Festival would not only commemorate Romulus and Remus, it also commemorated Julius Caesar, the former as founders of Rome, the latter supposedly as Rome's "savior" from republicanism.[2]

As custom required, the Lupercalia Festival of 44 B.C. involved a variety of activities. In the morning, goats and a dog were sacrificed by the priests of the order in the Lupercal shrine, the cave in the Palatine Hill. Two teams of young Roman nobles and magistrates then gathered in the crowded Forum to take part in an unusual footrace. This year, one of the teams was led by Mark Antony in his capacity as a consul.

The team members, all wearing goatskins sprinkled with the blood of the sacrificed animals, sat down to eat a sumptuous banquet, with the

teams on opposite sides of the long dining table. The banquet was traditionally a lighthearted affair, with team members poking fun at their
opponents across the table. The gaiety continued as the teams then
stripped to the waist, were anointed with oil, and assembled at a starting
line in the Forum.

Caesar, as high priest, took his place on the raised Rostra, or speaking platforms, in the Forum, to officially start the race. As he was entitled to do, he wore the triumphal garb he had earned from celebrating
a Triumph.[3] This consisted of a rich scarlet cloak and a tunic embroidered in gold with palm trees, a symbol of victory. He also wore the
laurel crown of a triumphant. As Caesar took his seat on the Rostra in
a golden chair placed there for him, he was flanked by the praetors and
the priests. Below, the competitors were given goatskin straps, which
they would carry throughout the race. On Caesar's "Go," and to the roar
of the watching crowd, the competitors dashed away, to run around the
base of the Palatine Hill and return to the starting point.

The runners' route, which was lined with the city populace, would
take them out one city gate, across the Campus Martius, or Field of
Mars, and back in through another gate. It was their privilege to strike
whomever they passed with their goatskin strap. But the runners faced
an unusual obstacle. It had become customary for Roman women of
childbearing age, including those of the highest birth, to step into the
path of the competitors with hands outstretched, "as boys in school
do to the master," said Plutarch, hoping to be struck by the straps.[4]
According to superstition, if the women were hit by the strap, those
who were barren would conceive, and those who were pregnant could
expect an easy delivery—this was an era when death during childbirth
was tragically very common.

As the race neared its end, the crowd parted, and Mark Antony came
running at the head of the competitors into the Forum. Contrary to
ancient custom, Antony ran up to the Rostra, where Caesar was seated.
Someone handed Antony a crown around which a laurel, another victory symbol, had been entwined. A number of Antony's friends had
gathered for this moment, and they hoisted him up, allowing Antony
to hold out the laurel crown to Caesar.[5] "The people offer this to you
through me," said Antony.[6]

The act of offering the crown generated an approving shout from
some members of the crowd surrounding the Rostra, "but only a
slight one, made by the few who were planted there" by Antony.[7]

"The majority booed," said Appian.[8] Caesar "drew aside to avoid it," declining to accept the crown, and in response, applause erupted from the majority of his audience.[9] Again Antony offered the crown to Caesar, and again Caesar waved it away. This time, only a few spectators applauded. For a third time, Antony offered the crown, and now Caesar came to his feet. "Jupiter alone is king of the Romans," he declared.[10] Caesar told Antony to take the crown to the Capitoline Mount and dedicate it to Jupiter, king of the gods and primary Roman divinity, in the massive and ancient Temple of Jupiter.

This should have been an end to the matter. But Antony's act of offering the crown to Caesar, coming in the wake of the affair of the crowned statues and dismissal of the tribunes, was not well received. Velleius Paterculus was to say that Antony "brought great odium upon Caesar" by offering him the crown.[11] According to Plutarch, Caesar himself was "very much discomposed by what had passed," and as the crown was being carried away to the Temple of Jupiter he pulled his cloak down from his neck, exposing his throat, and said to his closest companions that "he was ready to receive a stroke" of a blade "if any of them desired to give it."[12]

To make sure that no one had missed the fact that he had declined the offer of a kingly crown, Caesar subsequently had it inscribed in the official records that he had refused to accept the kingship when it was offered to him by the people through a consul.[13] But, again, the damage had been done. As men departed the Forum, many were in whispered conversation. The theatrical performance by Antony and Caesar at the Rostra had many convinced that it had been "deliberately arranged" and that Caesar was in reality "anxious for the name" of king, it being the one honor he had yet to accept, having secretly yearned for it since boyhood. Perhaps, Dio would muse, Caesar "wished to be somehow compelled to take it."[14]

Did Caesar and Antony concoct this crowning performance at the Rostra to test the public mood? If so, it backfired badly, arming a growing number of opponents with what they saw as proof that the Dictator actually wished to be made king of the Romans. Many Roman commentators, such as Dio, became convinced that "these events proved still more clearly that, although he pretended to shun the title, in reality he desired to assume it."[15]

Subtle political maneuvering such as this would have bored Caesar. He was a soldier at heart, and accustomed to decisive action.

Happiest at war, he was impatient for more glory and military action, and at this moment was focused on his next military campaign. Details of that campaign were well enough known at Rome; a number of senators and members of the Equestrian Order had been assigned to commands in the army that was forming on Caesar's orders to carry out the operation.

This campaign was to involve a preemptive war against the Getae, a warlike barbarian nation that lived north of the Danube River, beside the Caspian Sea. It was to be followed by an invasion of Rome's old eastern enemy Parthia to punish the Parthians for defeating Caesar's late colleague Marcus Crassus in 53 B.C. Caesar then intended marching around the Caspian Sea, through Germany, and across the Rhine into Gaul from the east. Caesar was preparing for a three-year campaign. While he was away, Rome would be administered by Master of Equestrians Lepidus and by consuls and praetors who had already been chosen years in advance by Caesar.

More than one hundred thousand troops, the single largest army ever put together by Caesar, involving sixteen legions and ten thousand cavalry, were to carry out this campaign.[16] As early as 47 B.C., Caesar had sent a legion from Egypt to Syria in preparation for a move against Parthia. By March 44 B.C., units assigned to the operation were assembling in Syria and Macedonia. A vast cache of arms and ammunition was being collected at Demetrias at Thessaly, Greece, not far from where the legions were encamped in Macedonia.[17]

Caesar intended starting his eastern campaign as early as possible in the spring, planning to depart Rome on March 19, the first day of the four-day Quatranalia Festival, an annual and ancient festival dedicated to the war god Mars. On the morning of March 19, a day sacred to both Mars and Minerva, the lustration ceremony would take place, over which Caesar must preside. This involved the anointing of military standards at Rome prior to the commencement of the year's military campaigning season. Caesar, other priests of the pontificate, and tribunes representing the army would attend a dance of the Salii priests of Mars in the Comitium, the Forum meeting chamber of the Comitia, the assembly of the common people. Following the priests' dance, the sacred *arma ancilia*, ancient weaponry dedicated to Mars hundreds of years before, which was kept year-round in a shrine to Mars at the Regia, the high priest's headquarters, would be purified with perfumes and decorated with garlands, as would the standards of representative military units.

Once he had dispensed with the ceremonial formalities required of a Roman commander in chief prior to going to war, Caesar planned to depart from the city later that same day, March 19, leaving behind all the petty politics, sycophancy, and backbiting of the capital, to concentrate on what he did best and liked best—military conquest.

# III

# FEBRUARY 22, 44 B.C.

## THE CARISTIA RECONCILIATION

O ver the past few mornings, graffiti and pamphlets had been appearing around Rome. The most prominent graffiti was on the Capitoline Mount, where there stood a brass statue of Junius Brutus, sword in hand. This Brutus, Rome's first consul, had famously removed from his throne Tarquinius, last king of Rome, in the sixth century B.C., and inaugurated the Roman Republic. And now there appeared scrawled on the pedestal of the statue of Brutus messages such as "O that we had a Brutus now!" and "If only Brutus were alive!"[1]

It was widely known that the family of esteemed forty-year-old Roman judge Marcus Junius Brutus claimed descent from Brutus, father of the Republic. During this week, when Marcus Brutus arrived at his tribunal, a raised platform on which his judge's bench was placed, to hear the latest cases in his capacity as city praetor, he found it covered with graffiti, including "You are asleep, Brutus" and "You are not a true Brutus." Similar sentiments were written in pamphlets that mysteriously appeared around the city overnight.[2]

All Rome knew that this referred to Caesar and his rumored thirst for kingship. Brutus was fully aware that it was aimed also at encouraging him to emulate his ancestor by doing something to stop Caesar from becoming king of the Romans. Even though Caesar's slaves would have quickly washed the graffiti away, its messages would have rapidly spread. And its import would not have been lost on a population astir ever since the incident outside the Porta Capena four weeks before and the more recent crowning affair during the Lupercalia Festival.

"Even the commons had come to disapprove of how things were going," said Suetonius, "and no longer hid their disgust at Caesar's tyrannical rule."[3] The glowing embers of popular discontent had been fanned by the many honors heaped on Caesar by a Senate he had personally appointed. Many of these acts, including Caesar's deification, were honors that, in the opinion of Suetonius, "as a mere mortal, he certainly should have declined." Not only was Caesar now celebrated as a god, he also was officially titled "Father of his Country," he was made censor for life, he was permitted to sit on a golden throne in the Senate House, and the month of Quinctilius was renamed July in his honor.[4] Some senators even "addressed him outright as Jupiter Julius," ranking him with Jupiter, king of the gods.[5]

On one particular day, after the Senate had passed a long list of such honors for Caesar, the entire body had hurried to inform him of its latest act of flattery. The hundreds of senators found him in Caesar's Forum, sitting in front of the Temple of Venus Genetrix. Prior to the Battle of Pharsalus, he had vowed to his patron deity Venus that he would build this temple at his own expense should he be victorious. Now he was installing two statues inside the temple. One was of Venus herself. Beside it would stand another, in gold, of Cleopatra, queen of Egypt.

Ever since 48 B.C., Cleopatra had been Caesar's principal mistress. When Caesar had departed from Egypt a year later, after fighting and winning a particularly grueling war against the Egyptians that had made Egypt a province of Rome in all but name, Cleopatra was pregnant. In 46 B.C., twenty-three-year-old Cleopatra had arrived at Rome. She had come with her "husband" and a large entourage. That husband was her younger brother Ptolemy XIV. Past Egyptian rulers who were brothers and sisters went through a marriage ceremony when they became king and queen that also made them husband and wife. There is no indication that this incestuous royal marriage was ever consummated. Cleopatra also had brought her newborn son with her to Rome. She had named him Ptolemy XV Caesar. In Egypt the boy was known as Caesarion, and people far and wide were convinced that this was Caesar's son. "Some Greek historians say that the boy closely resembled Caesar in features as well as in gait," Suetonius noted.[6]

At Rome, Cleopatra and her party had taken up residence in a villa owned by Caesar atop the Janiculum Hill, on the western bank of the Tiber outside Rome. Luxuriant gardens covered the hillside all the way down to the river; in his will, Caesar would bequeath these gardens to the people of Rome. From the villa on the hill, Cleopatra could look down into the city across the river. Leading members of the Senate trooped to Caesar's villa to cast their eyes on the vivacious young woman as they officially paid their respects to Caesar's guests, for Caesar had formally presented the queen and her brother to the Senate, in the Senate House, as "friends and allies of the Roman people."[7] "He would not allow her to return to Alexandria without high titles and rich presents," said Suetonius.[8]

Cleopatra had not come simply to pay a fleeting visit. She had "settled in Caesar's own house."[9] It appears that she was still there now, in March 44 B.C., with plans to accompany Caesar when he set off for the East in the middle of the month, then continue on back to Alexandria while he launched his military campaign.[10] Caesar himself was of course at liberty to regularly visit his own villa and to see Cleopatra. No one in Rome would openly criticize Caesar for keeping his exotic Egyptian mistress on the Janiculum, and his wife, Calpurnia, seems to have turned a blind eye to her presence.

But behind closed doors "he incurred the greatest censure from all because of his passion for Cleopatra," said Dio. Not so much the passion he had displayed for her when in Egypt, Dio noted, "but that which was displayed in Rome itself." Yet, even though Caesar "derived an ill repute" from this, "he was not at all concerned."[11] By placing a statue of his ladylove in the temple he was erecting for his goddess, Caesar was not only snubbing his nose at his critics, he also was ranking Cleopatra with a goddess, just as he himself was being ranked with the gods. The statue of Cleopatra would still be standing in that temple at Rome hundreds of years later.

As the senators flooded around Caesar outside the Temple of Venus, to their dismay he made no attempt to stand, but remained in his chair, as if he were superior to them. Like so many of the "sins" credited to Caesar during these weeks, to modern eyes this may seem no great crime. But in republican Rome, all Roman citizens were considered equal. Augustus, who would later become Rome's first emperor, would recognize this basic tenet, and to give his rule an egalitarian veneer he would adopt the title *princeps*, which literally means "first among equals."

Standing beside Caesar, the senator and eminent jurist Gaius Trebatius Testa, a friend of Cicero and a supporter of Caesar for the past ten years, is said to have suggested that as a courtesy, Caesar should rise to receive the senators. But Caesar's Spanish friend and business adviser Cornelius Balbus quickly spoke up, counseling Caesar to stay seated: "Will you not remember you are Caesar, and claim the honor which is due to your merit."[12]

Caesar obviously agreed with Balbus, for he "grimaced angrily" at Trebatius for suggesting he stand, and remained in his seat. Suetonius was to say that this "open insult to the Senate" by Caesar is what caused "Romans to hate him so bitterly."[13] Plutarch echoed the sentiment. "This treatment offended not only the Senate, but the commons too, as if they thought the affront on the Senate equally reflected on the whole Republic."[14]

Senators departed the scene looking visibly disconcerted by the affair. Too late Caesar appreciated "the false step he had made," and once he returned home he again dramatically offered his throat to any of his associates who felt he deserved the maximum penalty. Of course, they all assured him he had done nothing wrong. Afterward, said Plutarch, Caesar made the excuse that he had remained seated because of the "malady from which he suffered"—he was history's first recorded sufferer of epileptic seizures—claiming that he was more likely to bring on a seizure while standing.[15]

Some of Caesar's supporters would subsequently try to excuse his action that day by claiming that "owing to an attack of diarrhea he could not control the movements of his bowels and so had remained where he was in order to avoid a flux." Cassius Dio would write that this excuse failed to convince most people, for, not long after, Caesar was seen to walk home; a man suffering such severe diarrhea could have been expected to have been carried home in a litter. The upshot, said Dio, was that "most men suspected him of being inflated with pride, and hated him for his haughtiness."[16]

Before long, another of the many rumors about Caesar circulating around Rome would have met Marcus Brutus's ears. Now it was said that Lucius Cotta, the senator who was chief of the college of fifteen priests known as the Quindecimviri, which had responsibility for the safekeeping and interpretation of the Sibylline Books, would make a startling announcement to the Senate.[17] The Sibylline Books were three books of prophesies by a Greek prophetess, the Sibyl, acquired by Tarquinius Superbus, last king of Rome, and only consulted in times of emergency. According to a persistent rumor, Cotta would before long announce to the House that "the Sibyl had said the Parthians would never be defeated in any other way than by a king."[18] Then, so the rumor ran, Caesar's friends in the Senate would move that he be made king, to enable him to go east to conquer the Parthians in fulfillment of the sacred prediction. It was a rumor with a logical and persuasive ring to it.

In this rumor-rich atmosphere, Marcus Brutus this week received an approach from his brother-in-law Gaius Cassius Longinus, who would become known to history simply as Cassius. Brutus and Cassius had not been on speaking terms for months. While Brutus was famously the most easygoing and affable of men, Cassius was equally well known for his quick temper and dislike of injustice. And to Cassius's mind, he had been on the receiving end of an injustice, with Brutus promoted ahead of him by Julius Caesar.

Cassius was older than Brutus and more senior in terms of years spent in the senatorial order. Cassius also had extensive military experience, while Brutus had next to none. Yet Caesar had appointed Brutus to the post of *praetor urbanus*, city praetor, the most senior of the twenty chief magistrates of Rome, responsible for sitting in judgment in legal cases involving suits brought in Rome. Cassius had also received a praetorship from Caesar, that of peregrine praetor, but this was a less prestigious post. Caesar also had promised both men consulships, but had subsequently only announced that Brutus would be a consul, in four years' time.

None of this was Brutus's fault, but Cassius had blamed him for being the recipient of preferential treatment, or for acceding to it. That favored treatment had much to do with the fact that Brutus was the son of Servilia, the beautiful widowed half-sister of the famous orator Cato the Younger. In the past, Servilia had notoriously been Caesar's favorite mistress. One persistent rumor even made Caesar the father of Brutus. Some modern writers have ridiculed this, pointing out that Caesar was only fifteen when Servilia gave birth to Brutus. In fact, this does not preclude Caesar from fathering Brutus, for the Romans began their sex lives quite young. Roman women could legally marry at age thirteen, and frequently did, bearing children while still only children themselves. Roman men, meanwhile, were legally able to marry once they came of age at the end of their fifteenth year.

Those who dispute Caesar's paternity of Brutus also point out that some classical accounts of the affair between Caesar and Servilia date the relationship to some years after Brutus was born. Appian, however, says quite categorically that Caesar was "Servilia's lover when Brutus was born."[19] Whatever their blood relationship, if any, there is no doubting the fact that Caesar favored Brutus, if for no other reason than that he was Servilia's son. Following the Battle of Pharsalus, for example, during which Brutus had sided with Pompey and the Senate against Caesar, Caesar had instructed his commanders not to harm Brutus if they came across him, and to bring him safely to him; alternatively, if Brutus would not surrender, they were to permit him to escape.[20]

After Brutus surrendered to him in August 48 B.C., Caesar had entrusted him with the governorship of Cisalpine Gaul in 47 B.C., even while Caesar continued to wage war against those whom Brutus had up till then supported. When it came to the praetorships for 44 B.C., Plutarch reported that Caesar said to his friends, "Cassius has the strongest case, but we must let Brutus be the first praetor."[21] Cassius, feeling slighted by Caesar on Brutus's account, had vented his swift anger on Brutus, for he dare not vent it on Caesar.

But, now, out of the blue, Cassius had sought to reconcile with his brother-in-law—Cassius was married to Brutus's half-sister Junia Tertulla, to whom Brutus was very close. February 22 was when the Romans annually celebrated the Caristia holiday. This was a kind of thanksgiving day, when Roman families came together for reunion dinners, when they traditionally patched up quarrels and forgave offenses. This was an ideal and natural time for Cassius to initiate a reconciliation, and Brutus, on receiving an invitation for his family to dine with Cassius's family on the occasion of the Caristia, would have readily accepted.

The rift between Cassius and Brutus was well known, so the conciliatory nature of the holiday would have explained their meeting that evening after months of rancor between the pair. Nonetheless, considering Cassius's passionate nature and growing and undisguised disapproval of Caesar—Cassius was one of the few senators who had consistently voted against the many honors heaped on Caesar by the Senate over recent months—some outsiders may have been surprised by the brothers-in-law's unexpected get-together, despite their family ties.[22] Yet, for the moment, it drew little public attention.

Cassius, a tall, fit, lean man with a pallid complexion, should have been dead. When Marcus Crassus led his army of sixty thousand Roman soldiers into Mesopotamia in 53 B.C. to confront the Parthians, Cassius had marched as his quaestor, or chief of staff. When Crassus and his son Marcus perished at the Battle of Carrhae, where forty thousand

Romans were killed or captured by the Parthians in one of the most humiliating defeats in Roman history, young Cassius had not only fought his way out of the Parthian encirclement, he also had led twenty thousand Roman troops back to Syria and safety, and subsequently repelled Parthian assaults on Syria. His reputation as a hard man had been made by this.

Early in the Civil War, Cassius had served Pompey and the Senate as commander of the Syrian Fleet, surrendering his ships to Caesar following Pompey's defeat at Pharsalus. Again, Cassius's life was on the line—Caesar could have executed him. But Caesar had magnanimously forgiven Cassius, sparing his life and welcoming him into his fold. Despite this, wrote Plutarch, Cassius had grown to hate Caesar. Some would later attribute this hate to the fact that Caesar had confiscated a number of lions that Cassius had collected at the Greek city of Megara for use in spectacles at Rome. Caesar would have subsequently taken the credit for procuring the lions.[23]

First-century historian Plutarch was to defend Cassius, saying that those who gave the confiscation of the lions as Cassius's sole motive for hating Caesar were "much in the wrong. For Cassius had from his youth a natural hatred and rancor against the whole race of tyrants." Plutarch even gave an example of Cassius as a schoolboy coming to blows with the son of Sulla the Dictator for "extolling the sovereign power of his father."[24]

Cassius himself opens a window to his morals and motives, writing in late 45 B.C. to his friend Cicero the orator, "I trust people will realize how intense and universal is hatred for cruelty and love for worth and clemency, so that they will see how the prizes most sought and coveted by the wicked come to the good." He added a quote from the philosopher Epicurus, "Pleasure and peace of mind are won by virtue, justice, and right."[25] Certainly, Cassius would have felt that he had been led on by Caesar, who had promised the same rewards to both Brutus and himself.

In the early evening of February 22, Brutus, his wife, Porcia, and Porcia's adult son from an earlier marriage, Lucius Calpurnius Bibulus, would have traveled the short distance across the city from their house to Cassius's house, accompanied by an entourage of servants. Porcia, a petite, attractive, though delicate, woman, was the daughter of the late Marcus Cato, known to history as the revered orator Cato the Younger. Eloquent Cato, though a decade younger than both Caesar and Pompey, had taken on the mantle of the elder statesman in the 50s B.C., campaigning against corruption and opposing both Caesar and Pompey before siding with Pompey and the republican Senate in the Civil War. Cato had considered both Caesar and Pompey corrupt autocrats.[26]

To Caesar's dismay—for he was robbed of the satisfaction of granting one of his most forthright enemies a pardon—Cato had committed suicide rather than surrender following the Dictator's 46 B.C. victory at Thapsus in North Africa. Romans considered suicide a noble end, and Cato made himself a model of the virtuous Roman for generations to come. His reputation was such that first-century Roman writer Valerius Maximus was to say that "anyone who wants to describe an excellent, upright citizen must define him as a 'Cato.'"[27] This national esteem for Cato the defender of democracy reflected brightly on his daughter Porcia and son-in-law Brutus.

As tradition dictated, the diners would each have brought something to the Caristia dinner at Cassius's house, before sharing the meal in front of statues of Cassius's household gods, to whom offerings were made. The dinner took place in the house's triclinium, a dining room equipped with three couches around three sides of a square table. Three diners could recline on each couch, eating with their fingers as they took food and drink from the table, served by slaves from the table's fourth, open end. On special occasions such as the Caristia feast, a dozen or more courses were common, generally starting with an egg dish and ending with apples.

Once the dinner was over, "after the compliments of reconciliation had passed, and former kindnesses were renewed between them," Cassius took Brutus aside. The pair probably strolled in the house's internal garden. As they walked around the colonnade surrounding a carefully tended garden where a fountain may have trickled, Cassius took tall, handsome Brutus's arm and asked him whether he planned to attend the next sitting of the Senate, which was scheduled for a little over a week later, on March 1.[28] Before Brutus answered, Cassius added that it was rumored that Caesar's friends planned to move a motion at that sitting that Caesar be named king of the Romans.

"I will not be there," Brutus replied.

"But what if they should send for us?" Cassius asked.

"It will be my business, then, not to hold my peace, but to stand up boldly and die for the liberty of my country."[29]

To which Cassius said "with some emotion," "But what Roman would stand by and let you die?" Surely, he went on, Brutus was aware of his position in Roman society, aware of the pedestal that many leading Romans had placed him on. Cassius asked him if he thought it was weavers and shopkeepers who had written the messages on his tribunal, or the first and most powerful men of Rome. Those men expected money and spectacles and gladiators from other praetors, said Cassius, but from Marcus Brutus they expected, "as an hereditary debt, the eradication of tyranny." Cassius assured his brother-in-law that those men were also ready to "suffer anything" on Brutus's account if he were to show himself to be the man they thought he was and expected him to be.[30]

Brutus was unhappy with Caesar's autocratic rule, but unlike Cassius he did not despise Caesar. Brutus, said Plutarch, hated "the rule of oppression," while "Cassius hated the ruler."[31] Despite differing motives, Brutus and Cassius had the same desire, the restoration of republican government. Now Brutus agreed that something must be done to prevent Caesar from becoming king of the Romans, and that it must be done quickly, before Caesar departed from Rome on March 19 to launch his military campaign in the East. Once Caesar did that, he would be surrounded by loyal troops for the next three years. With this momentous declaration by Brutus, the plot to kill Caesar took root.

Cassius embraced Brutus, and the brothers-in-law agreed that they would discreetly sound out friends to see if others shared their view about the need to act against Caesar.[32] The first name that came to mind was that of Marcus Cicero, a respected member of the Senate with an extensive network of friends and great popularity among the common people. He also was "Brutus's principal confidant."[33] Cicero's very name would add luster to the conspiracy and attract men to the cause. Cicero had made no secret, among those closest to him, that he considered Caesar's rule oppressive. Cicero rarely bothered to attend Senate sittings now that they had descended into what might be characterized as meetings of the Caesar admiration society, with sycophantic senators vying with one another for Caesar's attention and approval like competitive children.

Yet, while Cicero was "very much trusted and loved" by the pair and might be expected to support their goal, they considered him "naturally timorous," a characteristic the brothers-in-law believed would be exacerbated by "the weariness and caution of old age." Their fear was that, being overly cautious by nature, Cicero would "blunt the edge of their forwardness and resolution."[34]

Cicero might think of countless logical reasons why a certain thing should not be done at a certain time to avoid the risk of disaster. After all, death potentially awaited those involved if the plot went wrong. So the pair agreed that it would be best to conceal the plot from Cicero, and that the type of men they must seek out had to be "bold and brave and despisers of death."[35]

As they parted, Cassius reminded Brutus of his declaration that he was prepared to die for the liberty of his country. "Is there a man among the nobility you would not win over with that sentiment?" Cassius asked.[36]

The violent death of Julius Caesar was one step closer.

# IV

# FEBRUARY 24, 44 B.C.

## PRESSURING BRUTUS

Just two days after the Caristia, another religious holiday was celebrated at Rome. This time it was the Regifugium Festival. Dedicated to Terminus, Roman god of boundaries, it commemorated the day, centuries before, when the original Brutus had acted to terminate the monarchy.

The latter-day Marcus Brutus had been a troubled man ever since his reconciliation with Cassius, with the matter they had discussed running through his mind night and day and the weight of history weighing heavily on his shoulders. On February 24, as he did every day, Brutus would have risen well before dawn and after a light breakfast, which for many Romans consisted merely of a glass of water or a piece of bread, welcomed the clients who crowded his vestibule. He would receive letters from friends abroad brought by visitors, pass the time of day with his clients, and pass out the cash that he regularly doled out among his poorer clientele, as he considered which, if any, of Rome's leading men could safely be approached on the subject of Caesar's removal.

Brutus knew that he must be very careful whom he spoke to and what he said. Fickle noblemen were known to run to Caesar seeking his favor by bringing tidings of plots real and imagined. To begin with, Brutus had to cast into a conversation, like a baited line in a murky pool, a casual question or two. Those questions must be carefully phrased so as not to give away his true intent. And then he must read the responses like an augur reading omens.

The previous day, Brutus found more pamphlets and graffiti on his tribunal when he arrived to conduct the assizes. The slogans continued in the same vein as before: "Brutus, have you been bribed?" "Brutus, are you a corpse?" "Would that you were with us now." "Your descendants are not worthy of you." "You are no descendant of *his*!" Brutus knew exactly what these messages referred to. He could not help but know, as anonymous letters also had begun to turn up at his door, along with letters from friends, all urging him to act in the interests of the Republic. As Appian noted, with each passing day "rumors about the kingship became all the more insistent."[1]

It is not impossible that his brother-in-law Cassius was behind this graffiti and letter campaign. Even if that were the case, the messages were read by many, the rumors heard by most, and their impact not lost on Brutus. During the Regifugium holiday, Brutus visited an old comrade, Gaius Ligarius, who was sick in bed. Ligarius, "one of Brutus's most intimate friends," had fought for the republican side against Caesar during the Civil War, and like Brutus and Cassius had been pardoned by Caesar. But Ligarius had recently made it known to Brutus that he was not grateful for Caesar's pardon when the price of that pardon was Caesar's oppressive rule.[2]

At the city house of Ligarius, his steward conducted Brutus into his bedroom. Finding Ligarius in his bed, pale and weak, Brutus exclaimed, "Oh, Ligarius, what a time you have chosen to be sick!"[3]

At this, Ligarius raised himself up on one elbow and reached out to Brutus, taking him by the hand. "But, oh, Brutus," he responded, "if you are involved in any scheme worthy of yourself, I am well."[4] No names had been mentioned in front of the servants, but no names were necessary.

Brutus had come for advice, but would have departed from his friend as much conflicted as when he arrived.

# V

# MARCH 1, 44 B.C., THE KALENDS OF MARCH

## DICTATOR FOR LIFE

On the Roman calendar, the first day of the month was known as the Kalends. Well before dawn on the Kalends of March, Julius Caesar walked the few yards from the Regia, the official residence and headquarters of the pontifex maximus on the Via Sacra, or Sacred Way, to the small, circular Temple of Vesta, goddess of hearth and home, which dated from the seventh century B.C. There, in predawn darkness lit by flickering torches, Caesar presided over the annual religious ceremony where the six vestal virgins rekindled the perpetual flame of Rome, symbol of Roman life.

The flame burned year-round inside the ancient temple, its circular design emulating the original round huts of Rome at the time of Romulus and Remus. The rekindling of Vesta's flame took place on March 1 because, earlier in Rome's history, March 1 was for centuries the Roman New Year's Day, and the rekindling was intended to bring good fortune to Rome and its people for the coming year.

It was one of the duties of the pontifex maximus to select new vestal virgins. The vestals were daughters of leading noble families. Entering the order between ages six and ten, they served for thirty years, with duties including guardianship of the eternal flame and the temple that housed it, preparing ritual food, and conducting the week-long Vestalia, or Festival of Vesta, each June. As their title implied, the vestals were required to remain virgins. They were permitted to marry once they left the order, but it was considered unlucky if they did.

A vestal who failed to carry out her duties could be beaten. A vestal found to have violated her vow of chastity—and there are several instances of this occurring—faced execution by being buried alive. On the other hand, vestals were revered by the Roman populace. To have a daughter serving as a vestal, and particularly as chief vestal, brought great honor to a Roman family. And in recompense for their restricted lives, the vestal virgins received numerous privileges: the carriage of the vestals was the only passenger vehicle permitted to use the streets of Rome in daylight, and white marble front-row benches would be reserved for them when the Colosseum was built so they could watch public spectacles from the best seats in the house; those benches can still be seen in the Colosseum today.

Once the ceremony at the Temple of Vesta had concluded, Caesar made his way to the temple where the day's sitting of the Senate was scheduled to take place, passing temples and the houses of priests, which, like the Regia, were being festooned by slaves with fresh laurels. The original Senate House had been burned to the ground during rioting prior to the Civil War. Caesar was building a new Senate House in the Forum, but until its completion the Senate met in various public buildings, frequently temples. While the leading men of Rome attended the Senate sitting today, their wives and daughters would be celebrating the Matronalia Festival. Forerunner of today's Mother's Day, the Matronalia celebrated the Roman mother, and during daylight hours its ceremonials were restricted to women.

As dawn broke over Rome, hundreds of senators arrived at the day's temporary Senate House. Caesar had increased the Senate's rolls to include nine hundred members, in part by granting membership in the Senatorial Order to foreign-born provincials, "including semi-civilized Gauls," as one critic wrote.[1] Caesar had even made a former army centurion a senator. This, too, had all brought Caesar much criticism. Traditionally, only noble natives of the city of Rome could sit in its Senate. An anonymous poster had recently gone up in Rome; referring to out-of-towners who had been made senators by Caesar, it declared: "Long live our country, but if any newly appointed senator inquires the way to the Senate House, let no one direct him there!"[2]

It could be argued that the resistance to Caesar's senatorial appointments was born of prejudice and age-old resistance to change, and that to be truly representative of the Roman people it was time for senators to be appointed from Rome's provinces. And some centurions in Caesar's day were actually members of the Equestrian Order, which was the traditional path to the Senate, so the elevation of a centurion to the Senate was perhaps not so exceptional.

Some modern authors have claimed that by broadening the base of the Senatorial Order, Caesar was acting through a desire to make the Senate more representative and egalitarian. In fact, Caesar was merely filling the Senate with men who would be beholden to him for their elevation and who would outnumber the aristocrats who sat in the House, thus ensuring that he always had a majority and the Senate acted as nothing more than a rubber stamp to his wishes.

Both Cassius and Brutus were among the throng of chattering senators who filled the chamber this morning. Like all around them, the pair was adorned in the *toga praetexta*, the white toga edged with a broad purple stripe that signified their senatorial rank. Brutus, who previously had not planned to attend, sat with his brother-in-law. Both dreaded the possibility that the rumored prediction about the Sibylline Books would be announced today, followed by a call for Caesar to be declared king. As serving praetors, the pair sat on wooden benches in the front row, together with the ex-consuls, the latter having the privilege of being called on by the presiding consul to speak next in debates following the current magistrates.

The presiding consul today would be Caesar. In addition to holding an unprecedented ten-year senatorial appointment as Dictator, he also was one of the two consuls for the year, with Mark Antony as his consular colleague. Even Caesar's appointments of consuls had come in for criticism. There was the obvious complaint that under the Republic the consuls had been elected by the people; now they were appointed by Caesar. Under the Republic, too, consuls had been appointed annually, giving their names to the year. Under Caesar, the primary consuls stepped aside after several months, to be replaced by *suffect*, or substitute, consuls chosen by the Dictator, enabling many more men to enjoy the consulship and the privileges it entailed, including the provision, at state expense, of twelve lictors, or attendants.

One such suffect consul appointed by Caesar, Quintus Maximus, who had served for three months, had, when he entered the theater on one occasion, been preceded by his chief lictor crying, as his job required, "Make way for the consul!" To this, many in the audience had protested, "He is no consul!"[3] When one of the previous consuls had died on New Year's Eve, Caesar had appointed a replacement for just the single day that remained before January 1, when the new consuls were due to take office. This one-day consulship, to many staid Romans, made a mockery of the office. To Caesar, it was one way of putting a member of the nobility in his debt.

"Make way for the Dictator!" came the heralding cry of Caesar's chief lictor. The men in the chamber fell silent and respectfully came to their feet. Caesar strode in, wearing his purple cloak and laurel crown of a triumphant. As custom required, before arriving, he had presided as a bird had been sacrificed and the augurs had examined its entrails. Unblemished entrails signified that the Senate's deliberations this day would go well. Caesar seems not to have enjoyed Senate sittings of late. Merely going through the motions for propriety's sake, he would have much preferred to be devoting his time to the final planning for the upcoming military campaign. Taking his place on the throne of gold and ivory voted to him by this Senate, Caesar opened proceedings.

A variety of motions were put and discussed that day. Then came a motion that, to many, would be the final nail in Caesar's coffin. This was not the motion feared by Cassius and Brutus, that Caesar should be declared king. Instead, it was proposed that Caesar be appointed Dictator for life. This was unheard of. Prior to Caesar's dictatorship, only twice in 170 years had the Roman Senate considered such an emergency to exist to make it necessary to appoint a Dictator. The last recipient of the dictatorial powers had been Cornelius Sulla, who had overthrown the consul Marius in a bitter civil war. In that civil war a young Caesar had supported Marius, and had narrowly escaped with his life when proscriptions ordered by Sulla had resulted in the execution of numerous political opponents. Yet, for all the severity of his rule, Sulla had given up the dictatorship, returned the Republic to the people, and gone into retirement.

After Caesar had pardoned many of those who had fought against him in the Civil War, and given a number official appointments, "the people hoped that he also would give them back democracy, just as Sulla had done."[4] The people were to be disappointed. Now it was being proposed that, against all precedent, Caesar be made Rome's sole ruler until the day he died. As if this were somehow different from being granted the title of king, and almost out of relief that kingship had not been proposed, the majority of senators voted in favor of the motion. Caesar was now Dictator for life.

There were two final motions put to the House before it rose. One required all senators to take an oath of loyalty to Caesar. The motion passed without dissent, with all senators vowing their loyalty. The final motion of the sitting was that all the senators and Equestrians of Rome would swear to act as the protectors of Caesar's life. Again, the motion passed unopposed, and the vow was taken.[5]

The House rose, the attendants flung open the doors, and in small groups the senators took their leave, talking among themselves. As Cassius and Brutus departed the Senate House, they would have agreed that in declaring Caesar Dictator for life the Senate had as good as made him their monarch. The only difference was in the title. The result was the same: Caesar was now ruler of the Romans for the remainder of his days.

Caesar, himself preparing to depart the chamber, noticed Brutus and Cassius leaving together, and saw that Cassius was animated with furtive conversation. Caesar was surprised. The fact that the two men had not been on speaking terms was common knowledge, and until now Caesar was unaware that they had reconciled. As he left the meeting place and walked toward his waiting litter, Caesar said to an aide, "What do you think Cassius is up to? I don't like him, he looks so pale."[6]

The litter returned Caesar to the Regia, where, during the day, his wife, Calpurnia, had played hostess to Matronalia celebrations with Rome's leading women. The Regia had been Caesar's home for the past eighteen years, ever since he had been popularly elected to the lifetime post of pontifex maximus. Prior to that, Caesar had lived in a modest house in Rome's disreputable Subura quarter.[7]

The roughly triangular-shaped Regia was one of Rome's oldest buildings. Its name means "royal" house; according to Roman tradition it had been built by the second king of Rome, Numa Pompilius (Romulus being the first), and was subsequently the residence of the kings of Rome. Under the Republic, the Regia had become the domain of the pontifex maximus. It was not a large building. Its three main, high-ceilinged rooms contained the sacred shrines to Mars and to Ops, a fertility goddess and wife of Saturn, and also Rome's religious archives. Caesar lived and worked there. The Regia, its servants, and its upkeep were provided by the State. Early in 44 B.C., Caesar had lavished golden decorations, ornaments, and statues on the building.[8]

The prestige of the post of pontifex maximus had attracted Caesar's candidacy. He was not a particularly religious man. In fact, in none of his writings, speeches, or acts did he show the slightest religiosity, unlike other writers and speakers of his time, who frequently invoked the help of the gods or praised them for their favorable intercession in human events.

To win the election to become pontifex maximus, Caesar had "used the most flagrant bribery," racking up "enormous debts" in bribing the voters. Suetonius says that as Caesar's mother had kissed him good-bye on the morning of the election, he told her that if he did not return as high priest, he would not return at all. Caesar's two opponents in this election were "much older and more distinguished than himself." Yet, when the votes were tallied, Caesar had won more votes from members of these two candidates' own tribes than from all the others; for election purposes all Roman citizens were members of voting tribes, the names of which they even included on their tombstones.[9]

This house, the Regia, and the Matronalia Festival had among them been the scene of one of the most sensational episodes in Caesar's tempestuous marital life. Years before, Mark Antony's handsome and debauched friend Publius Clodius had crept into the Regia one March 1 when the women were celebrating the Matronalia and seduced Caesar's second wife, Pompeia. Once this was revealed, it provoked a huge public scandal, and when Pompeia was accused of adultery by both her mother and sister, Caesar himself had refused to offer any evidence. "I cannot have any members of my household accused or even suspected," he had said.[10] But he divorced Pompeia nonetheless.

By 44 B.C. Clodius the seducer was long dead and the affair all but forgotten as Caesar and his current wife were joined at the Regia on the evening of the Matronalia by some of his closest colleagues and their wives for a celebratory dinner. Throughout the capital, Romans were enjoying the last hours of the high-spirited Matronalia Festival. Among the men who would have joined Caesar that evening would have been Lepidus, his Master of Equestrians; his business agent, Cornelius Balbus; and the Dictator's faithful assistant Aulus Hirtius, who was marked down by Caesar to be consul the following year. Perhaps other close friends of the Dictator, such as Gaius Oppius and Gaius Matius, also joined this gathering at the Regia.

Caesar's innermost circle no longer included Mark Antony. Even though Antony was Caesar's co-consul for the year, he had ceased to be the Dictator's favorite. Just prior to the Civil War, Pompey the Great had rated Antony, then just a tribune of the plebs with a good military record as a middle-ranking officer, as no more than a "feckless nobody."[11] During the Civil War, the government of Caesar "obtained a bad repute through his friends; and of his friends, Antony, as he had the largest trust, and committed the greatest errors, was thought the most deeply at fault."[12]

There was no doubting Antony's reliability as a soldier. Commanding Caesar's left wing at the 48 B.C. Battle of Pharsalus against Pompey, Antony had contributed significantly to Caesar's victory. But as an administrator, Antony was sadly lacking. "He was too lazy to pay attention to complaints," said Plutarch, "listened impatiently to petitions, and had an ill name for familiarity with other people's wives."[13]

As a youth, Antony had lived a life of wine, women, and song. The father of his best friend, Gaius Curio, had even banned him from his house because he considered Antony a bad influence on his son. In adulthood, Antony had continued to lead a dissolute life. But because of his loyalty, his family ties to Caesar, his military skills—of Caesar's commanders, Plutarch considered him, justifiably, "the best officer of all that served under him"—and the fact that many rank-and-file legionaries admired his fearlessness and military prowess, Caesar had at that time employed Antony as his deputy.[14]

In 48 B.C., following the victory at Pharsalus, Caesar had sent his own rebellious legions back to Rome with Antony while he himself pursued Pompey with several legions made up from Pompey's surrendered troops. Antony, as Caesar's then Master of Equestrians, had the task of ruling at Rome in Caesar's absence, but he had performed woefully in the role. Instead of diligently running the capital, Antony had made himself "absolutely odious" to all classes through "his drinking bouts at all hours, his wild expenses, his gross lovemaking." He spent the days "sleeping or walking off his debauches" and the nights "in banquets and at theaters." After attending the wedding of a comedian named Hippias, Antony had turned up drunk for a public speaking engagement next morning and proceeded to vomit in front of his audience.[15]

Antony had then come to blows with another of Caesar's favorites, Publius Cornelius Dolabella. Boastful, overweight young Dolabella— he was then only twenty-one years old—was considered "delightful company" by Caesar, who felt that Dolabella possessed "kindness of heart" and "goodwill."[16] Dolabella had supported Caesar from the outset of the Civil War, despite the fact that he had married the daughter of Marcus Cicero, who in turn had initially supported Pompey.

After Pharsalus, Dolabella had returned to Rome with Antony and the disgraced legions, taking up Caesar's appointment as one of the tribunes of the plebs. Dolabella, up to that time Antony's close friend, being "a young man and eager for change," decided to use his position to bring about the cancellation of all debts, including, of course, his own.[17]

To overcome the opposition of other tribunes, Dolabella wanted Antony's support, but Antony suddenly turned against him, for Antony was overcome "by a terrible suspicion that Dolabella was too familiar with his wife."[18] This was Antony's second wife, Antonia, who also was his cousin. Antony not only separated from Antonia over this, when he heard that Dolabella had seized the Forum and intended to force through his debt-cancellation law, he sought and received a vote of the Senate that Dolabella should be restrained by force of arms. He had then descended on the Forum with troops—one of the four mutinous legions camped outside Rome at that time was still responding to Antony's orders. A bloody fight had ensued, with casualties on both sides.

Antony had prevailed. Dolabella's bill failed to pass, much to the chagrin of many people who had been looking forward to their debts being canceled. As for Dolabella, he was charged with an unlawful act, with his fate to be decided by Caesar. When Caesar returned to Rome from Spain, he heard the case and acquitted Dolabella. He also removed Antony from office. From that time forward, Antony and Dolabella, once firm friends, were enemies.

Antony, meanwhile, had made a successful bid for Pompey's city mansion, in Rome's Carinae, or Keels district, when it was put up for auction on Caesar's orders. But when it came time for Antony to make payment, he complained bitterly. Antony himself was to write that he felt he should not have to pay "because he thought his former services had not been recompensed as they deserved." Caesar did not agree, forcing Antony to pay full price. For this reason, Antony was to say, he declined to accompany Caesar when he invaded North Africa that December to do battle with the republican forces that had assembled there.[19]

Antony had been out of office and out of favor for the remainder of the Civil War. In October 45 B.C., news reached Rome that Caesar was marching down through northwestern Italy on his way back from Spain. Having finally wrapped up the Civil War there in September, Caesar was returning at the head of thousands of cavalrymen and thousands of discharged soldiers who had been promised land in Italy by their

leader. When all of Rome's leading men had flooded out of the city to
meet Caesar on the road and escort him back to the capital, Antony
joined the exodus. Many went several days' distance north, but
Antony went farther than all the rest, traveling a hundred miles from
Rome to be the first to greet Caesar.

To Caesar, loyalty was everything. "Even as a young man Caesar was
well known for the devotion and loyalty he showed his dependants,"
said Suetonius, "and he showed consistent affection to his friends."[20]
Antony was a ruffian with a boyish charm that endeared him to five
wives, including, eventually, Cleopatra. On the road to Rome he begged
Caesar's forgiveness, and the Dictator softened, inviting Antony to join
him in his litter for the remainder of his journey back to the capital.

Caesar had subsequently rehabilitated Antony by appointing
him his co-consul for 44 B.C. But Antony, a man who held grudges,
remained a bitter opponent of Dolabella—so much so that, when early
in 44 B.C., Caesar had proposed in the Senate to resign his consulship for the year in favor of Dolabella, Antony, as Caesar's co-consul,
had stood up and "opposed it with all his might, saying much that was
bad against Dolabella, and receiving the like language in return" from
Dolabella. Caesar had abhorred the very public "indecency" of this
squabbling between his favorites, and postponed the matter.

Within a few weeks, when Caesar attempted once again to announce
that he was proclaiming Dolabella consul in his stead, Antony had again
objected, this time claiming, in his capacity as a priest, that the auspices
were unfavorable. In the face of Antony's intransigence, Caesar, "much
to Dolabella's vexation," had dropped the idea. But later, Caesar had
decreed that Dolabella would take up his consulship once he departed
for the East on March 19 to conduct the Getae and Parthian campaigns,
and Antony was unable to prevent it.[21] Leaving Antony and Dolabella
again at Rome together, with equal power as consuls, had its risks, but
this time Marcus Lepidus, as Master of Equestrians, would be standing
above and between the pair, armed with the authority of seniority.

Besides, Antony had promised Caesar that he would turn over a
new leaf and reform his private life, and to date he had kept his word.
He had remarried, this time to Fulvia, ambitious widow of Antony's late
friend and fellow carouser Clodius Pulcher, who had been murdered
in 52 B.C. And Antony had given the appearance of being cured of
"a good deal of his folly and extravagance," although he had yet to shed
all the excess weight gained during his late career of perpetual wining

and dining. With Antony and Dolabella not even inclined to be in the same room together, and with Caesar "about as much disgusted with the one as with the other" for falling out and disappointing him, the pair had ceased to be part of the Dictator's most intimate circle.[22]

As Caesar's invited guests dined with him on the evening of the Matronalia, an unidentified guest took the Dictator aside and warned him that it was rumored that Antony and Dolabella were plotting against him. Plutarch was to write that Caesar dismissed the suggestion. "It is not these well-fed, long-haired men that I fear," he responded, "but the pale and hungry-looking ones." He was referring to Cassius.[23]

Across town on March 1, pale, lean Cassius was dining with his brother-in-law. The Matronalia gave them the perfect excuse to spend time in each other's company out of the public eye and without raising suspicions. It is likely that Cassius brought his family to Brutus's house on this occasion, to return the compliment after their meal at Cassius's house during the Caristia. The nature of the holiday, when men honored both their wives and their mothers, combined with later events, suggest that it is probable that Brutus's widowed mother, Servilia, Caesar's former lover, also was present.[24]

As was customary on the Matronalia, the members of the two families would have exchanged gifts, with the men offering prayers for the well-being of their wives and mothers. As tradition required, the women would have worn their hair long and unbound, just this once, in public. Romans considered the custom of foreign women letting their hair hang long and loose to be barbaric, and Roman women went to great trouble to coif their hair in elaborate rolls, with the help of curling irons and the hairdressers on their household staff. But when celebrating the Matronalia the Roman *matrona* left her hair unbound and did not even wear anything knotted on her person, so that, symbolically, she did not hinder safe childbirth in the future.

After dinner, Brutus and Cassius would have adjourned, probably strolling in the mansion's internal courtyard garden. Wafting on the mild March night air from the streets outside would have been the sounds of revelry. During the day, the Salii, twenty-four priests of the religious college sacred to the god Mars, had danced through the streets of Rome—their title literally meant "leapers." Wearing ancient armor and carrying the sacred shields and spears of Mars, which according to legend had fallen to earth from heaven, they leaped about reciting a traditional chant, the *Carme saliare*. At the end of their progress through the streets, the Salii sat down to a gala feast, as they did every March 1. By night, all the people of Rome joined in the festivities of this traditional day of renewal.

In addition to the Matronalia feasting, gambling on dice and cards, which was otherwise strictly regulated, was permitted, and there was music and dancing in the streets. To the distant accompaniment of flutes and singing, clapping hands, and chattering and laughter from the city's streets, Cassius and Brutus gravely discussed the state of their world.

The appointment in the Senate that day of Caesar as Dictator for life would have shaken the pair, and galvanized their resolve. Caesar was now king in everything but name, and Rome was encumbered with what Cassius and Brutus believed to be an illegal and intolerable monarchy. As Dictator for life, Caesar could look forward to a lifetime of sole rule, with the likelihood that his son would lay a claim to be his successor. Caesar seemed to be preparing the way for the latter—one of the latest honors voted for him by the Senate was the right of his son, natural or adopted, to receive his post as pontifex maximus on Caesar's demise.[25]

Cassius would have reminded Brutus that time was running out. In eighteen days' time, Caesar would depart from Rome for the East, and with him would go any chance of terminating his autocratic rule. There was no argument that this rule was indeed autocratic; another of the latest honors bestowed on Caesar by the Senate was the power to declare any man who insulted him by word or deed an outlaw, without any right of defense or appeal by the accused.[26] Any comment, any act, a hint of displeasure, a disapproving look: these would be enough to be earn a man the status of outlaw. This, to lovers of democracy, was the last straw.

By this time, Brutus could see, and Cassius would have reiterated, that there was only one way to remove Caesar from power, permanently and irrevocably. Even if the Senate were by some miracle to oppose Caesar, he controlled the army. To the minds of the brothers-in-law, Caesar could only be stopped one way. Cassius and Brutus agreed: Caesar had to be killed.

# VI

# MARCH 2, 44 B.C.

## RECRUITING FELLOW ASSASSINS

To the Romans, the public bath was more than a place for cleaning the body. It was a center of public life. Since the third century B.C., wealthy Romans had built baths in their town houses and country villas, but by Caesar's time public baths, sometimes built by philanthropists, other times built by businessmen who charged for admittance, had begun to appear in cities and towns.

Within a decade of Caesar's death, 170 public baths were recorded at Rome.[1] Within several more centuries the number of public baths at Rome would approach 1,000.

In Caesar's day, men and women bathed separately. The complexes in which they bathed included cold, lukewarm, and hot baths, changing rooms, gymnasiums, and even exercise courts where leather balls were tossed around to work up a sweat. There were massage rooms, and rooms where naked customers were coated with mud that was then scraped off, supposedly as a means of invigorating the skin. The larger bath complexes boasted libraries, museums, and exhibition halls. Most had gardens surrounded by covered promenades.

Here, most afternoons, the Roman citizen would come to bathe, socialize, and discuss and debate. Here, Marcus Brutus was able to chat daily with leading men from all sides of Roman politics. Here, he could sound out potential affiliates in homicide, to decide who could or could not be safely admitted to the conspiracy. It took only one man to murder another, but Brutus was convinced that for the murder of Caesar to have legitimacy as a patriotic act of removal of a tyrant, a great number of Rome's leading men must jointly participate in the Dictator's execution.

Brutus's questions had to be carefully phrased. They could give no hint of what he and Cassius were plotting, in case the men he spoke to reported him to Caesar or in case someone else overheard the conversation and blew the whistle. Subtle philosophical questions posed while walking around a bathhouse promenade would be Brutus's way of testing the proverbial waters with his colleagues.

One man whom Brutus felt sure would be a likely recruit to the plot was Marcus Favonius. A friend and admirer of Brutus's late father-in-law, Cato the Younger, Favonius had been a republican praetor in 49 B.C. and had fought in Pompey's army at Pharsalus. When that battle turned against the republican side, Favonius had been just one of four men to accompany his dazed commander in chief, Pompey, as he made his escape, first on horseback and then by commandeered cargo vessel. Favonius had acted more like Pompey's personal servant on the flight across the eastern Mediterranean, and would have been present when Pompey was murdered by the Egyptians as he went to step ashore at Pelusium in Egypt. Surviving the republican defeats in North Africa and Spain, Favonius had been pardoned by Caesar. His devotion to both Cato and Pompey put him high on Brutus's list of potential collaborators.

Brutus was joined this day by Favonius, Statilius the Epicurean, and Marcus Antistius Labeo. When Brutus asked Favonius which he felt was worse, a civil war or an illegal monarchy, Favonius earnestly replied, "In my judgment a civil war is worse than the most illegal monarchy." This response prompted Brutus to back off; he decided not to make any further attempt to recruit Favonius.[2]

Another potential supporter also disappointed him. Talking with Statilius the Epicurean, Brutus asked whether it was wise for a man to put himself into troubles and danger on account of evil or foolish men. Statilius replied that such an act did not become a man who possessed any wisdom or discretion. But Labeo contradicted them both, declaiming against monarchy and stating his belief that it was worth a man putting himself in danger's way if it meant overcoming evil or foolish men.

Brutus made no reply, merely nodding, as if taking on board the conflicting points of view and planning to decide which he favored at some future time. But when he and Labeo were alone, suspecting that

Labeo had caught his drift, he risked disclosing the plot to him. To his relief, Labeo not only readily joined the conspiracy, he also undertook to recruit others of like mind.[3]

Other targets for recruitment were obvious. One such man was Pontius Aquila, a tribune of the plebs. Over the past several years, Caesar had conducted five Triumphs through the streets of Rome. In these theatrical victory parades of soldiers, spoils, and prisoners, Caesar had driven a golden chariot drawn by four horses and wearing the official garb of a triumphant, celebrating his victories in Gaul, Egypt, Pontus, Africa, and Spain. The man in the street had lapped up these Triumphs and the massive public banquets that followed them. But some of Rome's leading citizens had not been so impressed, for Triumphs were intended to celebrate victories over foreign enemies, whereas in Africa and Spain Caesar had been victorious in Civil War battles, primarily over Roman citizens, including friends and relatives of Rome's most prominent men.

Possibly that was why Pontius Aquila had remained seated on the benches of the tribunes of the plebs when Caesar drove by in his golden chariot in one of these Triumphs. Around Aquila, everyone else had respectfully come to their feet. Seeing this, Caesar had shouted, "Hey there, Aquila the tribune! Do you want me to restore the Republic?" Over the next few days, Caesar had sarcastically added to every undertaking he gave, "with the kind consent of Pontius Aquila."[4] Aquila, nursing his grievance with Caesar, humiliated by the Triumph affair, and affronted by Caesar's dismissal of his fellow tribunes Marullus and Caesetius, was quick to join the murder plot.

Some, like Aquila, were to join the conspiracy for personal reasons. Others acted to restore the Republic, despite its past faults, to liberate the people from a despot. Caesar's attitude to the Republic was widely known. Titus Ampius Balbus, a senator who had governed Asia and Cilicia before fighting on the republican side during the Civil War, was pardoned by Caesar and permitted to return from exile in 46 B.C., probably at the intercession of his friend Marcus Cicero. Ampius Balbus would later publish a book containing some of Caesar's public utterances. According to Ampius, Caesar had stated, "The Republic was nothing, a mere name without form or substance." On another instance, Caesar was supposed to have said that "Sulla was a dunce for resigning his dictatorship."[5] True or not, sayings such as these attributed to Caesar quickly gave weight to claims by republicans that while Caesar lived, the Republic was dead.

It was not as if Caesar had turned into a despot overnight. His earlier career had been marked by one attempt after another to subvert the Republic and win personal power. Suetonius was to report that as early as 65 B.C., Caesar had first contemplated urging the Latin colonists of Cisalpine Gaul to rise in revolt against the Senate. He later teamed up with Marcus Crassus and two other leading men to make "an even more daring attempt at revolution in Rome itself." According to Suetonius, these four conspirators had planned to attack the Senate House one New Year's Day and kill numerous senators before proclaiming Crassus Dictator, Caesar his Master of Equestrians, and the other two consuls. That plot had fallen to pieces when Crassus lost his nerve. On another occasion, Caesar was rumored to have plotted to use force to seize power with an ex-consul, Gnaeus Piso, but that scheme had collapsed when Piso died.[6]

No one at Rome could have been surprised that Caesar had eventually made a bid for sole power in 49 B.C. Now his one-man rule gave many a Roman reason to despise him. But how many leading men were prepared to put their lives on the line by joining this conspiracy against Caesar hatched by Cassius and Brutus?

# VII

# MARCH 7, 44 B.C.

## A VISIT FROM ONE OF CAESAR'S GENERALS

I t was the Nones of March, a day sacred to Vediovis, one of the oldest Roman deities, god of deceivers and protector of right causes. It is likely that the conspirators discreetly made offerings to Vediovis this day.

Marcus Brutus saw his clients that morning as usual, but his mind was by now totally preoccupied with the plot to kill Caesar, so much so that he had been having trouble sleeping. During the morning, Brutus received a note from Decimus Junius Brutus Albinus, a distant relative. Albinus, variously referred to as "Decimus" and "Brutus" in some classical texts, was "one of Caesar's most intimate associates" and had been his faithful follower for a number of years.[1] He also was a close friend of Mark Antony. In the note, Albinus asked for a private interview with Brutus. That a man so close to Caesar and Antony was asking to see him in private must have filled Brutus with trepidation. Had Caesar learned of the plot? Was he sending Albinus to see Brutus alone so he could deliver an ultimatum from Caesar? Brutus had a reply delivered to Albinus, agreeing to the meeting and setting a time.

Albinus had served as an army commander under Caesar both during the Gallic War and during the Civil War. While Caesar's governor of Transalpine Gaul in 49 B.C., Albinus had participated in a protracted siege of the city of Massilia, today's Marseilles, a city that had supported Rome's republican Senate and held out against Caesar's forces for months. Albinus also had commanded a Caesarian fleet that had taken on a combined fleet of republican warships and warships from Massilia, and routed it.

Plutarch considered Albinus "of no great courage," but Albinus had always served Caesar loyally and without question, and was well known for "the great confidence that Caesar put in him." As a reward, Caesar had marked Albinus for a consulship in two years' time, alongside Lucius Plancus, another faithful follower of the Dictator, who was currently supervising army veteran settlement in Gaul. In the meantime, Caesar had decreed that Albinus become governor of Cisalpine Gaul when that post became vacant at the end of that spring.[2]

Brutus did not have to wait long to find out what was on Albinus's mind. Albinus arrived alone at Brutus's city house, and when he was certain no one could overhear them, Albinus revealed to Brutus that he had been approached by Labeo and Cassius, who had told him of the plot to kill Caesar and invited him to participate. Albinus added that Labeo and Cassius had assured him that Brutus was not only party to the conspiracy, he also was a leader of it.[3]

Albinus would have looked questioningly at Brutus, and there would have been a nervous pause. When Brutus did not rush to deny the claim, Albinus went on to say that he had told that pair he would reserve his decision on the matter until he had determined from Brutus himself whether Brutus was genuinely a leader of the conspiracy. Then and only then would Albinus be prepared to join the plotters. This was why Albinus had asked for a private meeting.

The volatile Cassius, himself not the most popular of personalities, had soon discovered that Brutus's name was the key to winning supporters to the conspiracy. Once men knew that the noble, upright Brutus, a figure held in high regard even by Caesar, was one of the chief conspirators, a surprising variety of senators would agree to join the plot—"the most and the best were gained by the name of Brutus," said Plutarch. Now Brutus confirmed to Albinus that he was indeed all for the murder of Caesar and was prepared to take a leading role in the deed. On hearing this, a relieved Albinus "readily consented to partake in the action."[4]

If we are to believe all classical accounts, no deal was discussed or struck by the pair; Albinus neither asked for nor received anything in return for participating in the murder of the man he had loyally served for a decade, other than confirmation of the appointments already announced for him by Caesar. Albinus's great dissatisfaction with Caesar was his only motive, and that dissatisfaction must have become known to Cassius and Labeo for them to approach him, for on the surface he was the most loyal and trusted of the Dictator's lackeys.

Discussion next turned to how, where, and when the murder should be carried out. Cassius and Brutus had been discussing this, but with Caesar due to leave Rome in just twelve days, time was running out for the details to be ironed out. From the beginning, it was agreed that the murder should be carried out in a public place, with all the conspirators taking part to demonstrate to the Roman people that theirs was a unified, public-spirited act. The Forum was considered as a location. It was also suggested that Caesar be attacked on the Sacred Way going to or from his residence, or as he went to enter a city drama theater. "The conspirators wavered between these plans," said Suetonius, "until Caesar called a meeting of the Senate in the Theater of Pompey for the Ides of March."[5]

This sitting of the Senate on March 15 was intended to be its last meeting before Caesar's departure for the East on the nineteenth of the month. Both Brutus and Albinus had received notification of the sitting, and of its location. Albinus now told Brutus that he had been preparing a large troupe of gladiators for an upcoming public spectacle—apparently the Liberalia games scheduled for March 19, the day when Caesar intended leaving Rome. It occurred to Albinus that he could put on an exhibition by his gladiators for Caesar in the Theatre of Pompey following the Senate sitting—Caesar was a big fan of gladiators, even maintaining his own gladiatorial school.

Should the need arise, Albinus's gladiators could provide protection for the conspirators once Caesar had been killed, for no one really knew how the recently retired legionaries camped around the city would react to their commander in chief being murdered. These thousands of ex-soldiers, some still equipped with their arms, were camped in the temple precincts and holy sanctuaries of Rome, waiting to be allocated the fifty-to-sixty-acre land grants promised to them by Caesar when they had fought for him in the Civil War. Surveying teams were at this very moment busy throughout Italy mapping out the land grants.

Having returned from Spain with Caesar, a large number of these former soldiers, men from one particular legion, were occupying Tiber Island, in the middle of the Tiber River, outside the city walls. Long, narrow Tiber Island was a religious sanctuary that housed the Temple of Vediovis. The legion to which these men camped on Tiber Island belonged is not named by classical texts, but later events point to it being either the 7th or the 8th Legion.

Both these units had for some years been stationed in and most likely recruited in Spain, and had served with Caesar throughout the Gallic and Civil wars. Along with the 9th and 10th legions, also units with Spanish backgrounds, the 7th and the 8th were considered Caesar's best legions. But after defeating Pompey's legions at the 48 B.C. Battle of Pharsalus in Greece, all four of these legions had gone on strike, demanding their overdue discharge, financial bonuses, and land grants that Caesar had promised them. Caesar had given them none of these at the time. Instead, as he set off in pursuit of Pompey with his loyal cavalry and former Pompeian legionaries, he had sent the 7th, 8th, 9th, and 10th legions to Rome with Mark Antony. At Rome, the 8th, 9th, and 10th had rioted; only the 7th had continued to obey Antony's orders.

When Caesar had arrived back at Rome in late 47 B.C. after fighting a grueling war in Egypt and then swiftly defeating Pharnaces, king of the Bosporus, at Zela in Pontus, after which he had sent his famous message *Veni, vidi, vici*, or "I came, I saw, I conquered," Caesar had employed cohorts of the 7th Legion as his bodyguard in Rome. He had posted these Spanish legionaries around his residence and taken them with him when he addressed the other rebellious legions on the Campus Martius and brought them back under his control. Memories of these Spanish cohorts' role as Caesar's bodyguard at Rome would shortly spark a suggestion from the Dictator's friends.

Brutus agreed that involving Albinus's gladiators as protection for the conspirators against these retired legionaries in the city was an excellent plan, and Albinus departed their meeting assured that Brutus and Cassius would proceed with Caesar's murder no matter what, with Albinus undertaking to bring both his gladiators and more friends of Caesar to the plot.[6]

Albinus was not the only man close to the Dictator who had developed severe doubts about Caesar's rule. Another of Caesar's leading generals was among those now quickly recruited to the conspiracy. Gaius Trebonius had been a tribune of the plebs in 55 B.C. before serving as a general under Caesar in both the Gallic and Civil wars. Trebonius had efficiently governed Farther Spain in 47–46 B.C., receiving the reward of a suffect consulship from Caesar in 45 B.C. and appointment as governor of the province of Asia for this year of 44 B.C., an appointment he was soon due to take up.

In Caesar's own view Trebonius was a "humane" man who had displayed both "clemency and moderation."[7] Despite these qualities, and despite having received considerable rewards from Caesar for his loyal service, and without seeking or receiving any promises of rewards from the leaders of the conspiracy, Trebonius agreed to draw his blade against Caesar and, with the other conspirators, strike him down.

With the conspirators' numbers swelling with each passing day, and with the likes of Albinus and Trebonius not only agreeing to take part in the murder but also actively contributing suggestions on courses of action, Marcus Brutus should have been feeling more and more secure about the plot. But the enormity of what he and his fellow conspirators were planning made him uneasy. Failure to act would consign Roman democracy to history. Yet the murder of any man, let alone one to whom he and his mother were attached, went against all Brutus's principles.

During the day he was able to cover that uneasiness, but at night, as he lay in his bed beside his wife, Porcia, "he was not the same man," according to Plutarch. It was not so much that he feared the conspiracy would be discovered; the weight of expectations sat heavily on his shoulders, for he felt that "the noblest spirits of Rome for virtue, birth, or courage were depending on him" to carry the assassination through.[8]

The night following Albinus's visit, Brutus's sleep was again troubled as his conscience, self-doubt, and sense of honor wrestled in his tormented mind, and several times he jerked awake. Beside him, the sensitive Porcia could not help but notice, and she became convinced that Brutus's mind was agitated by "some dangerous and perplexing question." For the moment, Porcia said nothing. Instead, she decided to embark on a dangerous course of action.[9]

# VIII

# MARCH 9, 44 B.C.

## PORCIA'S SECRET

**B**rutus's wife, Porcia, was the daughter of the famous orator Marcus Porcius Cato, known to later generations as Cato the Younger. Brutus's mother, Servilia, was Cato's half-sister, which made Brutus and Porcia cousins. Porcia had been wed once before, marrying very young to a much older man. Porcia's first husband, Marcus Bibulus, commanding admiral of republican naval forces and a bitter enemy of Julius Caesar, had died in 48 B.C. during the Civil War, but not before giving her a son, the now young adult Lucius Bibulus.

Porcia's second marriage, to the handsome, erudite Brutus, had been a true love match. She was, said Plutarch, "a great lover of her husband." Usually, Brutus shared everything with his devoted wife, and his failure to communicate the cause of his troubled sleep worried and hurt her. Porcia was a thoroughly educated and well-read woman, addicted to the works of the great philosophers. Influenced by those learned men and by the example of her famous father, she had decided to do something to prove to her husband that he could trust her with the secret that was obviously burdening his mind.[1]

As Brutus was about to leave their house that morning, Porcia asked to speak with him in private. The servants were sent out; then, according to Plutarch, Porcia said, "Brutus, being the daughter of Cato, I was given to you in marriage not like a concubine to partake only in the common intercourse of bed and board, but to bear a part of all your fortune, good and bad." A perplexed Brutus agreed that was indeed the case. That being so, said Porcia, what evidence of her love for him could he receive if he would not allow her to share his "hidden griefs" nor to be "admitted to any of your counsels that require secrecy and trust"?[2]

Brutus would have been suddenly alarmed. What did his wife know?

"I know very well that women seem to be of too weak a nature to be trusted with secrets," Porcia went on. But, she said, she was the daughter of Cato and the wife of Brutus. She was the product of a virtuous birth and an excellent education, and had mixed in the company of Rome's good and honorable elite. To prove that she had what it took to keep a secret, no matter how painful, she now confided to Brutus, she had put herself to the test, and could positively assert that she had defied pain to keep a secret of her own.[3]

Brutus was half in dread that his wife somehow knew his murderous secret. Perhaps he had talked in his sleep. The other half of him was bewildered as he attempted to fathom what Porcia may have done. Now Porcia revealed her secret. Several days before, she had taken a small knife, the kind commonly used by Roman ladies to trim their fingernails, and had plunged it into the flesh of her thigh.

The wound Porcia created was deep; blood flowed freely, and the pain was intense. Methodically, Porcia had stanched the flow of blood with a bandage, but before long she was overcome by a fever that had her shivering. It had taken all her strength to control the shivers and to bear the pain. But for days she had kept the secret of her self-inflicted wound from both her husband and her staff. Plutarch was to write that Brutus was astonished at his wife's confession. Thinking he did not believe her, Porcia raised her dress to show him the wound in her thigh. Lifting his hands to heaven, Brutus "begged the assistance of the gods in his enterprise, that he might show himself a husband worthy of such a wife as Porcia."[4]

None of the conspirators had sought or given a sacred oath to keep the plot to themselves, but all had agreed that their security depended on refraining from speaking of it to anyone other than confirmed conspirators, and even then in circumstances that ensured no one overheard them. Not one of them had told their wives about the plot. But now Brutus, embracing his wife and congratulating her on her courage, confided his secret to her. Porcia became the only wife of a conspirator who knew about the plan to murder Caesar, and she swore to her husband that she would keep the secret as soundly as she had kept the secret of her self-inflicted stab wound.

That day, the Salii priests repeated their leaping, dancing, and chanting through the streets of Rome, then sat down to another sumptuous feast, as tradition required them to do. They would repeat the ritual for a third time that month, on the twenty-third day of March. During the day, too, Brutus met with several confederates and discussed the finer details of the plan they intended executing in just six days' time. A number of conspirators wanted to approach Mark Antony and bring him into the plot. It must have been obvious to many senators that Antony's relationship with Caesar, while repaired over the past few months, was not on a particularly strong footing, and that Antony seemed to be dissatisfied with having to play second fiddle to Lepidus.

The idea of recruiting Antony was knocked on the head by Trebonius. He was close to Antony; so close that, when word had reached Rome the previous October that Caesar was approaching Rome on his way back from Spain, Trebonius and Antony had set off together to meet the Dictator, and the pair had shared accommodation at roadside inns after each leg of the journey north. As Trebonius revealed to Brutus and Cassius, by that time, even before Caesar returned to Rome and was made Dictator for life, Trebonius was himself already thinking seriously about assassinating his leader. And in the privacy of their shared lodgings, Trebonius had dropped hints to Antony about combining to overthrow Caesar. Trebonius had been convinced that Antony "very well understood him," but Antony "did not encourage" him to take what he was proposing further. "However, he [Antony] had said nothing about it to Caesar, but kept the secret faithfully."[5]

If Antony was not to join them, several conspirators said, then they must also kill him at the same time that Caesar was struck down. This idea rapidly caught on, until it came to Brutus's ears. Brutus was quick to snuff it out. As he reminded his colleagues, the justification for murdering Caesar was that he had become a tyrant, and they were on the side of right because they were defending Rome's ancient laws, upon which Caesar had trampled. "Tyrannicide," the murder of a tyrannical leader, was not a crime under Roman law. But if they also killed Antony, it would look for all the world as if the conspirators' actual motive was revenge against Caesar and Antony for defeating Pompey. Brutus's view prevailed, and Antony's life was preserved, with unimagined consequences.

With Antony to be spared, it was agreed that it would pay the conspirators to physically separate him from Caesar on the day of the assassination. Antony was a man "whose bodily strength and high office made him formidable."[6] As an experienced soldier and powerfully built individual, Antony might succeed in defending Caesar, or in killing several of his assailants. Furthermore, as Caesar's co-consul, his presence beside the Dictator might deter some senators from striking Caesar, or he might rally others to his defense. Someone Antony knew and trusted would have to detain him in conversation outside the Senate building on the Ides of March as Caesar was entering. Antony needed delaying just long enough for the other conspirators to strike down Caesar inside the meeting hall. This task was delegated to Antony's friend Decimus Brutus Albinus.

Marcus Brutus discussed and agreed on these life-and-death matters knowing that his wife, alone among all the wives of the conspirators, was fully conversant with the plot to murder Caesar. While Brutus trusted Porcia implicitly, he did not tell Cassius or any of the others that Porcia knew. It must be remembered that most Roman men, even the most enlightened, felt that women were inferior, fickle, empty-headed, and untrustworthy beings. For Brutus to reveal that a woman was privy to their life-and-death secret might have been enough to panic some of his fellow plotters into doing something that would endanger the plot, and endanger the lives of them all.

# IX

# MARCH 14, 44 B.C., AFTERNOON

## CLEOPATRA AND THE EQUIRRIA

T wenty-five-year-old Cleopatra had brought her three-year-old son Caesarion with her to Rome. According to Suetonius, Mark Antony would confirm in the Senate that Caesarion was indeed Caesar's progeny. Suetonius also wrote that Caesar's close friends Gaius Oppius and Gaius Matius were similarly aware of the child's paternity. Just the same, Oppius later published a book in which he set out to prove that the boy was *not* Caesar's son.[1] But these claims and counterclaims came after Caesar's death, at a time when Caesarion became a political pawn, with his paternity an issue used by Antony and his opponents to further their own causes.

No one disputed that Cleopatra had a lengthy affair with Caesar, and there were those who were convinced that Caesar planned to divorce his current wife, Calpurnia, and marry Cleopatra. Under prevailing Roman law, Caesar was prevented from making Cleopatra his wife. That law banned Romans from marrying foreigners. Caesar was preparing a remedy for that obstacle, for in the writings of the Tribune of the Plebeians Helvius Cinna would be found the claim that Caesar had commissioned him to draw up a special bill for presentation to the Roman "commons," the Comitia, or assembly of the common people.

This Comitia served as a lower house to the Senate, rather like the lower house in a modern parliament. The tribunes of the plebeians were elected by the Comitia; some trials could be conducted in front of the Comitia; certain laws could be passed by the Comitia, and some decrees approved by it; this assembly even could declare war on Rome's enemies. According to Suetonius, Cinna the tribune revealed that Caesar had commissioned him to prepare legislation he was to present to the Comitia once the Dictator had set off for the East, legislation "legitimizing his marriage with any woman, or women, he pleased, 'for the procreation of children.'"[2]

Cleopatra had grown up in Egypt seducing and manipulating men, initially to survive, later to achieve her own political ambitions. Her lover prior to Caesar, for example, had been Pompey's eldest son, Gnaeus, when he was stationed in Alexandria. Now she would have had expectations that she would become Caesar's wife, and that her son Caesarion would become his legitimate heir and successor.

Officially, Cleopatra had come to Rome with her brother and son at the invitation of the Senate. Cassius Dio was to write that they "settled" in Caesar's villa on the far side of the Tiber, with Cleopatra and Ptolemy accepting the titles "Friends and Allies of the Roman People" from the Senate, honors given, of course, at Caesar's bidding. Many a senator, led by the praetors, would have paid Cleopatra and her brother official visits at her trans-Tiber resort, while the Dictator himself had the excuse of visiting his own villa when he went there. With Cleopatra and her brother living across the Tiber in Caesar's villa, month in, month out, "he derived an ill repute on account of both of them." Yet, "he was not at all concerned about this."[3]

Nor was he concerned by the persistent rumor currently swirling around Rome "that Caesar intended to move the seat of government to Troy or Alexandria" to be close to Cleopatra, "carrying off all the national resources, drafting every available man in Italy for military service, and letting his friends govern the city" of Rome.[4] Such a prospect would have horrified most Romans.

Cleopatra was no great beauty. The few surviving classical images of her depict a young woman with a good figure but a long, unattractive nose. But there is more to seductive power than good looks. Plutarch was to say that while Plato had described four different ways of flattery, Cleopatra possessed a thousand ways to flatter.[5] The skill to flatter men had been developed of necessity when she was growing up in a royal palace at Alexandria racked with plots, intrigues, and changing allegiances that had eventually seen her at war with her own siblings.

Cleopatra was also highly intelligent, well educated, and multitalented. The Egyptian royal family of this time was actually Macedonian, having descended from Alexander the Great's general Ptolemy, who, after Alexander's death, made himself Egypt's first king of the Macedonian line. These Egyptian royals spoke Greek as their native tongue, and as Plutarch was to note, few of them even bothered to learn Egyptian, the language spoken by their subjects. Cleopatra was the exception; not only did she learn to speak Egyptian like a native, she also was fluent in many of the languages of the East, Hebrew, Parthian, and Mede among them.[6]

Because Suetonius indicated, obscurely, that Cleopatra may have left Rome by this time to return to Alexandria, some modern authors have placed her back in Egypt by March 44 B.C. But having settled in Caesar's villa just outside urban Rome, and having only recently convinced Caesar to have Roman law changed so she could become his wife, there was no earthly reason for the wily Cleopatra to have gone back to the East. Egypt was now a kingdom in name only. Four Roman legions now occupied the country.[7]

Those legions were commanded by one of Caesar's favorites, a freedman's son—another source of complaint by the Dictator's critics.[8] Those occupying legions, and that freedman, were the true rulers of Egypt now. Living in Caesar's villa on the Janiculum, Cleopatra was close to Caesar, and close to the center of the government of the ancient world. From the Janiculum, she was able to use her talents to manipulate both, in her favor.

Inside the Janiculum villa on March 14, affairs would have been in a state of flux. Without doubt, Cleopatra, her brother the king, and their large entourage had plans to join Caesar's column when it left Rome in five days' time as he set off for his much-anticipated Getae and Parthian campaigns. Caesar would march overland to Macedonia, where half a dozen legions were at this moment awaiting the arrival of their commander in chief. Perhaps the Egyptian royals intended waiting in Macedonia, or maybe at Athens, while Caesar dealt with the Getae, or perhaps they planned to part company with him there and continue on to Alexandria.

As hundreds of servants busied themselves packing the king and queen's belongings for the journey back to the East, those at the villa on the Janiculum would have been attracted to the eastern windows by the distant roar of tens of thousands of massed voices from the other side of the Tiber. March 14 was another religious holiday on the Roman calendar. Called the Equirria, it was said to have been established by

Romulus himself. Dedicated to Mars, god of war, this was an equine festival celebrated by horse races of chariots drawn by teams of two horses, as opposed to the four-horse teams used in the most spectacular chariot-racing competitions.

For the Equirria Festival, the day's horse racing was conducted not at the usual venue, the Circus Maximus, but on a temporary racetrack mapped out on the Field of Mars, north of the city walls. Wooden stands had been erected around the long U-shaped track in the days leading up to the Equirria, and now the thousands of spectators lucky enough to secure tickets were cheering on their chosen teams.

For Romans, chariot racing had become more than a religious festivity, more even than a sport. It was almost a religion in itself. Four teams contested each race, one supplied by each of Rome's four racing corporations, the Greens, the Blues, the Reds, and the Whites. Many Romans were lifelong followers of one racing team or another, and it is from them that we have inherited the concept of and passion for sports teams. There was the added incentive that gambling on contests of physical skill such as chariot races was legal, and large amounts of money changed hands over every race.

With each chariot race, be it using two-horse teams or four, the object was to be first past the post after completing seven hectic circuits of the long, thin course, passing along the right side of the central spine that divided the track. That seven-lap circuit involved a total distance of about four miles. The stands were packed with excited spectators. The wealthy were armed with programs etched in ivory that listed the names of the drivers and horses for each race. To show which team they supported, spectators wore flowers, ribbons, and scarves in their team colors.

Among the spectators on this colorful day would have been the recently retired legionaries camped around the city, unarmed, but easily distinguishable by the berry-red military tunics still worn by many, which were a little shorter than the civilian tunic. In the official box, presiding over this festival to Mars, sat the most senior priest at Rome; today it would have been the pontifex maximus, Julius Caesar.

The roar of the crowd ebbed away. Another race had been run and won. The debris of an upturned chariot was quickly removed, an injured rider carried off, his bolting horses wrangled and led away. The spirits of the Roman people were high. Little did they know that before another day had passed their world would be turned upside down, like a crashing chariot, by the murder of their ruler.

## X

# MARCH 14, 44 B.C., EVENING

## THE BEST SORT OF DEATH

**A**fter returning from the races to his Via Sacra residence, Caesar may have gone to the bathhouse. Then, refreshed and dressed, he would have slipped into his litter. The litter, the preferred form of travel for the Roman elite, was like a bed with carrying poles, the top equipped with a frame supporting curtains that could be closed. Litter curtains were invariably closed when the modest Roman matron, wearing headdress and veil, was borne about. Caesar was carried by brawny slaves a short distance to the city mansion of Marcus Lepidus, the Dictator's Master of Equestrians and deputy. The precise location of Lepidus's home is unknown, but it is likely to have been on the Palatine Hill or the Aventine Hill, both then favored locations for the homes of the wealthy.

Caesar's litter crossed the city escorted by the twenty-four lictors to which he was entitled as Dictator. Lictors were often former centurions. In official processions, each lictor carried a bundle of rods tied with red ribbon surrounding an ax, symbolizing the Roman magistrate's right of punishment, his power over life and death. Under Roman law, a citizen condemned to execution for a capital crime was whipped with rods, then beheaded. On informal occasions such as this visit to a friend's house for a private dinner, a Dictator's lictors preceded the litter carrying wooden staves, clearing the way.

Caesar had not always been accompanied by such a small escort. The previous December, when he had visited the western coast of Italy for rest and recreation following his return from the war in Spain, he had been surrounded by an escort of two thousand horsemen. Many of these men had been the bearded, long-haired Germans of the loyal mounted bodyguard that had accompanied Caesar everywhere during the Gallic War and Civil War.

One of the people Caesar had called on during this sojourn on the western coast had been Cicero. The orator had written to a friend about the Dictator's stay at his seaside villa at Puteoli, on the Bay of Naples, on December 19: "The house was so thronged by the soldiers that there was hardly a spare room for Caesar himself to dine in. Two thousand men, no less!" These troops had pitched tents in the villa's garden, and a guard was placed on the house as if it were a military camp.[1]

By March, Caesar's trusty German bodyguards had left Italy, apparently allowed to go home to retirement by Caesar after their long service, in many cases having served him for as much as a decade. Two of Caesar's closest subordinates by this time, his longtime aide Aulus Hirtius and Gaius Pansa, both of whom Caesar had appointed consuls for the next year, urged him to maintain a strong bodyguard, for they "had always warned Caesar that he must hold by arms the position which he had won by arms."[2]

Hirtius and Pansa were undoubtedly the friends who, according to Appian, had wanted him to employ as his bodyguard in Rome a cohort or two of the retired Spanish legionaries now camped on Tiber Island and elsewhere around Rome. Cohorts from one of the Spanish legions, the 7th, had acted as his bodyguard when he returned to Rome between Civil War campaigns in 47 B.C. Appian said of Caesar's friends, "When they inquired if he would agree to having the Spanish cohorts as his bodyguard again, he said, 'There is no worse fate than to be continuously protected, for that means you are in constant fear.'"[3] Velleius Paterculus repeated the sentiment: "Caesar kept reiterating that he would rather die than live in fear."[4]

The ancient laws of Rome forbade armed men from entering the gates of the city in times of peace. The situation had been markedly different in 47 B.C.; a civil war was in progress then, and three rebellious, fully armed legions had been encamped on the Campus Martius, just outside the city walls, making a large armed escort a necessity. Now no such obvious threat existed. While Caesar had trampled on numerous ancient laws, to have been seen with an armed escort inside the city now, in peacetime, would have signaled his fear of assassination. Caesar was astute enough to realize that the appearance of fear gives hope to adversaries, and that by showing fear we often ignite the very thing we seek to protect ourselves against. The deflection of threat by a display of fearlessness is the basis of many a proverb.

It was known at this time that Caesar was not a well man. Suetonius reported that Caesar's health was in decline, while fellow historian Appian wrote, "He suffered from epileptic fits and sudden spasms, particularly when he was not busy."[5] Suetonius said that the knowledge of Caesar's declining health made some of his friends later suspect that he had dispensed with bodyguards because he no longer desired to live much longer.[6]

Yet Caesar was about to throw himself into a three-year military campaign, which was surely not something a man in poor health or with a death wish would undertake. Suetonius wrote that it also had been suggested that Caesar placed complete confidence in the decree made during the last sitting of the Senate in which all senators and Equestrians had vowed to act as his protectors. "A contrary view," Suetonius went on, "is that he deliberately exposed himself just this once to all the plots against his life which he knew had been formed."[7] Why Caesar would do that—through an intention to out those who wished him dead, or because of a death wish, perhaps—we are not told.

Yet Caesar seems to have genuinely believed that no Roman would strike against him. It was his view that the alternative to his dictatorship was chaos. Likewise, he believed that all thinking Romans shared his view and, for their own good, would do whatever they could to preserve his life and rule. It was almost as if Caesar considered his rule blessed by the gods. Suetonius wrote, "He is quoted as having often said: 'It is more important for Rome than for myself that I should survive. I have long been sated with power and glory, but should anything happen to me, Rome will enjoy no peace. A new civil war will break out under far worse conditions than the last.'"[8]

Even Caesar's lictors would have been left in an anteroom as he joined Lepidus in his dining room for the evening's repast on March 14. Lepidus had become Caesar's most trusted subordinate after favorites such as Antony and Dolabella had disappointed him. Lepidus was a man of good family, being the son of a consul. Ambitious, he had chosen to throw in his lot with the man he felt would win the Civil War, after Caesar had proven victorious against Pompey's legions in Spain. As a praetor in 49 B.C., Lepidus had led the Senate assembled at Rome by Caesar in proclaiming him Dictator for the first time. For his reward, Lepidus had received the governorship of Nearer Spain from Caesar. He had occupied that post in 48–47 B.C., showing both initiative and resolve in a difficult situation As a consequence, Caesar had appointed him his co-consul in 46 B.C.

Lepidus had married one of Marcus Brutus's half-sisters, another Junia—the women's clan name was Junius. Despite this family connection, Brutus was not close to Lepidus in the way he was close to his other brother-in-law, Cassius. Brutus would never have entertained the idea of approaching Lepidus to draw him into the murder conspiracy. No one, apart from Julius Caesar, felt that Lepidus could be entirely trusted. Lepidus was, in the opinion of Velleius Paterculus, "the most fickle of mankind."[9] Lepidus was considered by contemporaries to be such a weathercock, inclining in the direction of the prevailing political wind, that the conspirators feared that were the murder plot revealed to him by Brutus or another conspirator he would almost certainly rush to tell Caesar.

Coin portraits of Lepidus show a bony man with a large, angular nose, small chin, long neck, and thick hair brushed back. As he had demonstrated during his time in charge in Nearer Spain, he had tact and guile in sufficient measure to act as a conciliator. Compared to immature young Dolabella and boorish Antony, Lepidus would have seemed to Caesar, of all his leading subordinates, to have been almost statesmanlike.

This dinner hosted by Lepidus was an intimate affair, an opportunity for Caesar to relax out of the limelight after a day in front of the crowds at the races. Lepidus's only other dinner guest was Decimus Brutus Albinus—unbeknownst to him, one of the men plotting to kill Caesar. Not only did Caesar rank Albinus among his most trusted associates, it also would be revealed once the contents of his will became public that he considered him like family, making him his heir in the second degree—Roman heirs in the second degree inherited when heirs of the first degree were unable or unwilling to accept a bequest. Under the terms of this will, Caesar even made provision to adopt Albinus as his son should he inherit his estate.

With these two valued and trusted lieutenants, Caesar could drop his guard this evening. The meal they shared would not have been lavish. Unlike many wealthy Romans—Mark Antony, for example—Caesar was not known as a fussy eater or a man who enjoyed large banquets.

Just the opposite, in fact. According to Gaius Oppius, his aide through-out the Civil War, Caesar cared little for good food.[10] Caesar's was "a coarse diet," said Plutarch.[11] He had a soldier's plain taste. Nor did he like to be seen to be eating any better than his guests, on one occasion clapping his baker in irons for serving him better bread at dinner than that provided to his guests.[12]

A famous story related about Caesar by several classical authors told of the time he went to supper at the house of Valerius Leo at Mediolanum in Cisalpine Gaul, today's Milan in northern Italy. "A dish of asparagus was put before him on which his host instead of [olive] oil had poured sweet ointment," said Plutarch. "Caesar partook of it without any disgust, and reprimanded his friends for finding fault with it." 'It is enough not to eat what you did not like,' Caesar is reported to have said to his companions, "but he who reflects on another man's lack of breeding shows he lacks it as much himself.'"[13]

Only occasionally did Caesar eat and drink with abandon. Cicero wrote, of Caesar's reaction to the banquet the orator put on for him on December 19, 45 B.C., "He was following a course of emetics." That is, Caesar deliberately vomited up all he ate after the meal. This was prescribed by physicians of the day as a means of improving health. "And so [he] both ate and drank with uninhibited enjoyment. It was really a fine, well-appointed meal." Over dinner the Dictator and the orator had talked of mainly literary matters. "All in all, he was pleased, and enjoyed himself." Having to also feed Caesar's vast entourage had proven a burden to Cicero. It was, he wrote to a friend, "A visit, or should I call it a billeting, which as I said was troublesome to me but not disagreeable."[14]

With Caesar reclining on a dining couch in Lepidus's triclinium between Lepidus and Albinus as they ate, Caesar probably related a story about a recent visit from Cicero later repeated to Cicero by Gaius Matius, a friend of Caesar for many years. Cicero had gone to the Regia to seek a favor on behalf of one of his friends, Publius Sestius. Seeing Cicero sitting in the Regia vestibule, waiting to be summoned, Caesar had said to Matius, who was with him at the time, "There is Marcus Cicero sitting waiting and cannot get to see me at his own convenience. He is the most easygoing of mankind, but I don't doubt that he detests me."[15]

Caesar had been not far from the mark. Cicero, while keeping it to himself, at this time considered Caesar a "vile being" and a tyrant.[16] Had Brutus and the murder conspirators only known it, they could have signed Cicero up for the assassination plot without fear of negativity.

The Dictator, Cicero would write in April, had become the object of his "hatred and grief."[17]

The main subject of dinner conversation among Caesar, Lepidus, and Albinus on March 14 would undoubtedly have been Caesar's upcoming military campaign. All the preparations had been made. The legions had their marching orders, and they and thousands of cavalrymen from around Caesar's empire were honing their fighting skills with final training. Supplies were being readied. Weapons and ammunition had been manufactured and stockpiled. Many middle-ranking officers of Equestrian rank had already left Rome to join their units.

More senior officers would accompany Caesar when he departed the capital on March 19. Lepidus would remain at Rome. The position of Master of Equestrians made Lepidus the most powerful of all the Roman magistrates in Caesar's absence, with only the tribunes of the plebs retaining any real power. By the end of spring, other men among Caesar's subordinates also would depart from Rome to take up provincial commands; in Albinus's case, he was due to leave Rome for the governorship of Cisalpine Gaul, and under Roman law must depart the capital before spring ended.

Over dinner, it is likely that Caesar told Lepidus and Albinus how much he was looking forward to being joined on the campaign by his niece's son Gaius Octavius—Octavian, as he would be called by later historians. Now eighteen, Octavius had joined Caesar for the last stages of the war in Spain in 45 B.C. and, along with Albinus, had accompanied Caesar back to Rome in October. Caesar had then sent the youth to Apollonia in Epirus, western Greece, a renowned educational center. Caesar's plan for Octavius, said Velleius Paterculus, who later knew and served him, was "a view to training his remarkable talents by liberal studies" for six months at Apollonia, "with the intention of taking him with him as his companion in his contemplated wars with the Getae and the Parthians."[18]

Over the past few months, squadrons of cavalry had regularly ridden down to Apollonia from the legion camp in Macedonia to join Octavius, so he could train with them and improve his riding skills and javelin-throwing in preparation for the new military campaign.[19] Caesar had seen great potential in the youth and had come to consider young Octavius like a son, as his will would soon attest.

Caesar drank conservatively at Lepidus's dinner. He was noted for being an abstemious drinker. Cato the Younger had said of him, "Caesar was the only sober man who ever tried to wreck the Constitution."[20] But this did not prevent him from joining his companions in a cup or two of wine following their March 14 meal—many Romans diluted their wine by adding water, up to five times as much water as wine. Caesar never allowed his mind to be idle, often dictating two or more letters at the same time to several secretaries while traveling. Now, according to Plutarch, once the table had been cleared after the meal and the trio chatted over their wine cups, Caesar's male secretary brought him several letters to sign.

As he was signing, either Lepidus or Albinus, but more likely Albinus, put a philosophical question: "What sort of death is best?"

Caesar immediately answered, "A sudden one."[21]

Albinus, as he made his way back to his city *domus* in his litter that evening following dinner with the Dictator, would have reflected on the irony of Caesar's answer. Albinus and his fellow conspirators intended to give Caesar his preferred sudden death within hours.

# PART TWO

# THE MURDER

# XI

# MARCH 15, 44 B.C.,
# THE IDES OF MARCH

## CAESAR AWAKENS

O n Tiber Island, a strong and sudden breeze would have been making the torches that illuminated the single sacred standard behind which the retired legionaries marched flicker violently. Were this still a serving legion, legion trumpeters would be marking changes of watches every three hours, and three sentries would have taken station outside the *praetorium*, or headquarters, eight outside the quarters of the legion's duty tribune, ten at each of the camp gates, and one at every group of twenty tents.[1] But all was quiet on Tiber Island, as the former soldiers slumbered on.

Across the city, the breeze gusted so strongly at the Regia on the Via Sacra that all the window shutters and the door of Julius Caesar's bedchamber flew open.[2] The wind was so strong that it even rattled the sacred spears of Mars in the shrine next door to the Dictator's bedchamber.[3] Caesar, apparently a light sleeper, awoke with a start. Moonlight flooded into the room. Sitting up, Caesar looked at his wife, Calpurnia, lying, asleep still, beside him.[4]

Calpurnia was Caesar's third wife, having married him in 59 B.C. The first, Cornelia Cinnilla, his wife for close to fifteen years, had died in childbirth. Caesar's second wife had been Pompeia, granddaughter of Sulla the Dictator, whom he had divorced after six years following the Clodius incident. But if Cleopatra had her way, Caesar also would divorce Calpurnia and make the Egyptian queen his next wife. Divorce was, after all, simple for Romans. It was instant, at the wish of either party or both, and required no formality, documentation, or involvement from a third party.

Caesar was infamous for his rampant sexuality. According to Suetonius, Caesar had a long list of affairs with the wives of other leading men of Rome, including the senator Servius Sulpicius's wife, Postumia; the elderly general Aulus Gabinius's wife, Lollia; Marcus Crassus's wife, Tertulla; and Pompey the Great's wife, Mucia. He also had kept several mistresses at various times, including Eunoe, queen of Mauritania, not to mention Cleopatra.

"But Marcus Brutus's mother, Servilia, was the woman whom Caesar loved best," said Suetonius.[5] "And she [was] passionately in love with him," said Plutarch.[6] Their illicit relationship, which may or may not have spawned Brutus, had begun and ended in their youth, but had resumed when Caesar became consul in 61 B.C., when he separated from Pompeia. According to Suetonius, Caesar had at that time given Servilia a pearl worth 240,000 sesterces; its worth can be compared to the annual salary of Caesar's legionaries, of 900 sesterces. Between 49 and 45 B.C., during the Civil War, said Suetonius, Caesar had continued to give Servilia presents, "as well as knocking down certain valuable estates to her at a public auction for a song." It was even rumored, said Suetonius, that Servilia "was also suspected at the time of having prostituted her daughter Tertia to Caesar."[7]

Calpurnia must have known about Caesar's affairs and mistresses, which continued throughout their marriage, yet there is no record of her ever complaining about her husband's roving eye, to him or to anyone else. Normally a pragmatic, unemotional woman, she remained the constant, faithful, supportive wife through it all. It was common for wealthy and powerful Roman men to have numerous affairs, and like so many Roman wives, Calpurnia looked the other way as Caesar bedded his various conquests. What Calpurnia thought of her husband keeping Cleopatra just across the Tiber can only be imagined; perhaps it made her all the more determined not to give Caesar cause to divorce her.

Lying beside Caesar in the bed now, Calpurnia was murmuring to herself, and groaning; she was having a troubling dream.[8] Caesar let her sleep. After quietly closing the door and shutters, he returned to the bed, eased back down beside his wife, and went back to sleep.

# XII

# MARCH 15, 44 B.C.,
# THE IDES OF MARCH

## IN THE DARK BEFORE DAWN

**W**ell before sunrise, scores of members of Rome's male elite crowded noisily into Gaius Cassius's city house. Using the excuse of a party to celebrate the coming of age of his son, Cassius had organized a meeting where all the members of the conspiracy to murder Julius Caesar could meet en masse for the first time. Of the hundred or so senators and members of the Equestrian Order invited to Cassius's house this morning, more than sixty were party to the assassination plot.[1] This gathering would give the more committed plotters the opportunity to bolster the courage of their more nervous associates in crime and let them see the quality and number of the men who were prepared to strike a blow against kingship and for democracy.

In two days' time, on March 17, it would be the Liberalia, the religious festival when, traditionally, Rome's young men officially came of age. In Roman society, a youth came of age at the Liberalia closest to his sixteenth birthday, meaning that many actually came of age at fifteen. Just as an eighteenth birthday is a time when friends and family gather to celebrate the coming of age of their children today, the Romans, from whom we derive this coming-of-age custom, also made the Liberalia a time of celebration.

Cassius had brought the Liberalia party of his son forward by two days, apparently using the excuse of pressure of public business in the days leading up to Caesar's departure to the East for the early celebration. The real reason was, clearly, to provide the occasion for the meeting of all the assassination conspirators under the one roof without raising any suspicions.

Because some of those attending the party were not members of the conspiracy, those who were had to be careful what they said, speaking in innuendo to those whom they knew to be their fellow conspirators. This would have lent the affair a certain air of excitement, which, combined with apprehension about the success or failure of the venture, would have sent adrenaline pumping through the plotters' veins at a rapid rate.

As Cassius welcomed his guests, who would have included relatives, clients, and old friends, he was one of the few present who would have known the identity of each conspirator. The central core of conspiratorial leaders—Cassius, Brutus, Labeo, Albinus, and Trebonius—had been the plot's motivators and recruiters, and during the coming-of-age gathering those present would have carefully introduced plotters to one another using words and signs that revealed that each was in the same conspiratorial boat. The conspirators had come to the party ready for the day's business. Over a plain tunic they wore a white toga with a thick purple border. The toga was the tuxedo of the ancient world, worn only on official occasions, and the toga with a thick purple border was the sole preserve of members of the Roman Senate.

This toga, no more than a large piece of woolen cloth, was worn in a very particular way, so that the left arm was covered. Only the right arm was left exposed. This permitted the conspirators to conceal a dagger beneath the left arm. Before Marcus Brutus had left home that morning, his wife, Porcia, now privy to the murder plot, had helped him strap a dagger under his arm. Here, now, in Cassius's house, were the conspirators, wearing their togas and carrying their concealed murder weapons.

Apart from Cassius, Brutus, and Labeo, the conspirators included a number of men with similar backgrounds to themselves, supporters of the Republic and opponents of Caesar during the Civil War, men who had all been pardoned by Caesar during or after that war. They included the praetor Sextius Nasso, the senators Rubrius Ruga, Quintus Ligarius, and Marcus Spurius, the brothers Caecilius and Bucilianus, and the tribune of the plebs Pontius Aquila.[2]

From among Caesar's subordinates and supporters, in addition to Albinus and Trebonius, conspirators numbered leading senators such as Servius Sulpicius Galba, a praetor in 54 B.C., who had served Caesar faithfully throughout the Gallic and civil wars. Others from Caesar's own ranks included Lucius Tillius Cimber, Minucius Basilus, and the brothers Gaius and Publius Servilius Casca, who were both current tribunes of the plebs.[3]

Several of these men, from both camps, undoubtedly had personal axes to grind with Caesar: Aquila the humiliated tribune, for example. Likewise, it was rumored that Caesar had once seduced Galba's wife, reason enough for Galba to bear him a grudge. But others who were close to Caesar, such as Albinus and Trebonius, had no apparent reason to join the plot other than the stated motive of pulling down a tyrant and restoring the Republic. Even family members turned against Caesar—Lucius Cornelius Cinna, brother of Caesar's first wife, was still considered family by Caesar, who made him a praetor this year of 44 B.C. Yet Cinna, too, had become one of the assassins.

There were others in the crowd at Cassius's house who might have been invited to join the plot, men such Marcus Favonius, had their responses to guarded test questions not made the plotters wary of revealing the scheme to them. There can be no doubt that Cassius would have preferred to have made the much-admired elder statesman Marcus Cicero the spiritual leader of the plot, had Cicero not been inclined to philosophize when the times called for action. As it was, Cicero was currently away from Rome, staying at one of his many country estates.

Now, the coming-of-age ceremonial involving Cassius's son took place. It was called the *deposito barbae*. As the guests crowded into the reception room, Cassius's boy took a seat on a stool and was surrounded by proud and excited male slaves, servants of the Cassius household. A wrap of cambric or muslin was tied around the youth's neck before a servant wet the boy's face with water from a silver bowl. At this time, and until the second century, it was the custom for all Roman citizens to be clean-shaven. Only in the reign of the emperor Hadrian would beards, which were long common among "barbarians" such as the Germans, become universally fashionable. On the other hand, it was the Roman custom that boys who had not come of age never shaved. Their first shave came on the occasion of their coming-of-age party, when the full beard or few wispy hairs on their jaw were removed as part of the deposito barbae ceremony.

Cassius's personal barber, his *tonsor*, now stepped up and took an iron razor from a tray held by another servant. The barber would have made a great show of sharpening the razor on a whetstone, lubricating the blade by spitting on it. As the barber commenced to shave the youth, yet another servant stood by with a bowl containing spiderwebs soaked in oil and vinegar, which would be quickly applied to any nicks or cuts. But Cassius's barber would have been expert at his trade, and there would have been no need of the spiderwebs today. Each hair removed from the boy's face was placed in a small golden casket made specially for the deposito. When the last hair was removed, the barber closed the casket and, to the cheers and applause of the watching guests, turned and presented it to the proud father.

Cassius would then have left the room, taking the casket to the house's private chapel, which, in the homes of ancient Romans, could range from a small, dedicated room to just a wooden cupboard in a corner. The casket was deposited in the chapel as an offering to Capitoline Jupiter. In the *Satyricon*, first-century Roman author Petronius Arbiter has his hero place a deposito casket between the silver statuettes of his two *lares*, or household gods, and a statuette of the goddess Venus.

By the time Cassius returned to the gathering, his seated son's face had been washed and freshened with water and soft, sweet-smelling oil. Cassius called on the young man to stand, then took a plain white garment, the *toga virulus* (toga of manhood), and personally draped it on his son. To the applause of the guests, the servants then led the boy from the room. His father and all the guests fell in behind. The entire gathering then walked from Cassius's house to the Forum, where Cassius perambulated his son for all the world to see, clad in his manly gown for the first time, as was the custom. From there, with Cassius's chattering household servants escorting the young man home, Cassius and his guests set out for Pompey's Theater and the momentous Senate sitting.[4]

In groups large and small, and preceded by torch-bearing attendants, the senators bustled through the capital's streets. Around them, the city stirred, and other members of the House not invited to Cassius's celebration joined the exodus from the city, making their way on foot or carried in litters from the city proper to the temporary Senate House on the Field of Mars.

To replace the republican Senate, Caesar had stacked the House with men who would support him in return for their elevation. The precise number of senators who made their way to the Theater of Pompey on the Ides of March is not recorded, but it would have been many hundreds.

The first light of dawn was just beginning to streak the eastern horizon as the senators made their way from the suburbs and out of the northern city gates. The Roman day always began this early; Senate sittings invariably commenced at dawn, and could run all day until dusk, without a break.

Caesar had personally chosen the site for the day's sitting, the Theater of Pompey. Prior to the Civil War, Pompey the Great had erected this complex to house the city's first permanent drama theater, paying for it from his own pocket. It had been dedicated in 55 B.C., but by 44 B.C. the vast complex, which included four temples, including one, ironically, dedicated to Luck, and an art gallery, was still a work in progress. Rome's first emperor, Augustus, would complete the project.

By these Ides of March, the majority of the work had been done. The huge, roofless theater, built in tufa and travertine to the semicircular pattern established by the Greeks for their drama theaters, was already being used for drama, comedy, mime, poetry readings, and musical concerts, and could accommodate several thousand people on its tiered seating.[5]

Two pillared porticoes extended from the theater, running east either side of a garden to a lofty vestibule. The vestibule was fronted by a line of columns, from which a broad flight of stone steps ran down to the street. The theater's vestibule was so vast that large meetings could be held beneath its soaring roof. Today's sitting of the Senate was due to take place in this vestibule, which some later authors would call the Hall of Pompey; others, Pompey's Assembly Room; others still, the Portico of Pompey, or Pompey's Porch.

Today, Decimus Brutus Albinus's troupe of gladiators was onstage in the theater. Their number is unknown, but a troupe of several hundred was probable. Arriving well before sunup, the gladiators were rehearsing the exhibition that Albinus had promised to give Caesar once the business of the Senate was wrapped up. Because the wall behind the stage had yet to be completed, a temporary screen rose up behind the stage, preventing anyone on the porticoes or vestibule from seeing into the theater.

These gladiators, usually either slaves or prisoners of war, were trained for individual combat, in which they excelled. As later Civil War experience was to prove, generally, gladiators were no match for legionaries when the soldiers fought as a unit. The gladiators' standard weapons were sword, javelin, trident, and net. Some carried shields, and all wore armor of one type or another. Their skin shining with body oil and marked by scars from past combat, these physically fit, well-fed professional fighters made imposing figures.

In the theater's vestibule, slaves were making final preparations for the day's Senate sitting. Wooden benches had been arranged in several curving rows, facing a single, low-backed chair made of gold and ivory—the arms of which were probably solid elephant tusks—and decorated with precious stones. This throne had been crafted for Caesar on the orders of his Senate, just one of the many honors bestowed on him his since he had come to power. Caesar's throne had been put in position by the attendant whose sole task was its care.

Male secretaries at desks set to one side were preparing piles of wax writing tablets. It was Caesar who, in 59 B.C., when consul for the first time, had required that every word spoken in the Senate be recorded verbatim and kept in the official archives, the Tabularium. These Senate records were known as the Acta Senatus, and, at this time in Roman history, could be consulted at the Tabularium by the general public. The emperor Augustus would revoke this right, after which the Senate records could only be consulted with the emperor's permission.

The Senate secretaries used the Roman shorthand invented by Marcus Cicero's secretary, the freed slave Tiro, "by means of which," Seneca observed, "even a rapidly delivered speech is taken down."[6] Inscribed in wax, this shorthand would later be written out in full, in ink, on papyrus rolls, for filing and access at the Tabularium. These records would be destroyed in the famous A.D. 64 Great Fire of Rome; those that were originated after that date would fall victim to the fifth-century barbarian sack of Rome.

The other Senate staff included the water-clock attendants, who would have been checking that their devices were in working order. As soon as the sun was fully over the horizon, the water in the mechanisms would be permitted to begin to trickle, to record the passing of the first hour of the day. These devices were not particularly accurate. Seneca would quip, a century later, that all the philosophers of Rome were more likely to agree than the city's water clocks.[7] But at least the clocks gave an indication of time to senators cloistered in the Senate House all day.

Outside, at the bottom of the steps, security was provided by a company of members of the Equestrian Order, who traditionally guarded sittings of the Senate. By this time, the ancient Praetorian Guard had fallen into disuse; within months of Caesar's death Mark Antony would reform that famous corps, as his personal bodyguard unit. The task of the company of Equestrians today was to screen all persons entering the

Theater of Pompey. They would only grant admittance to the vestibule to senators. Unlike Rome's courts, there was no provision for a public gallery in the Senate.

At this time, senators were not searched for weapons. In the first century, several emperors would employ that practice, but in 44 B.C. the Equestrians providing security would of course have stopped any senator seen to have a weapon on his person; a sword, for example would have been virtually impossible to hide, even under a toga. Writing almost three hundred years later, Cassius Dio would claim that in the planning stage of the murder plot, the conspirators had intended to have "swords instead of documents brought into the chamber in boxes."[8] No other classical source mentions this. In the event, other classical sources spoke of daggers, not swords, as the weapons used by the murderers. Not even Dio actually described swords being used to kill Caesar on the Ides of March.

The first senators began to arrive in the vestibule, their voices echoing around the polished, yellow-white travertine marble walls. The conspirators among them would have attempted to hide their anxiety at what lay ahead, some engaging in overly enthusiastic conversation about trivial matters, others remaining silent and aloof. They had every reason to be tense; the conspirators had agreed among themselves that should Caesar fail to die as a result of their assassination attempt, or should the plot be discovered at the last moment, all would turn their concealed daggers on themselves and take their own lives, rather than be arrested and tortured for the names of other conspirators before being executed.[9]

This was normally a joyous day on the Roman calendar, for the Ides of March were sacred to Annae Perena, the personification of the succession of the years. Represented as an old woman, she was celebrated by men and women. One of the party games on Annae Perena's day required players to attempt to drink as many cups of wine as the years they wished to live. On a more formal note, public prayers and sacrifice would be observed, to ensure prosperity during the coming year. The murder conspirators would have been hoping that the grim venture they were embarked upon this day would prosper and that they would subsequently live to a ripe old age.

As the numbers of senators filling the vestibule continued to swell, Cassius and Brutus arrived, having walked all the way from the city preceded by the six lictors to which each was entitled as praetors. Inside the vestibule, a life-size statue of Pompey the Great, the theater's benefactor, stood on a plinth behind Caesar's throne. Like other statues of the time, the marble figure would have been painted over in lifelike colors. And, no doubt, this stone Pompey stood in the standard toga-clad pose common to most surviving statutes of Roman senators, with his right hand outstretched, as if he were delivering a speech.

For years, Pompey had been Caesar's close ally and son-in-law, having married Caesar's only child, Julia. It was after Julia's death, during childbirth in 54 B.C., that the pair's alliance had unraveled. Pompey, the Dictator Sulla's youngest general and one of Rome's greatest military commanders when Caesar was still only a callow youth, became the general defeated by Caesar to overthrow the Republic and seize sole power for himself.

More than one classical author reported that as Cassius stood there in the vestibule in the torchlight, he looked up to Pompey's stone face and "silently implored his assistance" in the forthcoming murder of Gaius Julius Caesar.[10]


Caesar rose well before dawn; there were official duties he must perform even before he presided over the sitting of the Senate, which was due to begin at sunup as usual.

Calpurnia rose at the same time. Either encouraged by Caesar or of her own volition, a concerned Calpurnia now revealed the contents of her troubling dream the night before. As Plutarch was to relate, there were several different accounts of the form that Calpurnia's dream took. According to one, passed on by Plutarch, she had dreamed that she was holding a bloodied Caesar in her arms and weeping over him. In another version of the dream, related by both Plutarch and Suetonius, the triangular gable ornament on the high priest's house, erected by the Senate as one of the many honors to Caesar, had come tumbling down. Suetonius, in his account, combined the two dreams, writing of the gable tumbling and Calpurnia nursing a bloodied Caesar.

Calpurnia begged Caesar not to leave their residence that day if it was at all possible, instead adjourning the Senate to another time. Seeing Caesar's disbelieving expression, she rushed to add that if he did not take the warning contained in her dream seriously, she was prepared to consult Caesar's fate "by sacrifices and other kinds of divination."[11]

Plutarch says that Caesar was unsettled by his wife's outburst, for he had never before encountered "any womanish superstition in Calpurnia."[12] His first task, presiding over the taking of official auspices for the day's sitting of the Senate, was to take place within the Regia's walls, so Caesar dressed for the business of the day and joined his religious attendants at the shrine of Mars inside the Regia, where the sacrificial altar stood. The entire month of March was sacred to Mars, so sacrificial auguries were made to him throughout the month.

It had become Caesar's habit to attend the Senate dressed in the outfit of a triumphant—the tunic decorated with golden palm branch motifs, a laurel crown, and a richly embroidered purple cloak. Caesar had gone further, inventing a new costume for himself for official occasions, having a new toga made in the style of the triumphant's cloak. When Caesar joined the priests taking the auspices, it was wearing his palm tunic, purple toga, and laurel crown—which, as Suetonius noted, effectively disguised his baldness.[13]

Chief among the augurs, or priests conducting the sacrifice, was an official with the title of *haruspex*—literally "diviner from entrails." It was the job of the haruspex to look for good or bad omens in the entrails of the bird or animal sacrificed at these ceremonies, and from these to pronounce the prospects of an enterprise. Entrails clear of blemishes were good omens, which promised a successful outcome.

Suetonius identified the haruspex on the Ides of March as Spurinna.[14] Cicero referred to Spurinna the haruspex eight months later, in a January 43 B.C. letter. Writing to a friend who had given up dining out, Cicero joked, "When I laid the facts before Spurinna and explained your former mode of life to him, he predicted that the entire Republic was threatened with grave danger unless you reverted to your old habits."[15]

When Shakespeare wrote his account of this day in his play *Julius Caesar*, he turned Spurinna the haruspex into a nameless soothsayer, which Tudor and subsequent audiences erroneously took to be a fortune-teller of the crystal ball variety. Spurinna the haruspex had conducted several official divinations for Caesar since the Dictator's return to Rome, and on one of those occasions he had warned Caesar that he was in danger and that "the danger threatening him would not come later than the Ides of March."[16]

Despite the fact that Caesar was high priest of Rome, "religious scruples never deterred him" from anything, according to Suetonius.[17]

Acquisition of the post of pontifex maximus had been purely to satisfy Caesar's political ambitions at the time. As a consequence, while he went through the motions of the role of chief priest, as a rule he was not influenced by the predictions of the augurs. As Caesar joined the augurs with predawn darkness still cloaking Rome on the morning of March 15, he chided Spurinna: "Where are your prophesies now? The Ides of March have come. Do you not see that the day which you feared is come, and that I am still alive?"[18]

"Yes, it is come," Spurinna ominously replied, "but it is not yet passed."[19]

With his characteristic impatience, Caesar instructed the augurs to proceed with the sacrifice. As the Dictator watched, a bird was taken from a cage. The type of bird involved on this occasion is not mentioned in classical texts, but for a similar sacrifice in the presence of the emperor Caligula eighty-four years later, a flamingo would be used. As the bird was held by the haruspex's assistants, its throat was slit, its chest opened, and its innards removed and inspected. According to Appian, Spurinna announced that the sacrificial bird was "without a head to the intestines," referring to a projecting part of the liver. "This is a portent of death," the haruspex gravely pronounced.[20]

Caesar made light of the divination, laughing and saying, "Much the same happened to me in Spain when I was fighting Pompeius."[21] He was referring to a sacrifice he made prior to going to battle against Pompey the Great's eldest son, Gnaeus, at Munda in Spain in 45 B.C.

Spurinna did not think it a laughing matter. "On that occasion, too, you were in extreme danger," he said. This was true; the Battle of Munda had turned on a knife edge, and Caesar had come perilously close to losing it, only securing victory by personally leading an uphill charge that had faltered. "But now the portent is even more deadly," Spurinna added.[22]

At any other time, this evil portent was excuse enough for the Senate sitting to be called off until another day. But Caesar wanted to have the day's sitting, the last prior to his intended departure from Rome in four days' time, out of the way, so he could concentrate on final preparations for the march to Macedonia and the military campaign that would follow. So the Dictator ordered the augurs to carry out a second sacrifice. A second bird was taken from a cage and killed over the altar. Once he had studied the bird's entrails, Spurinna the haruspex announced that this victim's entrails were also impure, and he counseled Caesar not to conduct any official business that day.

Again Caesar thought of Calpurnia's dream, and of her heartfelt plea for him not to leave the house that day. There was also a dream of Caesar's own. Suetonius and Dio would both claim that Caesar also had experienced an unusual dream on the night of March 14–15. In that dream, they said, Caesar had soared above the clouds and shaken hands with Jupiter, chief among the Roman gods. The dreams, the inauspicious omens from two sacrifices, and his wife's plea for him to stay home all combined to unnerve the Dictator.

Caesar sent a messenger scurrying along the city's stone-paved streets to deliver a message to the house of Mark Antony in the Carinae district, summoning Antony to come to him at once at the Regia. Caesar had decided to send Antony to the Senate at dawn, in his capacity as his co-consul and deputy president of the Senate, to announce that the day's sitting was being postponed until another date.

# XIII

# MARCH 15, 44 B.C., THE IDES OF MARCH

## CAESAR MUST SUFFER CAESAR'S FATE

The vestibule at Pompey's Theater was overflowing with senators; the marble walls echoed with chatter. This being Caesar's last appearance in the Senate prior to his departure for the East, a great many members had made an effort to attend. Some senators were outside Italy serving in official capacities, men such as Asinius Pollio, who had crossed the Rubicon with Caesar in January 49 B.C. and who was currently serving as governor of Farther Spain. Other senators, such as Cicero, were away from Rome on personal business, while others, such as Brutus's friend Ligarius, were too ill to attend the sitting.

The sun rose over the Eternal City, and, at the Theater of Pompey, there was no sign of the Dictator. After some time, a runner was sent to the Regia to announce that the Senate was ready to sit, and to find out what was keeping Caesar; Dio wrote that the senators "called for Caesar."[1] In the meantime, all the praetors present offered to hear suits from citizens who wished to present them for adjudication, as the praetors were obliged to do by Roman law.

Each praetor dealt with different areas of law. Caesar had doubled the number of praetors to twenty, allowing him many more positions of favor to endow on men who pleased him. Among the current year's praetors was Mark Antony's younger brother Gaius. But Marcus Brutus, as city praetor, was the most sought-after by litigants. Now temporary law courts were set up under the colonnades behind the theater by the praetors' lictors, and announcements made to the crowd now milling around the theater complex that suits would be heard.[2]

Brutus was about to seat himself on his tribunal to hear a case when the runner returned from the Regia with the information that, after the portents of two sacrifices had been negative, Caesar intended sending Antony to adjourn the sitting of the Senate. On hearing this, the attendant in charge of Caesar's golden throne "carried it out of the Senate, thinking that there now would be no need of it."[3]

This news that Caesar was not coming to the sitting caused consternation among the conspirators, until it was suggested that Decimus Brutus Albinus, "as one supposed to be his devoted friend," should be sent to the Regia to convince Caesar to come to the Senate House, even if it was only to personally adjourn the sitting.[4] It was probably the cool-headed Cassius who came up with this suggestion, or perhaps it was Albinus himself, being "one in whom Caesar had such confidence that he had made him his second heir."[5]

With the Senate water clocks showing that the day was well into the second Roman hour, Albinus set off on his mission to Caesar at the Regia.

When Albinus arrived at the Regia on the Via Sacra, he would have seen Caesar's litter and its bearers standing in readiness in the Forum outside, and, behind it, Mark Antony's litter, indicating that Antony was at the Regia. When Albinus was eventually ushered into the Dictator's presence, he found Mark Antony in conversation with a seated Caesar. Apparently it had taken some time for Caesar's messenger to locate Antony, or at least for Antony to answer the summons to come to Caesar at the Regia.

When Albinus politely asked the cause of the Dictator's delay, Caesar told him of his wife's dream overnight and of the two negative divinations that morning. In response, Albinus "spoke scoffingly and in mockery of the diviners." Continuing on the offensive, Albinus "blamed" Caesar for giving his critics in the Senate an opportunity to claim that he had offended the House; after all, "they had met on his summons."[6]

Antony would later claim that he counseled Caesar against attending the sitting. Seeing that the Dictator was inclined toward Antony's view, Albinus became highly inventive and persuasive. According to

Appian, Albinus claimed that his fellow senators "were ready to vote unanimously that he [Caesar] should be declared king of all the provinces outside Italy, and might wear a crown in all places but Italy, by sea and land."[7]

This succeeded in winning Caesar's attention. Albinus went on, with a nod in Antony's direction, "If anyone should be sent to tell them they might break up for the present, and meet again when Calpurnia should chance to have better dreams, what would your enemies say?" Caesar probably now had a pained expression on his face. "Or who with any patience would listen to your friends," Albinus continued, "if they should presume to defend your government as being neither arbitrary nor tyrannical?"[8]

Albinus reached out and, taking the Dictator by the hand, helped him to his feet. As Caesar rose, Albinus told him that if he was convinced that the day was ill-starred, the decent thing for him to do under the circumstances would be to go to the Senate and adjourn it in person, which at least showed respect for the Senate.[9]

With these words, and holding Caesar by the hand, said Plutarch, Albinus "conducted him forth."[10] As Antony trailed along behind like a pet dog, Albinus led Caesar from the Regia. "For," as Appian was to write, "Caesar must suffer Caesar's fate."[11]

At Marcus Brutus's house, his wife, Porcia, very much aware of what her husband planned to do that morning, and equally aware that Caesar was supposed to present himself at the Senate sitting at dawn, became more and more worried as the sun rose higher in the morning sky and no word came that the deed had been done, that Caesar had been dispatched. The only construction that Porcia could put on this was that something had gone wrong with the murder plan and that consequently something had happened to Brutus.

The highly strung Porcia, said Plutarch, "being extremely disturbed with expectation of the event, and unable to bear the greatness of her anxiety, could scarcely remain indoors." She was so on edge that she would jump "at every little noise or voice she heard." As staff came in from early morning shopping at the shops of the Basilica Aemilia in the Forum, Porcia asked them what Brutus was doing, but none had any news to convey. Sitting with the ladies of her entourage, probably spinning, a common pastime for Roman matrons, Porcia "sent one messenger after another to inquire" about what was happening, but each returned to say that there was no word of either the master or of Caesar.[12]

"After long expectation and waiting, the strength of her constitution could hold out no more." The blood had drained from Porcia's face. So choked with emotion had she become, she could no longer speak. And then she fainted. The women with her let out a scream of horror and crowded around her. Houses in Rome were built side by side, without any intervening gardens or lawns—neighbors of Porcia and Brutus heard the women scream next door, and sent staff to Brutus's door to find out what had taken place. "The report was soon spread about that Porcia was dead."[13]

But Porcia was not dead. With the help of her ladies, she regained consciousness. But she looked so ghastly that Brutus's steward, who would have had orders from his master to keep Porcia and members of the household well away from the Senate House that morning, decided that Brutus must be told.

Under a colonnade at the Theater of Pompey, the praetors who were party to the conspiracy were hearing civil suits and making judgments. They "did not only calmly hear all who made application to them and pleaded against each other before them," wrote Plutarch, the conspiratorial praetors, like their colleagues, acted as if they were "free from all other thoughts," and "decided causes with as much accuracy and judgment as they had heard them with attention and patience."[14]

For all his attention and patience, Brutus found himself dealing with a difficult litigant. Brutus had just ruled against the man in a civil suit, and the unsuccessful litigant was not happy. "With great clamor" this man protested Brutus's decision and declared that he would appeal to Caesar. Brutus looked around at all who were present and said, "Caesar does not hinder me, nor will he hinder me, from ruling according to the laws."[15]

As lictors hustled the litigant away, Brutus rose and stepped down from his tribunal. Outsite, he joined Cassius on the theater steps, looking back toward the city and the buildings on the Capitoline Mount, knowing that Caesar's house was just below the hill and that Caesar was probably still there. None of the hundreds of senators who had assembled at the theater had gone home; Caesar had called this sitting of the House, and until he advised otherwise, they had to wait for him.

The conspirators' nerves were being tested to the limit by the wait, which was stretching into hours. This delay inevitably bred the fear that the plot had been discovered and that at any moment the game would be up. The tribune of the plebs Gaius Casca was particularly keyed up, for he had asked for the right to strike the first blow at Caesar, a request that Brutus and Cassius had granted. It is likely that Casca's colleagues the tribunes of the plebs Marullus and Flavus, who had been dismissed and banished by Caesar over the incident concerning the crowned statue, had been Casca's friends, and he was intent on seeking revenge on their behalf.

Out of the crowd in the theater vestibule, a senator came up to Casca and shook his hand. "You concealed the secret from us, although you are my friend," said the senator with an ambiguous expression, "but Brutus has told me everything."[16]

Casca paled, with the dread of discovery overwhelming him. As later events were to prove, Casca was a person whose instincts for self-preservation were finely honed. His mind raced. He looked dumbly at the man, unable to speak, and apparently thinking that, although he had not seen this fellow at Cassius's house that morning, he must be a fellow conspirator. Casca was "so near" to letting out the secret by welcoming the man as a comrade assassin when the senator laughed, obviously amused by Casca's dumbfounded reaction.[17]

"How is it that you are so rich all of a sudden that you can stand for election as an aedile?" said the senator.[18]

The relieved Casca broke into a smile and made light of the business. Once the man had moved away, Casca went looking for Cassius and Brutus. Finding them standing together on the theater steps, he shared his frightening little encounter with them.

It was not long after Casca had related his tale to them that Brutus and Cassius were approached by a senator named Popillius Laenas, who was not a party to the conspiracy. Laenas, "having saluted them more earnestly than usual," leaned close to the pair and whispered, "My wishes are with you, that you may accomplish what you design. And I advise you to make no delay, for the thing is now no secret."[19]

As Laenas moved away, Brutus and Cassius looked at each other in shared alarm, suspecting that word of the murder plot must have escaped the bounds of the conspiratorial ring. But before they could fully absorb this, one of Brutus's lictors brought him word that there was a messenger from Brutus's house at the foot of the steps. The messenger had brought Brutus word "that his wife was dying."[20]

Plutarch wrote that "when Brutus received this news he was extremely troubled, not without reason." But Brutus knew his emotional wife all too well, and guessed that the strain of waiting on news of the assassination had proven too great for her. As much as he loved Porcia, Brutus was not prepared to deviate from his course. As Plutarch wrote, Brutus "was not carried away with his private concern" for his wife and was not prepared "to quit his public purpose."[21]

Brutus would have sent a message back to his house that all was well with him and that his business had been a little delayed but would soon be accomplished.

According to Cassius Dio, who was a highly superstitious Roman author particularly attracted to omens, as Albinus was leading Caesar out the door of the Regia and they were passing though the house's vestibule, a bust of Caesar fell from its plinth and smashed on the floor, but Caesar took no notice.[22]

Outside the Regia, in the Forum, Caesar's litter was waiting, with its bearers and the Dictator's twenty-four lictors in readiness, as they would have been since well before dawn. A crowd of onlookers quickly grew. Behind Caesar's litter, Mark Antony's litter also sat on the pavement, awaiting its passenger.

Caesar clambered into his litter, which was hoisted onto the shoulders of the brawny slaves whose task it was to bear the Dictator. Most of these slaves would have been relatively young, but strong. Ahead of the litter, the two dozen lictors formed up in two rows, each man carrying a cylindrical fasces. Antony also took his position, in his own litter, as his twelve lictors formed up in front of it. At the command of Caesar's chief lictor, the little pedestrian convoy set off. Albinus joined the crowd that fell in behind the pair of conveyances. The time was close to 10:00 A.M.[23]

The little procession proceeded down the Forum toward the Rostra. There, Marcus Lepidus was waiting. Lepidus would have been in his toga, and had obviously been waiting to accompany Caesar to the Senate sitting. At the Rostra, Caesar ordered his bearers to halt, after which he alighted, then stood briefly conversing with Lepidus. Caesar apparently told Lepidus that he did not intend spending long at the Theater of Pompey, and advised his deputy not to bother accompanying him, as he would soon return, but to await him there. As Caesar slid back into his litter and set off again, Lepidus remained behind in the Forum.

There is no record of what Calpurnia thought of her husband venturing out of the house after previously assuring her he would not stir that day. Her fears for her husband's safety were compounded when, not long after Caesar had departed from the Regia, she was informed that the servant of a leading personage had arrived at the Regia and was asking to see her on a matter of grave importance. When Calpurnia agreed, the servant was ushered into her presence.

The man, without doubt a freedman, proceeded to beg Calpurnia to keep him safe there at the Regia until Caesar returned. "He had matters of great importance to communicate to him," he told Calpurnia. The servant said that he had arrived at the Regia just as Caesar was leaving, but the crush of people around Caesar's litter had prevented him from approaching. The servant would not reveal to Calpurnia the nature of the information he had for Caesar, or even who his master was. But Calpurnia was sufficiently concerned to tell the Regia staff to permit the man to wait in the vestibule until her husband returned.[24]

As the litters passed from the Forum, the crowd fell in behind them. This, said Appian, was a "large throng made up of inhabitants of the capital, foreigners, and numerous slaves and ex-slaves."[25]

From the Forum, the informal procession proceeded along the Street of the Banker, passing the City Prison, which stood on the left, at the base of the Capitoline Mount. Caesar had plans to build a massive theater here, using the natural slope of the hillside, to outshine Pompey's Theater.[26] The litters passed out the city gate that opened onto the Flaminian Way, and traveled along this for a little distance until reaching a three-way intersection. Turning left, the litters and their large following headed west toward the Tiber, alongside the Villa Publicus, a vast, grassy space dedicated to public use, toward the Pompeian Theater complex.

In the enthusiastic crowd surging along behind the two litters was a Greek teacher of rhetoric named Artemidorus of Cnidus. He was friendly with Brutus and a member of his circle and, according to Plutarch, via that connection "came into the secret" of the murder conspiracy.[27] As Brutus and Cassius had quite deliberately only recruited members of the Senate into the plot, on the basis that each conspirator had to agree to strike a blow at Caesar in the Senate on the Ides of March as part of their admission to this exclusive and murderous "society," Artemidorus would not have been approached to join the conspiracy. Either a conspirator had loose lips, or the Greek teacher had overheard parties to the plot talking.

Artemidorus also was on close terms with Caesar, who, when a young man, had stayed with him in Cnidus, which was a famous Greek center of learning not far from the island of Cos.[28] Artemidorus had jotted recently discovered details of the plot onto a sheet of papyrus. This he had rolled up and sealed with his personal wax seal, as was the custom. His intention was to hand this note to Caesar, but the size of the crowd surrounding the Dictator had till now prevented him. As the litters were set down at the foot of the flight of stone steps leading up to the theater vestibule, and Caesar stepped out, Artemidorus saw members of the waiting crowd surge around him, with various people handing petitions of one kind or another to Caesar.[29]

The Greek teacher observed that the Dictator did not read any of these petitions; he merely handed them to his staff behind him. Determined that Caesar must read the warning contained in his note and not just pass it on the way he had done with the petitions, Artemidorus pushed his way through the throng until he reached Caesar. Holding out the little roll of parchment, he urged, "Read this, Caesar, alone and quickly, for it contains a matter of great importance which vitally concerns you."[30]

Having apparently recognized Artemidorus, Caesar took the note, opened it, and several times tried to read it, but he was "hindered by the crowd of those who came to speak with him." To Artemidorus's frustration, Caesar gave up his attempt to read the note in the jostling throng. After speaking with several people, Caesar began to climb the steps with the roll of parchment in his hand still.[31]

When word arrived at the theater that Caesar was coming, the majority of the waiting senators retired inside the vestibule and took their seats.

Cassius and Brutus were among a few who lingered at the top of the steps. The conspiracy's leaders wanted to be certain that all now went to plan before they took their places inside. The key to the plot's immediate success lay with keeping Mark Antony detained outside the Senate chamber.

Plutarch, in his *Caesar*, has Albinus waylaying Antony as per the original plan, but in his *Marcus Brutus* he writes that "Trebonius, in the meanwhile, engaged Antony's attention at the door, and kept him in talk outside." Appian and Dio both concur that it was Trebonius, another close friend of Antony, who now struck up the delaying conversation with the powerful consul and purposely detained him outside.[32] Knowing that Caesar intended to quickly adjourn the sitting and would therefore spend only a few minutes in the chamber, Antony decided not to bother going inside, and was content to engage in conversation with Trebonius until the Dictator reemerged.

As Cassius and Brutus were about to hurry into the chamber, they saw the senator Popillius Laenas, the man who had earlier shaken the pair by telling them that he knew what they were up to, stop Caesar at the bottom of the steps and talk to him at length, with Caesar seeming very attentive. Due to the hubbub of the crowd, neither Cassius nor Brutus could hear what was passing between Laenas and Caesar. Other conspirators at the top of the steps also witnessed this meeting. All immediately thought the game was up, that Laenas was informing on them, "and, looking at each one another, agreed from the looks on each other's faces that they should not stay to be taken, but should all kill themselves."[33]

Plutarch says that Cassius and several others were actually in the process of reaching under their togas to draw their daggers and do away with themselves when Brutus realized that Laenas, from his expression and gestures, was not informing Caesar of a treasonous plot to kill him but was earnestly petitioning him for a favor. Brutus quickly looked to Cassius. There were too many nonconspirators around them for him to say anything, so Brutus simply smiled broadly and nodded toward Laenas and Caesar. Seeing his smile, Cassius and the others stopped short in the act of drawing their blades, and followed Brutus's gaze to Laenas.[34] When "they saw him embrace Caesar at the end," wrote Appian, "they recovered their courage."[35]

Laenas kissed Caesar's hand and drew aside.[36] As Caesar began to climb the steps, Cassius, Brutus, and the others withdrew within to take their places in the Senate chamber.

# XIV

# MARCH 15, 44 B.C., THE IDES OF MARCH

## THE CRIME

**C**ountless conversations were filling the air in the vestibule of Pompey's Theater when the Dictator's chief lictor appeared at the door and, with raised voice, announced Julius Caesar's entrance. The hall quickly fell silent as all the members of the Senate respectfully came to their feet.

The front row of the assembly was reserved for the most senior members of the House, among them the current year's praetors, including Cassius, Brutus, and other conspirators, as well as Caesarians such as Antony's brother Gaius, and pro-Caesar men set down for senior appointments once Caesar left Rome, among them Dolabella, Hirtius, and Pansa. Other senators and tribunes engaged in the plot against Caesar had positioned themselves as close to the Dictator's golden throne as possible.

Caesar, wearing his gold-embroidered palm tunic, unique purple toga, and laurel-branch crown, entered the chamber and walked to his throne, which its attendant had hurriedly restored to its position at the front of the chamber just in time. The sixty-plus conspirators then bustled forward "and all crowded round about him."[1] Caesar eased himself onto his chair and adjusted his toga. The five primary classical accounts of Caesar's murder vary slightly from version to version in some details, but all basically corroborate one another. The following description of Caesar's murder is an amalgam of those accounts.

The plotters had agreed that one of their number, Lucius Tillius Cimber, would pretend to implore Caesar to agree to allow his brother, whom Caesar had exiled, to return home to Rome. This Cimber did, as, crowding around the throne, "they all joined their prayers with his," said Plutarch, "and took Caesar by the hand and kissed his head and his breast."[2] Caesar, obviously irritated by this, "would not agree at all," Appian wrote, "and wished to defer a decision."[3] "When he saw they would not desist," Caesar "violently" rose to his feet.[4] "Cimber then took hold of Caesar's purple toga as though he were still pleading with him," then pulled it down over his arms, "shouting, 'What are you waiting for, friends?'"[5]

The shocked Caesar exclaimed, "This is violence!"[6]

All, or most, of the other conspirators pulled out their concealed daggers. Gaius Casca, who had asked for the privilege of drawing first blood, was standing behind Caesar and went to strike him over the shoulder, aiming for the throat. Caesar, meanwhile, had wrenched his toga out of Cimber's hands.[7] Instinctively, Caesar grabbed Casca's wrist, staying his blow.

"Vile Casca!" Caesar exclaimed. "What does this mean?"[8]

Suetonius, the least reliable of the classical sources in many respects, would claim that Caesar now stabbed Casca with his stylus, driving it right through Casca's arm.[9] The stylus was a small penknife used by Romans to write on notebooks made up of one or two sheets of beeswax with a wooden backing. The sharp end of the stylus was used to inscribe words or images on the wax, while the blunt end was used to erase them. The stylus and the notebook—which would fit in the palm of the hand—were carried in a cloth or leather bag attached to the belt.

No other classical author mentions Caesar using a stylus to defend himself, and, unless he already had one in his hand, it seems highly improbable that he had the time to reach to his waist, open a bag on his belt, and withdraw a stylus, when he was at that time wrenching his toga free of Cimber's grip and then grabbing Casca's wrist. Suetonius's tale about the stylus seems, at best, questionable.

With Caesar gripping his arm and the dagger, Gaius Casca desperately looked around to his brother Publius, a fellow conspirator. "Brother, help!" Casca yelped in Greek.[10]

Almost immediately, Caesar received a vicious stab wound in the side, apparently from Publius Casca. Other conspirators followed suit, raining frantic blows on Caesar, who continued to retain his hold on Gaius Casca's arm. "Some say that he fought and resisted," Plutarch wrote, "shifting his body to avoid the blows and calling out for help."[11] But no help came. According to Appian, despite the Dictator's avoiding tactics, Bucilianus plunged his dagger into Caesar's back. Cassius's dagger struck Caesar in the face, Brutus's in the thigh.[12]

Caesar, in shock, looked at Brutus. The Dictator spoke several words, in Greek. There are various version of precisely what he said. There is Shakespeare's famous line, in *Julius Caesar*, "*Et tu, Brute?*" meaning, "And you, Brutus?" Of the classical sources, Suetonius and Dio both reported that Caesar cried out, "You, too, my child?"[13]

In the short, sharp killing frenzy, as blades flew and blood ran, some of the conspirators' blows missed altogether, while "in the scuffle many of them struck each other with their daggers."[14] Brutus was jabbed in the hand—apparently the right, his weapon hand—"and all of them were covered with blood."[15]

Having all made their almost ritualistic strikes, the assassins stood back. Caesar let go of his grip on Casca's arm and staggered a few feet until his strength gave out. He collapsed at the foot of the statue of Pompey the Great. The irony of this would not escape classical authors. "Pompey himself seemed to have presided, as it were, over the revenge enacted against his adversary," Plutarch was to remark. Caesar, knowing that he was mortally wounded, dragged his toga up around his head, determined not to let his enemies see his face as he breathed his last.[16]

Hundreds of stunned senators, all still on their feet, had witnessed the attack on Caesar. Now that he had fallen, chaos erupted in the chamber. Certain that the assassins would murder every man associated with the Dictator, or even all who had not taken part in the conspiracy, the vast majority of men in the House fled in panic, streaming out the exits and down the steps to the street outside.

"Run! Bolt doors! Bolt doors!" Dio says they bellowed in their terror to the crowd waiting outside.[17] Bystanders and senators swiftly melded into an undisciplined mob that fled in panic back to the city. Appian alone would claim that "some senators were injured and others lost their lives in the pandemonium," with none of the supposedly dead senators being identified.[18]

Mark Antony was standing outside with Gaius Trebonius when the throng came pouring from the Senate chamber in tumult and flooded down the steps. He would have looked questioningly at Trebonius, and Trebonius would have calmly and deliberately informed him that Gaius Julius Caesar was a dead man. Realizing that there had been a conspiracy to murder Caesar and that his own good friend Trebonius was a party to that conspiracy, Antony immediately "concluded that the plot was against himself as well as against Caesar."[19]

According to Appian, Antony himself later said, "I was not yet clear about the conspiracy or the number of its targets."[20] So Antony dove into the fleeing crowd to make himself scarce. At his first opportunity, said Plutarch, Antony, discarding his stand-out senatorial toga, "took a servant's garment, and hid himself."[21]

Brutus had planned to give a prepared speech to the Senate once Caesar had been cut down, explaining why the conspirators had acted in this way and announcing that they proposed to immediately reinstate the Republic. But the mass exodus made this impossible. Albinus, meanwhile, had hurried to the theater proper and summoned his gladiators, who, fully armed, ran to the Senate chamber.[22] Albinus's gladiators apparently distributed swords among the conspirators, for many of the assassins were soon reported carrying them. If the swords did not come from the gladiators, then Dio's claim that swords were smuggled into the theater complex in round document cases had a basis in fact, and these swords were now accessed. Either way, several classical sources now put swords in assassins' hands.

Some senators who had not participated in the assassination had not fled, but instead joined the conspirators. Chief among these was Marcus Favonius, whom Brutus had left out of the plot after the discouraging response to his initial veiled approach. Favonius, it turned out, fully endorsed the murder of Caesar, and became one of the most committed Liberators, as the conspirators quickly became known—because they had, in their opinion, and in the opinion of their supporters, liberated Rome from the tyranny of Gaius Julius Caesar.

Other senators who now spontaneously joined the Liberators included Lucius Cornelius Lentulus Spinther, son of one of Pompey's generals, as well as Gaius Octavius, Marcus Aquinus, and Quintus Patiscus. Another was the ex-praetor Lucius Staius Murcus, who was due to take up Caesar's appointment as governor of Syria this year. The latter three had all supported Caesar during the Civil War. Most surprising of all, Publius Dolabella, Caesar's youthful pet and consul-designate, also threw his lot in with Brutus, Cassius, and the other assassins. These new recruits, too, were soon flourishing swords.[23]

With the Senate House having emptied of most of its senators, and the opportunity for speech-making lost, Brutus and Cassius agreed that their best course now was to march to the Capitoline Mount, a walled religious sanctuary in the heart of the city that could be defended in an emergency, from where Brutus could deliver the speech he had intended making in the Senate chamber. In case of trouble, the Liberators removed their togas and wound them around their left arms to serve as shields of a sort.

They had swords in their right hands now instead of the daggers they had used to strike Caesar down. Appian said that these swords were "bloody," but Appian himself described how Caesar had been killed with daggers.[24] Plutarch more accurately wrote that it was the hands of the assassins that were bloody. These hands, covered with Caesar's blood, he said, they showed to passersby, while their swords were "naked."[25]

Accompanied by Albinus's well-armed gladiators, the assassins and their new senatorial recruits departed the chamber and hurried down the steps outside. En masse, they set off along the now nearly deserted street, retracing the route that Caesar had taken from the Forum to reach Pompey's Theater. As they went, the Liberators brandished the swords and shouted "that they had destroyed a tyrant and a king." Caesar himself was left where he had fallen.[26]

One of the senators in the Liberators' party found a cap lying on the ground, dropped by a fleeing freedman. These leather caps, on which the caps worn by revolutionaries during the French Revolution in a much later period in history would be modeled, were worn to show the world that the wearer was a slave who had gained his freedom. Seeing the symbolism of the cap, the senator took a spear from one of the gladiators and carried the cap aloft on the end of it, calling out that all Romans had now been freed from the slavery of Julius Caesar. Heading into the city, the Liberators urged everyone they met along the road "to embrace the Republic of their ancestors, and reminded them of the first Brutus and the oath they [the Roman people] had sworn at that time against the kings of long ago."[27]

Once the assassination party, several hundred strong, was out of sight, people began to emerge from hiding places near the Theater of Pompey. One of the first to come out from hiding was Artemidorus of Cnidus, the Greek logic teacher. Having unsuccessfully attempted to warn Caesar about the murder plot, and fearing the worst for the Dictator, Artemidorus ran up the theater steps and entered the vestibule.[28] The vast marble hall, deserted now, echoed to the Greek's footsteps. The wooden Senate benches were no doubt now jumbled, with some overturned in the rush by senators to escape the chamber. The water clocks and the desks of the secretaries had probably been tipped over in the panic. The Dictator's golden throne was still in its place, soiled now with Julius Caesar's blood.

Artemidorus edged closer to a bloodied bundle lying at the foot of the statue of Pompey the Great. The base of the statue, too, was bloodied. Artemidorus realized that he was looking at the dead body of Julius Caesar, with the Dictator's cloak dragged up over his head. Later Roman historian Cassius Dio would comment on the irony of the place where Caesar fell—"Inasmuch as he had been slain in Pompey's edifice and near the statue which at that time stood there." (Pompey's statue was later relocated by the emperor Augustus.) Dio wrote that Caesar "seemed in a way to have afforded his rival his revenge."[29]

As the terrified Artemidorus withdrew from the vestibule, three of Caesar's litter-bearers warily entered. The trio of slaves lifted up their master's bloodied body and carried it out to the litter in the street. Loading Caesar's corpse into the conveyance, the three bearers raised it up, two at one end, one at the other, and with difficulty headed back to the city, bound for the Regia, with one of the dead Dictator's arms hanging limply over the side.[30]

# XV

# MARCH 15, 44 B.C.

## THE GATHERING STORM

C aesar's deputy Marcus Lepidus, waiting in the Forum for Caesar's return, saw a wave of people come rushing from the direction of the Field of Mars. There was unadulterated panic. People were shouting and waving their arms about. Lepidus froze as he heard people call out that Julius Caesar had been murdered at Pompey's Portico. And then Lepidus sprang into action.[1]

Appian reported that Lepidus, "when he heard what had happened, dashed across to the island in the Tiber, where he had a legion."[2] This was the legion of retired troops, the 7th or 8th. There were several bridges across the Tiber. The nearest, the Pons Aemilius, was undoubtedly the one that Lepidus used. Crossing the Aemilian bridge, Lepidus had only to hurry a short distance up the western bank of the Tiber to the Pons Cestius. Recrossing the river via this bridge, he reached Tiber Island.

A serving legion at this time in Roman history was commanded by six military tribunes, young gentlemen officers in their twenties who were members of the Equestrian Order. On campaign, one of these military tribunes commanded the legion for two months, while the other five each commanded two of the ten cohorts, so that each had a turn in overall command over the period of twelve months. In the imperial era, this system would be radically changed, with a dedicated commander of senatorial rank allocated to each legion, for postings of three to four years at a time; a single military tribune would serve as his deputy.

The military tribunes of this legion on Tiber Island would have gone home once their men were discharged, so that on March 15, 44 B.C., the unit's former centurions were in charge when Master of Equestrians Lepidus came panting onto Tiber Island. Lepidus ordered the men of the legion to accompany him at once to the Field of Mars.[3] Forming up in their old cohorts and grabbing up what arms they had retained, these men followed Lepidus across the Pons Fabricius to the Field of Mars, where they would have formed up in neat ranks on the grass of the Villa Publica, facing the city. Here, the armed former legionaries were outside the *pomerium*, the ancient, sacred boundary of the city of Rome said to have been drawn by Romulus himself, and inside which it was unlawful for any man to carry arms.

Some of the ex-legionaries would have worn chain-mail armored leather vests over standard-issue tunics. On some men's heads were jockey-style legionary helmets of iron and bronze, their horsehair plumes wafting in the late-winter breeze. On their right hip many men had a sheathed short sword, the *gladius*; on their left, a dagger, the *pugio*. On the left arm, some carried a large, rectangular convex shield; made of wood, it was covered with leather, and on the leather was painted the emblem of their legion. In the case of "Spanish" legions serving under Caesar, the unit emblem was a bull.

Lepidus took the former legionaries to the Field of Mars, said Appian, "to hold them in greater readiness for Antony's orders, deferring to Antony because the latter was closer to Caesar and also a consul."[4] Lepidus, while senior to Antony when Caesar was alive, now had absolutely no authority—according to Roman law, a Master of Equestrians' appointment ended the moment his Dictator ceased to hold office. Caesar, with his death, certainly no longer held office. Lepidus, now without any legal standing, had to defer to Antony, whose post as a consul was unaffected by the Dictator's death.

Two problems now emerged for Lepidus. Antony was in hiding, in fear for his life, and in no position to deliver orders to the ex-soldiers. The second problem was that the former legionaries soon learned that Caesar was dead. And they realized that, accordingly, Lepidus no longer had any power to command them. The ex-soldiers and their centurions now conferred. "When they considered what to do," said Appian, "their impulse was to take revenge for what Caesar had suffered, but they feared that the Senate would be on the side of the assassins, and decided to await further developments."[5]

After spending some time on the Field of Mars, the retired soldiers marched back to their camp on Tiber Island. Lepidus, now fearing for his life the same way Antony did, melted away and went into hiding in the city. According to Plutarch, "Antony and Lepidus, Caesar's most faithful friends, got off privately and hid themselves in some friends' houses," where they would spend that night.[6]

Writing three hundred years later, Cassius Dio, the classical author most removed from these events, would claim that Lepidus occupied the Forum that night with soldiers and at dawn the next day delivered a speech against the assassins.[7] This claim is not substantiated by any other classical source; none confirms that Lepidus took troops to the Forum on the night of March 15. In fact, it is a claim contradicted by Plutarch, who says that Lepidus stayed in hiding with friends that night. And with Lepidus by then deprived of all official authority by Caesar's death, it is highly unlikely that the troops would have followed him at that point. Dio seems to have confused various other accounts, one of which more credibly puts Lepidus in the Forum with troops two days later, but not on the evening of March 15.


The first that Caesar's wife, Calpurnia, would have known about the Dictator's murder would have been when the three slaves who had struggled to take his litter from the Theater of Pompey and back into the city carried his body into the Regia late on the morning of March 15. The servant who had been waiting at the Regia to pass on vital information to Caesar would now have fled in terror. The horror of Caesar's wife as his body was brought in, especially after she had begged Caesar not to leave the house that day, can only be imagined.

Caesar's physician, Antistius, was sent for. Antistius carried out a postmortem on Caesar's body, the first postmortem on a historical figure in recorded history. The physician found that Caesar had received twenty-three stab wounds. Of these, he would report, none had been fatal except for a stab to the chest.[8] Over the coming days, Caesar's body would remain at the Regia.


The Liberators, with their gladiator escort, arrived at the hilltop Capitoline complex after marching from the Field of Mars, and took possession of it. Far from thinking about fleeing Rome to escape arrest as murderers, said Plutarch, they passed into the city "with an air of confidence and assurance." Along the way they were joined by many sympathizers attracted by their call for the restoration of the Republic.[9]

By this time, the tumult and the wild panic had subsided. The streets of Rome had become deserted. Appian was to report that in the city, in expectation of Caesar's assassins going on a murderous rampage, "everybody barred their doors and prepared to defend themselves from their rooftops." He added that "many foreigners and ordinary inhabitants of Rome were also killed" and that "the goods displayed for sale were looted."[10] But Plutarch contradicted him by stating that there was no bloodshed other than Caesar's murder, and this was confirmed by both Suetonius and Dio. Plutarch also noted that there was "no plundering of the goods in the streets."[11]

The position of the Liberators was precarious. Albinus's gladiators numbered perhaps several hundred armed men. But there were several thousand armed former legionaries on Tiber Island, and there was no telling what they would do or who they would follow. More than that, Appian pointed out that "there were also a large number of discharged soldiers in the city" itself. These men, like those on Tiber Island, who had served in Caesar's legions during the Civil War, "were going to go out and settle in large groups on land and property taken from others"—former supporters of Pompey and the old republican Senate—an act instigated by Caesar and approved by his Senate, which, in Appian's opinion, "was in contravention of justice."[12]

These ex-soldiers "were now encamped in the sanctuaries and sacred precincts" of the capital "under a single standard and a single officer appointed to supervise the new settlement" program.[13] In addition, there were other former soldiers in the city who "had already been settled in colonies but had come back to Rome to escort Caesar on his way when he left" on March 19 to commence his Getae and Parthian campaigns.[14] Appian estimated that these ex-soldiers in the city, including those on Tiber Island, numbered "tens of thousands."[15]

After consulting among themselves at the Capitol, Brutus, Cassius, and the other assassins decided to distribute bribes among the ordinary people, thinking that they would thus cement the support of those who did not have a "love of freedom" nor were necessarily "longing for the Republic." Their agents went about the city, handing out money and encouraging people to come to the Capitoline Mount to hear Marcus

Brutus speak, and a large crowd very soon came surging up to the Capitol and assembled.[16]

Appian, who was apt to confuse the timing and order of some of the events he chronicled, wrote that Lucius Cornelius Cinna, the brother-in-law of Caesar, spoke first, followed by Publius Dolabella, Caesar's young favorite and the consul-elect. Plutarch tells it slightly differently, with Cinna speaking last and Dolabella not speaking publicly at all at that juncture. Plutarch's version of events makes much more sense. According to him, Brutus spoke first at this gathering on the Capitol. This he had intended to do in the Senate House. Probably standing on the steps of the huge Temple of Jupiter Capitolinus, Rome's oldest and most sacred temple, Brutus read, or recited from memory, a speech he had prepared days earlier. In May, Brutus would send this speech to his friend Marcus Cicero the orator, asking him to make any corrections to it that he felt necessary, prior to it being published for mass consumption.

"The speech is a most eloquent composition," Cicero would tell a friend in a May 18 letter. "The wording and the turn of the sentences could not be bettered. But if I had been handling the material I would have put more fire into it, considering the nature of the theme and the role of the speaker."[17] So elegant Brutus gave his elegant speech, but a speech lacking fire. Nonetheless, it was a speech that proved "very popular" with the pro-assassination crowd on the Capitol, "and proper for the state that affairs were then in," in the opinion of Plutarch. The crowd applauded, and called for the Liberators to come down to the Forum and address the city as a whole.[18]

Both Plutarch and Appian wrote that, taking confidence from this reception, Brutus and the other assassins came down from the Capitoline Mount during the afternoon, escorted by Albinus's gladiators. A much larger crowd, of mixed allegiances and emotions, gathered in the Forum. "Many of the most eminent men, accompanying Brutus, conducted him in their midst with great honor from the Capitol and placed him on the Rostra," said Plutarch. The members of this enlarged crowd of thousands "were struck with reverence" for Brutus and "heard him silently and attentively" as he apparently repeated the speech he made on the Capitol.[19]

According to Appian, Cassius also spoke, as would be expected. He praised Brutus as an honorable man, congratulated Rome on having regained its freedom, and thanked Albinus for providing his gladiators in the hour of need. Cassius called for the recall of Pompey's surviving son Sextus to Rome, and also of the two tribunes, Marullus and Flavus, "who were in exile after being stripped of office by Caesar."[20]

Cinna, a serving praetor and Caesar's brother-in-law, now made his way to the Rostra. Because of his close family connection to Caesar, many members of the crowd were surprised to see the assassins give way to him. As he climbed the steps to the Rostra to speak, Cinna "threw off his praetor's insignia," which appears to have taken the form of a crimson waistband, "despising it as the gift of a despot," that despot being his brother-in-law Julius Caesar.[21]

From the Rostra, looking out across the throng, Cinna "called Caesar a despot, and the men who had killed him tyrannicides." This term, tyrannicides, in Roman law applied to those who killed a tyrant in defense of Roman democracy, and was an honorable title. Conversely, a person convicted of being a tyrant was deprived of all civic rights, even the right of a funeral, cremation, and the interment of his remains.

Cinna praised Caesar's murder as an act resembling those of the Romans' noblest ancestors, and told the crowd that they should be grateful to the men who did it. According to Appian, those who had been bribed applauded Cinna.[22] But, Plutarch wrote, others "broke out in a sudden rage, and railed at him in such language that the whole party thought fit to again withdraw to the Capitol."[23]

Dark clouds had been forming over the city ever since Caesar's murder, and late in the day a thunderstorm erupted over Rome, with booming thunder that shook walls and flashing bolts of lightning that lit the gloomy metropolis's dark corners with brief flashes of silvered light. Heavy rain then lashed the rooftops and deserted streets.[24] The more superstitious Romans, skulking in their homes behind locked doors, would take this to mean that the gods were angry at Caesar's death, or at least at the manner of it.

Safe from both inclement weather and physical attack under a temple roof, Brutus, on the Capitoline Mount, "expecting to be besieged" by the mob, sent away all those other than the conspirators who had taken part in Caesar's assassination, feeling it unfair that those who had not shared the deed should have to share the danger.[25] There at the Capitoline complex, with their gladiator protectors, and themselves armed in expectation of an assault, the sixty or so original conspirators "spent the day and night."[26]

Ordinarily, the city of Rome was a bustle of activity at night. Caesar himself had introduced traffic regulations that kept the merchants' wagons and builders' carts off the streets in daylight hours. This meant that from dusk till daylight the streets were alive with vehicles coming and going, giving ancient Rome the reputation as "the city that never sleeps," a title much later appropriated by New York City. On the night of March 15–16, 44 B.C., Rome was deathly still. None of the usual hub-bub. Nothing stirred.

On the Capitol, Brutus, Cassius, and their colleagues spent a sleep-deprived night, expecting to be attacked at any moment. In the suburbs, all doors were securely bolted. In the houses of friends they could trust, Mark Antony and Marcus Lepidus, themselves afraid of assassination if they ventured back to their own homes, spent the hours of darkness. At the house of Marcus Brutus, his wife, Porcia, would have been almost demented in her worry for the welfare of her husband on the Capitol. In the colonnades of temples and sanctuaries throughout the city, ex-soldiers would have sat in groups sourly lamenting the death of their commander, Caesar, worrying that the land grants he had promised them would not now be forthcoming, and discussing whom they would support in the power vacuum that was now Rome.

At the Regia at the head of the Forum Romanum, the widow Calpurnia wept over the body of her dead Caesar.

PART THREE

# AFTERMATH AND RETRIBUTION

# XVI

# MARCH 16, 44 B.C.

## PLEADING FOR THE REPUBLIC

T he city awoke, well before dawn as usual, with many among the population probably wondering whether they had dreamed that Caesar was dead, that he had indeed been cut down in the Theater of Pompey the previous day.

As the sun rose over the eerily quiet city, it became clear to Mark Antony and Marcus Lepidus, hiding with friends, that "the conspirators had assembled on the Capitol and had no further design on anyone," so the pair slipped back to their own homes.[1] On the Capitoline Mount, Brutus and Cassius stayed put, still wary about leaving the security of the sanctuary.

Some of the conspirators' friends and relatives, "who were now able to reach the sanctuary for the first time," brought them food, drink, and word that all was quiet in the city. From these men, a delegation was chosen to seek out Antony and Lepidus. As the sole remaining consul, Antony was now the most senior official of the Roman state. Lepidus, as the former Master of Equestrians, could potentially command the loyalty of the armed ex-legionaries on Tiber Island, who had obeyed his initial summons the previous morning, and also of the disarmed former soldiers elsewhere in the city. The Liberators' delegates were instructed to "discuss how to secure unity, plan for political freedom, and avert the disasters that would overtake their country if they failed to agree."[2]

This delegation duly met with Antony and Lepidus during the day. That pair must have exchanged notes and agreed on a shared strategy prior to meeting with the delegates, for they presented a unified front. In these discussions, the Liberators' delegates deliberately refrained from praising the murder of Caesar, but they asked that it be accepted now that the deed had been done, and suggested that they all move on. They urged that compassion be shown to the perpetrators of the murder. If anyone was to be pitied, they said, it was Rome. Antony and Lepidus, said Appian, wanted to avenge Caesar, and would have preferred to have seen the assassins arrested and executed. But they "were nervous that the rest of the Senate was swinging toward" the Liberators.[3]

Appian said that Antony and Lepidus were particularly worried about the assassin Albinus. The province that he was due to take command of, Cisalpine Gaul, bordered Italy, and contained several legions, with which Albinus could control affairs at Rome. Antony and Lepidus decided to see how events turned out, in the meantime trying to devise a way of winning control of the legions in Cisalpine Gaul.[4]

"We shall take no action that stems from private enmity," Antony told the delegates, even though, as Antony reminded them, he and Lepidus had sworn an oath to both protect Caesar and avenge him. "We shall examine the matter with you in the Senate and shall deem whatever course you may jointly approve to leave the community unpolluted."[5]

Antony issued an edict, as consul, and sent runners all around the city to promulgate it, calling a meeting of the Senate for dawn the next day. Still wary of being cut down in the Senate chamber the same way that Caesar had been, or perhaps on the way to or from the Senate, Antony specified that the House meet at the Temple of Tellus, the Temple of Earth, which was close to his house.

Antony also issued orders, as consul, that the magistrates post guards in the city during the hours of darkness—these would have been slaves or freedmen, or perhaps the magistrates' lictors—and "to place their official seats at intervals in public and preside though it were daytime." Fires were duly lit throughout the city, but little legal business was done that night, with many of the magistrates being Liberators. In the light of the fires "the associates of the murderers went hurrying round all night to the houses of the senators, pleading for them and the Republic of their ancestors." At the same time, delegates of the ex-soldiers in the city used the opportunity to also visit members of the Senate, "issuing threats" that the land grants either given or promised to them had better not be withdrawn.[6]

All through the night, tension gripped the city.

# XVII

# MARCH 17, 44 B.C.

## THE JOSTLE FOR CONTROL

D awn was not far off, and most of the senators of Rome, apart from the members of the Liberator party camped on the Capitoline Mount, were hurrying through the city streets, heading for the Temple of Tellus. Brutus, Cassius, and their colleagues would not attend, as they did not trust Antony, fearing that in convening a sitting of the Senate he was setting a deadly ambush for them.

One of the hundreds of leading men making for the temple was the unpopular praetor Cinna, Caesar's brother-in-law, who had spoken in favor of the assassins. He was spotted by a mixture of city residents and some of the ex-soldiers. Cursing him and throwing stones at him, they chased Cinna down the street. When the desperate Cinna took refuge in a house and barred the door, the mob gathered wood and piled it up at the house's door. Cinna's pursuers were on the point of setting the wood alight when Marcus Lepidus arrived on the scene with a party of soldiers, probably men from Tiber Island.[1]

The appearance of troops quickly dispersed the mob, and a shaken Cinna was able to continue on his way. Lepidus, too, made his way to the temple, where the Senate was due to sit. Although there is no further reference to the body of soldiers who had been accompanying Lepidus, it is likely that he posted them around the Temple of Tellus, to provide Antony and himself with protection from the potential interference from the Liberators' force of gladiators while the pair attended the Senate sitting, for Lepidus and Antony were just as nervous about their opponents' intentions.

Inside the Temple of Tellus, the temporary Senate benches filled up, and with the sun climbing above the eastern horizon, Mark Antony, sitting in the president's chair at the front of the chamber, called the Senate to order. The first speakers, current magistrates and former consuls, made it swiftly obvious that the vast majority of senators sympathized with Caesar's assassins and were in favor of a return to the Republic. They sought to help the Liberators, proposing that they be invited to come down from the Capitol and take their seats in the Senate chamber; a resolution to this effect was passed by a great majority. "Antony made no attempt to block this resolution," said Appian, "knowing they would not come. And they did not."[2] As the sitting continued, the nervous Liberators remained on the Capitoline Mount.

Senate motions were then proposed by some members granting honors to Brutus, Cassius, and their fellow assassins. Other speakers were not in favor of granting honors, because, they said, the Liberators did not want honors, for their actions had not been motivated by a quest for rewards; they proposed that the assassins be simply saluted as benefactors of Rome. Others opposed even this, and moved that the Senate should merely vote to spare the lives of all the men involved in the assassination. Others again, while openly aghast at the murder of Caesar, were prepared to pardon the murderers because they represented Rome's greatest families. All through this, Mark Antony sat and listened without saying a word, gauging the strength of the political wind in one direction and another, sizing up who was in favor of what.[3]

One unidentified senator now declared that they must all vote in favor of one of two motions—"either they declared Caesar a tyrant or they granted the murderers immunity" from prosecution. With Caesar likely to be officially declared a tyrant, a host of speakers rushed to disassociate themselves from their past support of him, saying that they could not be held responsible for decrees of Caesar they had endorsed while he was alive, claiming they had been forced to do so because "they had come to fear for their own lives after the death of Pompey and the subsequent death of thousands of others."[4]

Here, Mark Antony saw his opportunity, "and decided to upset their arguments by playing on their own fears and their concerns for themselves." For, as Antony well knew, like himself these men had been appointed to their existing or future posts by Caesar—consulships and the other magistracies of Rome, priesthoods, governorships of the provinces, and army commands, extending over the next five years. Antony called for silence. When he had it, he said, "Those who have asked for a vote on Caesar should be aware of this—if he held office legally and was our elected leader, all his acts and decisions remain valid. But if our decision is that he was an upstart who ruled by force, his body is cast out unburied beyond the borders of his country and all his acts are invalidated."[5]

Of course, Caesar had never been elected to rule over the Romans, and had indeed seized and maintained power by force, in which case his reign had been illegal, and he could validly have now been declared a tyrant under Roman law. But here was Antony's street cunning at work, for if Caesar were adjudged a tyrant, then all his appointments were, by definition, illegal. Antony now informed his fellow senators that if they truly felt that Caesar's rule was illegal and tyrannical then they must all willingly resign their existing or future appointments made by this tyrant Caesar. When they all indicated they were willing to do this, said Antony, he would put the question of whether Caesar was a tyrant to a vote.[6]

This brought a clamorous response. Many senators immediately leaped to their feet, loudly protesting that they should not have to submit themselves to elections, preferring instead to hold on to the appointments they already had. Some of these men had received their appointments from Caesar in contravention of the laws that set minimum ages for various posts. Publius Dolabella was chief among these— Caesar had made Dolabella a consul to succeed him even though Dolabella was now only twenty-five. Under republican Roman law, a man had to be forty-two years of age before he could be a consul, and even then the law required him to be elected, not appointed.

According to both Appian and Dio, in the Forum on the afternoon of the Ides of March, Dolabella had spoken in favor of Caesar's murder. Appian said that Dolabella had even claimed to have previously known about the plot, declaring that while he had not actually plunged a dagger into Caesar, he would have done so had he been afforded the opportunity. Appian added that some of those in the Forum that day would later assert that Dolabella had gone on to propose that forthwith the Ides of March be celebrated as Rome's birthday, in recognition of the fact that the Republic had been reborn this day of Caesar's murder.[7]

Now, at the Temple of Tellus sitting of the Senate, said Appian, Dolabella changed his tune. Desperate to hold on to the consulship that

Caesar had promised him, young Dolabella had seized Caesar's abandoned fasces and insignia of office.[8] Now he claimed that with Caesar dead, his appointment had automatically come into effect. Antony did not speak against Dolabella's assumption of consular office—he or Lepidus may have even counseled it, to turn Dolabella out of the Liberators' corner. There being no precedent for this, many senators were unsure whether Dolabella was now legally a consul.

To keep his consulship, Dolabella rose and spoke against those who were in favor of voting for the murderers and against Caesar. His adversaries countered that *they* were prepared to surrender their magistracies, as they were confident that, in elections, the public would restore their posts to them. The praetors among them even made a show of removing their insignia of office and laying it aside.[9] Dolabella, of course, had no such hope of receiving his consulship through a popular vote, for under the old law the twenty-five-year-old was not entitled to run in a consular election for another seventeen years.

While this rancorous debate was continuing, with Dolabella holding the floor and, in Antony's view, entitled to preside as his co-consul, Antony and Lepidus slipped from the chamber in response to messages sent from outside. A vast, noisy crowd had gathered around the temple, and when the consul and former Master of Equestrians were seen on the steps, people shouted questions at them. Antony, wearing his senatorial toga, raised his right hand for quiet, and eventually the shouting died away. As silence reigned, and Antony was about to speak, someone in the crowd yelled, "Be careful they don't do it to you!"[10] Clearly, he was referring to the murder of Caesar.

In answer to this, Antony undid a little of his tunic, to reveal to the crowd that beneath it he was wearing a protective breastplate. This promoted a new wave of shouting, with some members of the crowd calling to him that he should take revenge for Caesar's murder. These sentiments were countered, and outnumbered, by other voices, which called for the preservation of peace.[11]

Antony, identifying the members of this peace party in the crowd, called back to them, "This is what we are debating, how to have peace and make it last. For it is difficult to find a guarantee of it now, when hundreds of vows and solemn curses were useless even to Caesar." Turning to those who had called for vengeance, he commended them for their loyalty to Caesar and said that he would have lined up with them had he not been the sole remaining consul and duty-bound to take the expedient course. "For that is what those men inside urge on us."[12]

Members of the crowd favoring revenge then called on Lepidus to share his views, but others cried that he should come down to the Forum, where everyone could hear him. "Thinking that the populace was already swinging his way," Lepidus set off for the Forum, followed by the crowd, while Antony rejoined the Senate sitting. Once Lepidus reached the Forum and mounted the Rostra, "he groaned and wept in full view for a long time" to make a show of his grief at Caesar's murder. Then he began to speak, telling the by now vast crowd spread around the Rostra that the last time he stood on this very spot it had been the morning of the Ides of March, with Caesar. Yet here he was now, forced to ask the people what they wanted him to do about Caesar's murder.[13]

"Avenge Caesar!" a number of people called from the crowd.

"Peace for the city!" others cried.

"Of course," Lepidus replied to the latter. "But what kind of peace do you mean? What oaths can make it safe? We all took the traditional oaths to Caesar, and we trampled them underfoot."[14]

When those seeking vengeance persisted, Lepidus responded that the Senate was at that very moment debating the question of what action was to be taken, but that the majority were not for vengeance, for the sake of all who survived Caesar. Someone urged him to forget the Senate and personally keep his vow to avenge Caesar. That was his inclination, he said in answer, but acting alone would achieve nothing. Other members of the crowd now praised him for his restraint, and, perhaps at Lepidus's instigation, called for him to be elected pontifex maximus in Caesar's place. Lepidus, clearly in favor of the idea, asked them to kindly remember that proposition later, if they still thought he deserved the post. With many members of the crowd urging him to support peace, he departed the Rostra and hurried back to the Senate sitting.[15]

When Lepidus resumed his seat in the Senate, Dolabella was still speaking, having delivered a long, tiresome speech about why he should now hold the consulate that Caesar had intended for him. In Appian's opinion, Dolabella had been "holding forth in a disgraceful way about his office."[16]

Antony, said Appian, had watched Dolabella with amusement, for the pair had until now been bitterly at odds. When Antony had tired of the speech-making, and knowing that the crowd outside had quieted and could not be expected to influence affairs any further, he called for silence.[17] Antony was later to say, "I considered that we Caesarians could safely survive only if Caesar were not judged a tyrant. Now our enemies and the Senate itself were gripped by a similar fear, that if Caesar were *not* a tyrant, then they would be guilty of murder."[18]

Once the Senate had come to order, Antony rose to his feet. Looking around the worried faces on the packed benches, he said, "Gentlemen, my equals in rank, I expressed no view while you were debating the fate of our citizens who have broken the law." Now he inserted his opinions into the debate, speaking with "unusual deep intensity and urgency." If those who held appointments made by Caesar resigned them, he said, they would be acknowledging that they had obtained them undeservedly. And if they gave up what Caesar had given them as undeserved, so too must every city in Rome's empire surrender honors and rights bestowed by Caesar. They would also have to deprive the retired soldiers of the land they had been given or expected to be given by Caesar.[19]

As for declaring Caesar a tyrant, Antony said, "Do you think that the men who served in Caesar's army will stand and watch while his body is dragged in the dust and broken and thrown aside unburied? For these are the penalties prescribed for tyrants by the law." He warned his fellow senators to have nothing to do with such proceedings. "I propose that we ratify all Caesar's acts and projects." At the same time, he said, they should vote to spare the murderers by granting a general amnesty to all involved in Caesar's assassination, provided that their friends and family in the Senate agreed to acknowledge that it was a favor to them.[20]

Antony would later explain that facing violent argument in the Senate from those who wished to see Caesar declared a tyrant and his assassins granted honors, "I therefore gave way to them when the amnesty was proposed in place of the honors, so that I could obtain the things I wanted in exchange."[21]

The amnesty was agreed by a large majority, with the pro-Liberator senators inserting "in the public interest" preceding the wording of the enabling resolution where it referred to recognizing all of Caesar's acts. At the forceful requests of the leaders of the ex-soldiers in the city, another motion was then passed validating all the previous land grants to Caesar's former soldiers, and a third resolution did the same for all proposed land grants to ex-soldiers. Antony then adjourned the momentous sitting.

Most of the senators were in no hurry to leave the House, preferring to wait until the crowd outside dispersed, for there was the fear that those members of the public who had called for vengeance would not be happy that the Senate had pardoned Caesar's assassins, and would attack them for it. The members stood in the temple talking in groups, with one particularly large group forming around Lucius Calpurnius Piso, Caesar's father-in-law. A consul in 58 B.C. and a neutral during the Civil War, Piso was by law entrusted with Caesar's will and had charge of his funeral arrangements. Pro-Liberator senators now urged Piso not to make the contents of Caesar's will public or give Caesar's body a public burial, in case these things incited a fresh public disturbance. When Piso would not agree to this, some of the senators around him threatened to launch legal action against him for defrauding the Roman public of a large sum of money when he was in office.

Piso, not surprisingly, was affronted, and loudly called to Mark Antony to reconvene the sitting. "They are stopping me from burying the pontifex maximus," he cried, and "threatening me if I reveal the contents of the will." Piso said that the decision regarding a funeral was Antony's as consul, "but in the case of the will, it is mine."[22]

This sponsored an angry shouting match across the chamber between those who did not wish to see Caesar's will made public and those who did. Among the latter, said Appian, were members who had hopes of being beneficiaries of the will. Antony reconvened the sitting as Piso had demanded, and once the senators had resumed their seats and order had been restored, a motion was put, and passed by a majority vote, that the contents of Caesar's will be made public, and that Caesar be the recipient of a state funeral. With the passing of this resolution, the Senate again rose, this time for the last time that day.

A proclamation from Antony now called a meeting of the Comitia next day, to endorse the Senate's resolutions.

Word of all that had taken place in the Senate that morning was quickly conveyed to Brutus, Cassius, and the others on the Capitol. Brutus and Cassius immediately issued a proclamation calling a public meeting on the Capitoline Mount, and a large crowd duly assembled there.

Brutus addressed them. Without referring specifically to the debate and resolutions in the Senate that morning, he put a case that he and his colleagues could not be condemned for breaking their oaths to safeguard Caesar, for Caesar, he said, had become a despot. Brutus reminded his listeners that even Sulla the Dictator had, after destroying his political enemies, returned the Roman people's democratic rights and stepped down. Caesar, on the other hand, had been about to embark on a new military campaign, having deprived the Roman people of democratic elections for the next five years. He reminded the crowd of how, ignoring the law that protected them, Caesar had removed and banished the tribunes Marullus and Flavus.

Brutus then asked those members of his audience who were ex-soldiers and had received or expected to receive land grants from Caesar to identify themselves. Many men in front of him raised their hands. Brutus praised them, and said they were entitled to their land. But, he said, the process implemented by Caesar's agents, who had ousted thousands of farmers from their land to redistribute it to Caesar's ex-soldiers, was unjust and gave rise to uncertain title. Brutus and his associates would correct that act of Caesarian despotism, he said, by paying dispossessed farmers for their land from the public purse, "so that you may own your allotments not merely with good title but also without incurring hostility."[23]

This went down well, and the crowd dispersed feeling "full of admiration" for Brutus and his companions, "because they seemed to be undaunted and very much on the people's side."[24] That night, the Liberators remained encamped on the Capitoline Mount with their gladiator guard. Progress had been made; the Liberators had won the Senate amnesty for their deed, and the public, most importantly Caesar's ex-soldiers, seemed to be softening their attitude toward the murder of the Dictator. But the people remained divided.

Another uneasy night passed in the Eternal City.

# XVIII

# MARCH 18, 44 B.C.

## THE LIBERATORS GAIN THE ADVANTAGE

Marcus Cicero had arrived back in the capital. Summoned by a note informing him of Caesar's death, he had returned from one of his many country estates. It turned out that Cicero was overjoyed at Caesar's murder. Yet, as he wrote to his best friend, Titus Pomponius Atticus, he considered it "a fine deed, but half done." Had Cicero been consulted prior to the Dictator's assassination, he would have counseled dispatching Mark Antony at the same time. Antony, to Cicero's mind, posed a major threat to the restoration of the Republic, and a dagger to his heart on the Ides of March would have been a great service to the Roman people. In Cicero's view, a living, breathing Mark Antony was a major obstacle to the return of democracy.[1] Cicero was to be proven all too correct.

The Comitia met first thing that morning, to ratify the previous day's Senate resolution granting amnesty to Caesar's killers. Cicero joined the assembly, and after the resolution was read aloud he gave a powerful, carefully wrought speech in favor of the amnesty. Cassius Dio, writing of Cicero's address three hundred years later, put a long, invented speech in Cicero's mouth. But in saying that Cicero called on his listeners to regard the murder of Caesar as a hailstorm or deluge that had done its damage and then quickly passed, and to accordingly consign the event to oblivion, the third-century historian was probably not far from the mark.[2]

Cicero had said, according to Dio, that anybody could lay much of the blame for Caesar's death at the feet of Caesar himself. Even if some people thought that his killers deserved punishment, Cicero implied that the two factors canceled each other out.[3] And this was a view that quickly caught on, for Cicero was considered one of Rome's most influential figures, and many a Roman would have been waiting to hear what position he took on the assassination. So once Cicero signaled that he supported amnesty for the murderers, so, too, would a large swath of the population.

The members of the Comitia, commoners all, influenced by Cicero's speech and pleased with the turn of events, which presaged reconciliation and peace between the Caesarians and the Liberators, wholeheartedly supported the amnesty. The Comitia subsequently sent a message up to the Capitol, inviting Brutus, Cassius, and the other Liberators down from the sanctuary.

The Liberators were still suspicious of Antony and Lepidus, and demanded hostages to guarantee their safety before they would set foot outside the Capitoline complex. So, pressed by Senate and commoners, Antony sent his three-year-old son Antyllus, and Lepidus sent his teenage son Marcus Lepidus the Younger. Both boys were retained on the Capitoline Mount, under the watchful guard of Albinus's gladiators, as Brutus, Cassius, and the others finally came down from their place of refuge.

When the Liberators' party was seen coming down into the Forum, there was much gleeful shouting and applause from many thousands of waiting Romans, Caesar's former soldiers among them. Antony and Dolabella, while still personal enemies, had, as the two recognized consuls now, become enforced allies against the Liberators. From the Rostra, this pair tried to make speeches to the crowd as each attempted to gain control of affairs and sway the population his way. But both were shouted down, as the people urged them to first shake Brutus and Cassius and their colleagues by the hand and reconcile with them.

The two consuls, whose "resolution was severely shaken" by the crowd reaction, had no choice but to comply with the shouted demands, and there were handshakes all round among Antony, Dolabella, Brutus, Cassius, and the other Liberators. Despite the outward signs of reconciliation, Antony and Dolabella were far from happy, for, as Appian observed, the Liberators seemed to have gained "the political advantage over them."[4]

Antony and Lepidus, anxious not to be relegated to the role of bystanders by the swelling popularity of the Liberators, extended invitations to Brutus and Cassius to dine with them and discuss the future. All the remaining members of the Liberator faction were invited to dinner by friends and acquaintances among the senators. That evening, Brutus dined with Antony at Antony's house, and Cassius with Lepidus at Lepidus's house. Meanwhile, the sons of Antony and Lepidus remained hostages on the Capitoline Mount.

Brutus went to Antony's house in the city's Carinae district very much aware that this had previously been the city house of Pompey the Great and that Antony had taken special delight in acquiring it after Pompey's murder by the Egyptians in 48 B.C. Antony would have learned that on the eve of the Civil War, Pompey had considered him nothing but "a feckless nobody."[5]

According to Cassius Dio, a wary Antony said to Brutus soon after the chief Liberator arrived at the Carinae house for their dinner engagement, only half in jest, "Have you perchance a dagger under your arm even now?"

"Yes," Brutus replied, "and a large one, should you, too, desire to make yourself a tyrant."[6]

As the four men ate at the homes of Antony and Lepidus and guardedly discussed the next possible steps, the one thing on which they fully concurred was the need to remove armed men from the city without delay. For the Liberators' part, they would agree to Albinus's gladiators—their one physical safeguard—being withdrawn from Rome only if Antony and Lepidus agreed that the retired veterans of Caesar's legions then at Rome who already had land allotted to them were "sent out immediately to the colonies," further reducing the number of potential belligerents at the capital.[7]

That night, after dinner, Brutus and Cassius returned to their homes, and both men reunited with their worried wives. Porcia in particular must have been frantic for her husband's safety over the past four days. With the Liberators unharmed and safe in their own houses, it was then, it would seem, that the sons of Antony and Lepidus were freed by the gladiators at the Capitol and allowed to return to their families.

Caesar's assassins slept in their own beds that night, for the first time since the murder, but with their doors securely bolted and guarded.

# XIX

# MARCH 19, 44 B.C.

## CAESAR'S WILL

T his was the day on which Caesar had planned to depart from Rome to launch his wars on the Getae and the Parthians. In Macedonia and Syria, the legions and cavalry units assigned to that campaign were encamped, their men going through their drills in anticipation of Caesar's imminent arrival, and in ignorance of the fact that their commander in chief was lying dead at the Regia in Rome, awaiting a funeral and cremation.

It being the first day of the Quinquatria Festival, later in the day the Salii would still dance in the Comitium as custom required, and the *arma ancialia* would be sanctified under the watchful eye of the *celerum* tribunes, representing the army, and all the pontiffs bar the dead pontifex maximus. Across the empire, army commanders would be presiding over similar ceremonies as the standards of the legions were sanctified in preparation for the year's planned military campaigns.

As dawn approached, all the members of the Senate flooded to the Temple of Tellus for another sitting of the House. Today, Brutus, Cassius, and the more than sixty senators and tribunes of the plebs who had participated in the murder of Caesar were joining their fellow senators for the first time since the fateful morning of the Ides of March. As the sun rose, and with Brutus, Cassius, Albinus, and the other Liberators sitting on the benches in front of him with their peers, Mark Antony called the sitting to order.

There followed a succession of fulsome speeches in praise of Antony for having prevented a new civil war through his temperate and conciliatory behavior as consul. A vote of thanks to Antony passed without opposition. From the other side of the House, similar speeches were given in praise of Brutus, Cassius, and their colleagues as protectors of democracy.

Antony then turned the Senate's attention to the matters of Caesar's will and the Dictator's funeral—which had already been delayed longer than was the custom of the Romans. Antony asked Piso to have the will brought to the House to be read. Piso hurried away to fetch the document. While Caesar lived it had been kept at the House of the Vestals in the Forum, in the safekeeping of the chief vestal virgin. But Caesar's elephant seal had already been broken—according to Suetonius the will had been read at Antony's house, meaning that Antony, Piso, and probably also Lepidus were aware of its contents.[1]

In Piso's absence, Antony proposed to the Senate "that the body should not have a private or dishonorable interment," on the grounds that this might "further exasperate the people."[2] More than that, Antony proposed that Caesar's funeral depart from Roman custom and be conducted within the city walls. In the same way that Roman priests were not permitted to touch the dead, funerals were normally banned from inside cities and towns for fear of polluting the abodes of the living. Similarly, all Roman crypts and tombs were outside built-up areas, usually lining the roads into metropolises.

Cassius quickly came to his feet and violently opposed a public funeral for Caesar within the city. He could see political advantage for Antony, Lepidus, Dolabella, and other Caesarians in such a public and potentially stage-managed event. He wanted a small, private affair, devoid of both crowds and of opportunities to exploit Caesar's death. Cassius also had wanted to destroy Caesar's will, and to kill Mark Antony on the Ides of March, but had been dissuaded by brother-in-law Brutus. To Cassius's exasperation, Brutus now rose to speak in support of Antony's proposal of a public funeral in the city. Brutus, for his part, saw this as a concession to Antony that would help cement the rift between the pro- and anti-Caesar factions. But, as Plutarch was to write, in doing this, Brutus made "a total and irrevocable error."[3]

With Brutus, recognized as the leading assassin, and also the current city praetor, supporting this departure from precedent, the Senate voted to give Caesar the state funeral in the Forum of Rome that Antony had called for, followed by cremation of the Dictator's body beside the tomb of his daughter, Julia, outside the city walls on the Field of Mars. In addition, the Senate chose Antony to deliver the funeral oration, "as a consul for a consul, a friend for a friend, and kinsman for a kinsman."[4] Caesar's funeral was set for the following day.

Now the Dictator's last will and testament arrived. The vast crowd that had again gathered outside the temple saw the document borne ceremoniously into the building by Caesar's father-in-law, and immediately realized what it was. Many in the throng bayed for it to be read aloud for all to hear.[5] They were not to be disappointed.

Silence descended on the Senate as Piso, standing before his expectant peers, unraveled the papyrus document. Senators leaned forward and pricked up their ears. Caesar had rewritten his will just six months before, at his country villa near Lavicum, not long after his return to Rome from Spain. His previous will had been written more than a decade earlier. In that will, Caesar had left the bulk of his estate to his son-in-law Pompey the Great, loving husband of his only child, Julia, and, at that time, Caesar's loyal and supportive ally. At the height of their alliance, Pompey had even read portions of that will to his troops to show how close he and Caesar were.[6]

As Piso's listeners now heard, Caesar's new will contained several surprises. The first was that Caesar had left two thirds of his estate to his grand-nephew Gaius Octavius, son of his sister's daughter, and had adopted him as his son. The balance of the estate went to Octavius's cousins Lucius Pinarius and Quintus Pedius. Mark Antony was named chief executor of the will. This bequest meant that eighteen-year-old Octavius, who was at this moment in Greece, could take Caesar's name, and from this time forward would be entitled to call himself Gaius Julius Caesar Octavianus. Much later, historians would contract the young man's new last name to Octavian.

Caesar's will contained more surprises. He had bequeathed his gardens on the Janiculum Hill to the people of Rome, for perpetual public use. Had Cleopatra and her party indeed been resident at Caesar's villa outside the city on the Janiculum at the time of the Dictator's murder, they would almost certainly have departed that same day, to escape the explosion of violence that seemed likely to erupt in Rome. Cleopatra's column of wagons, litters, and multitudes of pedestrian servants would have hurried away with almost indecent haste, heading for the East, bound for Alexandria, home, and safety.

In addition to giving the people his gardens, Caesar also left three hundred sesterces to every adult male Roman citizen living in Rome at that time. To an individual, this was a not insignificant amount, the equivalent of four months' pay for a soldier in Rome's legions. Word of these bequests to the people both perplexed and disturbed the crowd outside the meeting place, once news of them was relayed outside by Caesarian senators who left the sitting to curry favor with the mob by announcing the will's contents. Ever since the assassination, Brutus and the other Liberators had been telling the Roman people that Caesar had been a despot. Yet here, said Appian, "they were now faced with the testamentary provisions of a public-spirited citizen."[7]

When it also was revealed that Caesar had named as his principal heir in the second degree Decimus Brutus Albinus—the same Albinus who had turned against Caesar and been chief among his assassins, what's more providing his gladiators as bodyguards to the Liberators—many people became incensed. Under Roman law, had Octavius been unable or unwilling to accept Caesar's bequest, two thirds of the estate would have gone to Albinus, and he could have become Caesar's adopted son. The crowd became restive. "They thought it monstrous and sacrilegious that Decimus Brutus [Albinus] should have plotted against Caesar when he had been named as a son," said Appian.[8]

News of the contents of Caesar's will quickly spread throughout the city, and the public mood, which had become one of acceptance of the necessity of the removal of Caesar the despot, began a transformation. In some quarters, especially among Caesar's retired soldiers, resentment grew. Overnight, Caesar came to be seen as a benefactor rather than a despot, and "the whole city was fired with a wonderful affection for him, and a passionate sense of the loss of him."[9]

# XX

# MARCH 20, 44 B.C.

## CAESAR'S FUNERAL

The Forum was packed, shoulder-to-shoulder, with men and women who had come to pay their last respects to Julius Caesar. Caesar's body was carried from the Regia on an ivory couch spread with purple and gold cloth. It would have come out feet first, in accordance with an ancient Roman belief that this ensured that the spirit of the deceased would be less likely to return. A funeral procession led by Piso, Caesar's father-in-law, moved through the Forum the short distance to the Rostra. The pallbearers were magistrates and former magistrates, and the bier was followed by professional mourners who wailed with practiced grief, and singers who sang funeral dirges, as was the custom. The couch, bearing Caesar's body, was carefully and reverently placed on the Rostra.[1]

According to Appian, a large body of armed men gathered to guard the corpse—a number of the retired legionaries. "Wailing and lamentation arose again for a long time, and the armed men clashed their weapons." Finally, with the dramatic scene set, Mark Antony mounted the rear steps to the Rostra and took his place beside the funeral couch.[2]

With a herald standing close by, Antony looked out over the solemn gathering. Cassius Dio would credit Antony with a lengthy, articulate speech on this occasion, but it was the historian's invention. Sixteen hundred years later, Shakespeare would put his famous "Friends, Romans, countrymen" speech in Antony's mouth, but that, too, although inspired, was a fiction. While Antony was a street-smart political player, all the indications are that he was in fact a poor public speaker. His writings were even less elegant; letters of his to Octavian reveal a vulgar, boorish man possessed of neither style nor wit, indicating that Antony did not have the capacity to compose a brilliant speech of the kind credited to him by some later writers.

Suetonius and Appian seem to have the most accurate takes on how Antony eulogized the fallen Dictator. Suetonius wrote, "He instructed a herald to read, first, the recent decree simultaneously voting Caesar all divine and human honors, and then the oath by which the entire Senate had pledged themselves to watch over his safety. Antony added a very few words of comment."[3] Appian elaborated on those few words, saying that Antony reminded his audience of the key contents of those decrees, which referred to Caesar as "sacrosanct," "inviolate," "father of his country," "benefactor," and "leader."[4]

Appian continued that Antony, stretching his hand toward the temples standing on the Capitoline Mount behind him, loudly called, "O Jupiter, god of our ancestors, and you other gods, for my part I am prepared to defend Caesar according to my oath and the terms of the curse I called down on myself." The vow taken only weeks before by all senators, including Brutus and Cassius, had stated that any man who took the oath and subsequently failed to defend Caesar would be accursed forevermore. "But since it is the view of my peers that we have decided what will be for the best, I pray that it *will* be for the best."[5]

Numerous senators in the crowd called out in protest at this, so Antony said, to calm them, "We must attend to the present instead of the past," and proceeded to recite a customary funeral chant for Caesar, in his priestly capacity. But once he had completed the chant, he held up the clothes that Caesar had worn on the Ides of March, complete with dried bloodstains and rents caused by the blades of the assassins' daggers.[6] According to Plutarch, Antony declared that those who had performed this foul deed were "villains and bloody murderers."[7] Incited by this, many in the crowd erupted, some wailing in lamentation, while others yelled and raised their fists, fired with anger and indignation.[8] This uproar prompted those Liberators and their supporters who were present to hastily withdraw.

A horde of men swept up onto the Rostra, took up Caesar's bier, and attempted to carry it up onto the Capitoline Mount, intending to cremate it there on Rome's most sacred ground, against all precedent. But the priests deliberately and stubbornly barred their way, so the mob turned around and carried the ivory couch across the Forum and set it down just outside the Regia, Caesar's residence. They then rampaged around the Forum, stripping chairs, tables, and benches from the many shops lining the market arcades, creating a massive funeral pyre in front of the Regia. The couch, bearing Caesar, was then placed on top of the pyre. Someone—no one knew who—brought fire and set the wood alight. And soon, the pyre was burning fiercely.

From the crowd surrounding the pyre, retired soldiers threw their bravery decorations onto the blaze. Women tossed their jewelry and children's breastplates and ceremonial robes into the fire. Mourners who had been wearing the robes used by Caesar in all his Triumphs removed them and added them to the conflagration. The crowd swelled, as people who had kept away from the funeral were summoned by the astonishing news of a crematory fire in the Forum.

"Public grief was enhanced by crowds of foreigners lamenting in their own fashion," said Suetonius, "especially Jews, who came flocking to the Forum."[9] Caesar was especially popular with Jews after he had granted special dispensations to them throughout the Empire, in gratitude to Jewish fighters who had helped him win the war in Egypt in 48–47 B.C. Those dispensations included relieving Jews from military service with the Roman army because their religion forbade them to bear arms or travel on their Sabbath day, and permitting them to celebrate certain Jewish feasts. At the time of Caesar's death those measures had not been committed to law, so this demonstration of grief was partly designed to convince Rome's leaders to ratify the dispensations to the Jews.

As the growing crowd watched, the body of Gaius Iulius Caesar, Dictator of Rome, conqueror of Gaul, victor over Pompey the Great and his father-in-law Scipio and King Juba of Numidia, victor over Pharnaces, ruler of the Bosporan Kingdom, conqueror of the Egyptians, victor over Pompey's sons Gnaeus and Sextus, initiator of Rome's first daily newspaper and first traffic laws, and reformer of the Roman calendar, was consumed by flames.

By the time that only his blackened bones remained, those Liberators who had attended the funeral had long since slipped away from the Forum, returned to their homes, brought their families around them, and bolted their doors. It was a wise retreat, for once Caesar's body had been consumed, a number of people grabbed up burning brands from the funeral pyre and ran throughout the city, bent on burning down the houses of Caesar's assassins and incinerating the occupants.

Helvius Cinna, a minor poet and friend of Caesar, was the tribune of the plebs who earlier in the year had led the call for the banishment of fellow tribunes Marullus and Flavus for punishing those who had crowned Caesar's statue. Cinna had been suffering from a fever and had not left his bed to attend Caesar's funeral. During the night, Cinna had experienced a feverish dream in which Julius Caesar had come to him and invited him to dine; when Cinna had declined the invitation, Caesar had taken his hand and forced him to go, although Cinna had hung back all the way.

This dream was still fresh in Cinna's mind when, during the morning, word reached him that Caesar's body was burning in the Forum marketplace, close by the Regia, and not on the distant Field of Mars, as expected. Having been a friend and supporter of the Dictator, Cinna decided to make the effort to go to the nearby Forum out of respect for Caesar. Cinna dragged himself from his bed, although a little apprehensive after his odd dream the night before.

Weakly making his way through the streets toward the Forum with several servants, Cinna was met by wild-eyed men running with burning brands in their hands, fresh from Caesar's funeral pyre. One of these men asked Cinna his name. When Cinna gave it, the man passed it onto his colleagues. The hotheads, mistaking the tribune Cinna for the praetor Cornelius Cinna, who had taken part in Caesar's murder and who had delivered a bitter speech against Caesar in the Forum the day after the assassination, "immediately seized him and tore him limb from limb upon the spot," ignoring his cries that he was a friend of Caesar.[10] The mob then "paraded the streets with his head stuck on the point of a spear."[11]

This was the most damage that the rioters were able to do. With the Liberators' doors closed and bolted, and the occupants ready to repel them from the rooftops, the mob failed in its bid to burn down their houses, despite igniting several fires across the city. The Roman city house had no ground-floor windows facing the street, so that if confronted with a closed door, the rioters had no other way to gain entry. And no Liberator was foolish enough to venture out into the street in daylight.

The message that it was not safe to remain in the capital was made clear to the Liberators by this riot. Once night fell, many of the assassins and their families discreetly left the city and headed for country estates—their own or those of friends. Brutus, Cassius, and their families headed south-southwest for the coastal town of Antium,

modern-day Anzio, a year-round resort for wealthy Romans on a penin-
sula jutting into the Tyrrhenian Sea.

Among the assassins and those who had thrown in their lot with
them since the murder were several men due to take up Caesar's appointments as officials in the provinces before the spring was out, and these
men, including Trebonius, who was slated to become governor of Asia,
and Murcus, whose allotted province was Syria, soon set off for the
comparative safety of their new foreign seats.[12]

Gaius Casca, the tribune of the plebs who had sought the right to
aim the first blow at Caesar on the Ides of March, was so frightened by
this latest turn of events that he published a statement declaring that
he had not participated in the stabbing of Caesar. This was technically
true—the Dictator had held his arm throughout the time that others
were striking their blows at Caesar, so that Casca had never actually
drawn blood. More than making this hairsplitting defense, Casca wrote
that the Casca who was known to have been one of the assassins of
Caesar was in fact Publius, his brother.[13]

Mark Antony had adeptly turned the tables on the Liberators with
his funeral oration, and here, with Casca's spineless and traitorous statement, was the first sign of the unraveling of the bonds that had bound
the conspirators.

# XXI

# MARCH 21, 44 B.C.

## ANTONY CONSOLIDATES HIS GRIP

A s soon as Mark Antony learned that Brutus, Cassius, and other leading Liberators had left town overnight, he moved quickly to consolidate power. One of his first acts was to visit the Regia with his lictors. He would have previously consoled Calpurnia, Caesar's widow, over her loss; this time he had come on business.

As consul, Antony asked Calpurnia to hand over all of Caesar's papers from the Regia archive, together with his seal. Among those papers were drafts for future decrees that Caesar had been planning just prior to his death. Calpurnia instructed Caesar's secretary Quintus Faberius to comply with Antony's request. Antony also called on Calpurnia to hand over Caesar's gold coin and valuables, which he promised to keep safe. These were worth ten million sesterces.[1] Under Roman law, a widow could as a rule inherit only the equivalent of her wedding dowry from her dead husband's estate, making Caesar's bequests to his male heirs the norm. This also meant that Calpurnia had no lawful reason not to hand over the contents of Caesar's estate to Antony, who was both a consul and executor of Caesar's estate.

At the same time, Antony removed seven hundred thousand sesterces that Caesar had lodged in the shrine to Ops in the Regia.[2] Antony, wielding unquestionable authority as a consul, and supported in his administration by his brothers Gaius, a praetor, and Lucius, a tribune of the plebs, now had Caesar's riches and implements of power in his hands. And he fully intended exploiting them.

For the moment, there were still sufficient senators remaining in the city, Cicero among them, who were for order and against anarchy. At the day's Senate sitting a resolution was approved by which an investigation was launched into the riot that had followed Caesar's funeral. This investigation would result in several men being arrested for attempting to set fire to the houses of the Liberators. No arrests were made in the case of the murder of the unfortunate Helvius Cinna.

That evening, Decimus Brutus Albinus received a visit from consul-elect Aulus Hirtius. Albinus had remained at Rome; he at least had his gladiators to protect him. Hirtius, who had served as Caesar's aide throughout the Civil War and was marked down to become a consul in 43 B.C., was very much in the Caesarian camp and was felt to have some influence with Mark Antony. But he also was close to some of the Liberators, including Albinus. So Albinus took the opportunity to quiz Hirtius on Antony's intentions.

Next morning, Albinus would write to Brutus and Cassius at Antium, "Let me tell you how we stand. Yesterday evening Hirtius was at my house. He made Antony's disposition clear." That disposition, said Albinus, was "as bad and treacherous as can be." Antony had told Hirtius that he could not permit Albinus to take up his appointment as governor of Cisalpine Gaul.[3] Cisalpine Gaul was a wealthy province, but more important than that, it was garrisoned by three legions. That wealth, and that army of eighteen thousand men, right on Italy's doorstep, were not things that Antony was prepared to let fall into Albinus's hands. As would soon become clear, Antony had his eye on Cisalpine Gaul for himself.

Hirtius told Albinus that Antony "thinks none of us is safe in Rome with the soldiers and populace in their present agitated state of mind." Albinus wrote to Brutus and Cassius, "I expect you can see the falsehood of both contentions." Hirtius made it evident to Albinus that Antony was afraid that if the Liberators' position was enhanced even moderately, Antony and those who followed him "would have no further part to play in public affairs." Considering himself in a predicament, Albinus asked Hirtius to seek free commissions from the Senate for himself and for the rest of the Liberators, which would allow them to leave Italy, officially on Senate business.[4]

"I can get that agreed to," Hirtius assured Albinus.[5]

But Albinus had no confidence that Hirtius would succeed, "in view of the general insolence and vilification of us," as he wrote to his friends. "Even if they give us what we ask, I think it will not be long before we are branded as public enemies, or placed under a prohibition order." Albinus, clearly intimidated by Antony, had lost hope of overcoming him, for he believed that Antony, who had power as a consul, and his ally Lepidus between them commanded the allegiance of the military and the ex-military. "I think we must give way to fortune, leave Italy, go to live in Rhodes or anywhere under the sun," he wrote despairingly to his colleagues.[6]

To Albinus's mind, the matter of who governed Rome would be decided by military might. With Antony preventing Albinus from taking up command of the legions in Cisalpine Gaul, and expecting all of Caesar's former legions to throw their loyalty behind Antony and Lepidus, Albinus could see just two slender hopes for the Liberators gaining military support. One was via Pompey the Great's youngest son, Sextus Pompeius, who, leading a small but faithful band of followers, was still fighting a guerrilla war in western Spain against Caesar's governor there, Pollio.

The other potential supporter was Caecilius Bassus. The year before, Bassus, an affirmed republican and former subordinate of Pompey the Great, had led a mutiny of a legion left in Syria by Caesar, in the process killing the governor, Caesar's relative Sextus Julius Caesar, and took over control of the province. Caesar had appointed Lucius Staius Murcus to recover Syria for him. Murcus, who had joined the Liberators immediately following Caesar's murders, had only just set out for the East to take up that appointment. Albinus hoped that Bassus would throw the weight of the legions in Syria behind the Liberators.

In Albinus's view, whether they linked up with young Pompey or with Bassus, the Liberators would have to leave Italy to build their armed support, living in the meantime in exile. "I imagine their hands will be strengthened when this news about Caesar gets through," Albinus wrote to Brutus and Cassius of Pompeius and Bassus. "It will be time enough for us to join them when we know what their power amounts to."[7]

Hirtius departed from Albinus's house undertaking to return by mid-morning the next day with news of what concessions, if any, Antony would agree to. The news would not be good. Antony was in the box seat. He had no need to make any concessions to his political opponents, and he would make none.

# XXII

# MARCH 24, 44 B.C.

## ENTER OCTAVIUS

It was in the evening that eighteen-year-old Octavius, studying at Apollonia in Epirus, received the news from Italy that his great-uncle had been slain in the Senate House at Rome. That first message he received was brief, and failed to tell him how Caesar had been killed, or by whom, or why. He was simply informed that Caesar had been killed by those who were closest to him.[1]

Very shortly after, centurions serving with the six legions encamped in Macedonia, north of Epirus, came riding into Apollonia. These legion officers, who had frequently visited Octavius over the past six months because of his family connection with Caesar, also had heard that the Dictator had fallen. They came to vow their allegiance to Octavius, and urged him to accept their services and those of their men, and to return to Macedonia with them for safety's sake.

Two of Octavius's friends were studying with him at Apollonia. One was nineteen-year-old Marcus Vipsanius Agrippa, a bright young man of obscure background. The other, Quintus Salvidienus Rufus, while a young member of the Equestrian Order, had no ancestors of note of whom he could boast. Octavius, Suetonius was to observe, chose his friends for their loyalty rather than their connections, and was in turn staunchly loyal to them. Both Agrippa and Salvidienus now strongly advised Octavius to accept the centurions' offer.[2]

But Octavius preferred to wait for more details of what had taken place at Rome before he took any step that might rebound against him. "He felt fearful, and wondered whether the deed [Caesar's murder] had the support of the whole Senate," Appian would write, suggesting that Octavius was aware of Caesar's broad underlying unpopularity with Rome's leading men. Equally, Octavius worried "whether the ordinary people were pleased" with Caesar's death.[3] Likewise, Octavius seems to have been aware that Caesar had lost his popularity with the ordinary people. If it proved to be the case that both the Senate and the man in the street supported Caesar's murder, Octavius knew that since he was a relative of Caesar, his own life could well be in danger.

The next communication came in a brief letter from Octavius's mother, Atia, and stepfather, Lucius Marcius Philippus, at Rome. This told him no more about the assassination than he already knew, and failed to inform him that Caesar had made him his principal heir in his will; their letter seems to have been written prior to the contents of Caesar's will being made public on March 19. In this letter, Octavius's mother and stepfather counseled him to "choose the less dangerous course of behaving more like a private person" than a relative of Caesar, and urged him to "come quickly and circumspectly to them at Rome."[4]

Accompanied by Agrippa and Salvidienus, Octavius immediately set off north, to hire a boat and cross the Strait of Otranto to Italy.[5]

# XXIII

# MARCH 27, 44 B.C.

## THE NAME OF CAESAR

O ctavius, Agrippa, Salvidienus, and a handful of servants were carried across to Italy from the Greek coast in a small boat hired for the urgent journey. The craft was probably one of the six-oared fishing boats that were common in these times. Warned by his mother and stepfather to be as inconspicuous as possible, instead of putting into Brundisium, the major port from which he had left Italy to travel to Greece six months before, and a city in which troops were known to be quartered, Octavius had the boat land him and his party at the little fishing village of Lupiae, nearby.[1]

From Lupiae, Octavius sent messengers galloping to Rome to obtain more information from his family. He sent other servants to Brundisium to sound out the mood of the troops in the city and to ensure that no trap had been laid for him there by Caesar's murderers. From Rome came a package of documents by hurried return. This package contained a much more detailed letter from his mother and stepfather, a copy of Caesar's will, and copies of senatorial decrees published since the Ides of March. Now Octavius learned that Caesar had made him his son and principal heir, learned the identities of the assassins, and discovered that they and Caesar's friends had come to an accommodation since the murder that had seen the conspirators pardoned.[2]

In their latest letter, Atia and Philippus "warned him still more solemnly to beware [of] Caesar's enemies, because he was Caesar's [adopted] son and heir, and advised him to renounce both the inheritance and the adoption."[3] At age three Octavius had lost his father, Gaius Octavius, who had fallen ill and died in 63 B.C. while on his way back to Italy after serving as governor of Macedonia. Atia had married Philippus, a consul, in 56 B.C., when her son Octavius was five. But despite having been raised by Philippus, Octavius had never been close to his step-father. By age sixteen he had become Caesar's favorite, and had returned his great-uncle's affection.

Now, said Velleius Paterculus, who knew and served under Octavius in later years, Octavius "preferred to trust the judgment, concerning himself, of a great-uncle, who was Caesar, rather than that of a stepfa-ther, saying that he had no right to think himself unworthy of the name which Caesar had thought him worthy."[4] This decision was confirmed for Octavius when he set off from Lupiae to Brundisium and was met on the road by soldiers from Brundisium whose job was to provide security for official baggage, military pay, and tax revenues that passed through the city to and from the provinces. These men spontaneously greeted him as Caesar's son. Once in Brundisium he made a temple sacrifice to Caesar's memory and formally adopted his name.[5] He was no longer Gaius Octavius, but Gaius Julius Caesar Octavianus—Octavian, as we know him.

Word quickly spread that Caesar's adopted son was in Brundisium, and people began flocking to the city to pay their respects to him. Some did so merely out of regard for the late Caesar. Others were Caesar's retired former soldiers, or slaves or ex-slaves of the Dictator. Encouraged by this, Octavian and his friends set off on the road for Rome, "accompanied by a remarkable crowd which increased every day." At each of the military colonies he passed through, Octavian received a hearty welcome from Caesar's retired veterans resident there. These men expressed their grief at Caesar's murder and vented their frustration over the fact that Antony had failed to avenge his fallen leader with the blood of the assassins.[6]

But at other towns along the way Octavian found that the welcome was not so warm; in nonmilitary communities sympathy was strongly with Brutus and the Liberators, and against Caesar.[7] Undaunted, Octavian pushed on toward Rome.

# XXIV

# APRIL 7, 44 B.C.

## WISE OPPIUS

I n the Roman calendar, much of April was occupied with the celebration of public holidays. With the Senate adjourned for the Ludi
Megalenses holiday, and with the eight-day Ludi Ceriales holiday
due to run soon through the middle of the month, Marcus Cicero had
decided to leave Rome and spend much of the month in the country.

In the Senate, Cicero had taken the lead in attempts to rein in bids
for power from Antony, Lepidus, and Dolabella, and by and large he had
been successful. Influenced by Cicero, the Senate had not voted to deprive
Albinus of his governorship of Cisalpine Gaul, contrary to Antony's plan.
But by way of compensation it had granted Antony, as consul, permission to raise a military force to maintain law and order at the capital.
There was after all strong precedent—in times past, the praetors and then
the consuls had maintained such a force at Rome. Cicero feared Antony
most, because of his authority as consul and the direction he was taking. All this time, ever since Caesar's funeral, Brutus, Cassius, and the
other leading Liberators had lain low in the country and played no part in
political affairs at the capital, relying on Cicero and other public-spirited
senators to look after their interests and the interests of democracy.

Leaving Rome on the morning of April 7, Cicero made a stop at the
country villa, not far south of the capital, of Gaius Oppius. An Equestrian,
Oppius had faithfully served on Caesar's staff right through the conquest of Gaul and the Civil War, maintaining his friendship with Cicero

throughout that time. Not only was Cicero in quest of refreshment and a respite from his journey, he also was intent on gauging Oppius's view of the state of public affairs, Oppius being a confirmed Caesarian.

Oppius was depressed. "Our problems are insoluble," he frankly informed Cicero. "For, if a man of Caesar's genius could find no way out, who will find one now?" When Cicero replied that he tended to agree with his friend, Oppius, with relish, declared, "Rome is finished! The Gauls will be up within three weeks."[1]

Oppius had been at Caesar's side throughout the subjugation of Gaul. He had seen the Gauls rise in revolt under Vercingetorix in 52 B.C., and bore witness to the fact that it had only been with difficulty and great loss of life that Caesar had quelled that uprising. With Caesar gone, and with Rome divided against itself, Oppius rightly saw this as the ideal time for the Gauls to again attempt to throw out their Roman overlords. It is in fact remarkable that Gaul remained peaceful throughout the ructions that Rome went through following Caesar's death.

Cicero asked Oppius to whom he had spoken since the Ides of March, and Oppius replied that he had only seen Marcus Lepidus in the past twenty-three days. After speaking with Lepidus, Oppius had come to a pessimistic conclusion. "It cannot all just pass quietly off," he told Cicero.[2]

"Wise Oppius!" Cicero glumly wrote to his friend Atticus that night. "He regrets Caesar no less, but says nothing which any honest man could take wrongly."[3]

The next day, Cicero would resume his journey to his seaside villa at Puteoli.

# XXV

# APRIL 10, 44 B.C.

## CAESAR'S HEIR

I t was the last day of the Ludi Megalenses, a religious festival in honor of the goddess Cybele, the Great Mother. That morning, a number of members of the Senate, led by Lucius Piso, Caesar's father-in-law, met at the Temple of Concord on the Capitol. They were there to witness the committing to law of Caesar's intended measure granting Jews freedom from service with the Roman army, for Piso was determined that the late Dictator's wishes be adhered to in all things.

Caesar's dispensations had been endorsed by a recent sitting of the Senate presided over by Antony and Dolabella, at which four Jewish ambassadors sent from Jerusalem by Hyrcanus I, the Jewish high priest, had been presented to the House by the consuls. "They both introduced Hyrcanus's ambassadors into it, and spoke of what they desired, and made a league of friendship with them. The Senate also decreed to grant them all they requested." And now the law was inscribed on brass tablets at the temple, to be displayed for all the world to see.[1]

Late that afternoon, young Octavian's party came up the Appian Way from Brundisium and arrived outside Rome. Eleven weeks before, Julius Caesar had ridden along this same road, over these same cambered paving stones, on his way back from Alba Longa and on his way to the first of the controversial incidents that would lead to his death. Word of Octavian's approach had spread through the city in the preceding days, and he was met beyond the Servian Walls by a vast, enthusiastic crowd that spilled out of the city to escort him into the capital.

The exact date of Octavian's arrival at Rome is not recorded. However, the courts were operating the next day, and it is recorded that Octavian attended the courts the day after his arrival at Rome, meaning that Octavian must have arrived on April 10, for between April 4 and 19, public holidays prevented official business from being conducted on every day but April 11. The courts would not thereafter reopen until April 20. Other events rule out a later, April 19 arrival.[2]

The city was in good humor on April 10; there had been chariot racing at the Circus Maximus during the day, the last festivity connected with the Ludi Megalenses. A day at the races always cheered the population, as much because gambling was permitted on the race outcomes as for the rough and tumble of the competition among the four racing factions.

With the sun setting in the west behind Octavian, "at the moment of his entering the city men saw above his head the orb of the sun with a circle about it, colored like the rainbow." This, Velleius would write, seemed "to place a crown on the head of one destined soon for greatness."[3] Octavian went directly to his mother's house in the city. His family was of course pleased and relieved to see him, but "his mother, Atia, and Philippus, his stepfather, disliked the thought of his assuming the name of Caesar, whose fortune had aroused such jealousy."[4]

In the event, Octavian showed that he was so single-minded in his determination to take up his inheritance and seek revenge for Caesar's murder that Atia "wished him all good fortune" with his plans. At the same time, "she advised him to proceed craftily and patiently for the moment."[5] Crafty he would be, but Octavian ignored his mother's advice about being patient. That evening, Octavian sent messages to his friends, asking them to join him in the Forum at dawn the next day, urging them to bring as many companions as they could muster.[6] April 11 was the lone business day prior to the commencement of the long Ludi Ceriales festival holiday; it offered Octavian a one-day window to publicly advance his claim as Caesar's heir.

# XXVI

# APRIL 11, 44 B.C.

## OCTAVIAN MEETS WITH ANTONY

As the sun rose over Rome, Octavian was joined in the Forum by Agrippa, Salvidienus, and many other friends. On the south-eastern side of the Forum, in the Julian Basilica, a massive colonnaded building erected by Caesar, the praetors were holding court during the single business day that separated the Ludi Megalenses and Ludi Ceriales festivals. There, Octavian sought out Mark Antony's brother Gaius, one of the praetors, who was, at Antony's direction, carrying out the formal duties of the city praetor in Brutus's absence.

Octavian informed Gaius Antonius that he wished to make a legal declaration. As the praetor's legal clerks noted down his words in shorthand on wax tablets, young Octavian declared that he accepted adoption as Caesar's son. In front of Octavian's massed friends, Mark Antony's brother Gaius officially witnessed the declaration.

Learning that Mark Antony was at that moment in the Gardens of Pompey, which Caesar had given to Antony, Octavian then made his way directly there and announced that Caesar wished to see the consul Antony—Octavian was now using his adoptive father's name. He was kept waiting outside the gate to the walled gardens for some time. Octavian himself would later put the delay down to Antony's aversion to him.[1]

Finally, Octavian, and Octavian alone, was admitted to Pompey the Great's former gardens and led to the consul. Several day before, while on his way to Rome, at Tarracina, fifty miles from the capital, Octavian had learned that Antony was acting like a monarch of old. Using Caesar's seal and papers, Antony had "made many erasures and many substitutions." Then, under the heading "Memoranda of Caesar," he had issued a host of decrees including these erasures and substitutions, claiming them to have been prepared by Caesar prior to his death. In this way he had recalled men exiled by Caesar, and enrolled into the Senate others who were Antony's own supporters. Other men he deprived of money and offices. Others still he granted citizenship in return for payment. And all the while "pretending that in doing so he was carrying out Caesar's wishes."[2]

Antony also had recently implemented some other cunning measures. To cement his alliance with Marcus Lepidus, Antony had betrothed one of his daughters, Antonia, to Lepidus's son, Marcus Lepidus the Younger.[3] And with the office of pontifex maximus vacant with the death of Caesar, Antony issued a decree transferring the election of the high priest from the people to the college of priests, of which he was a member. He then had the priests elect Marcus Lepidus pontifex maximus, a post Lepidus would hold for life. Rushing through the ceremony, Antony personally consecrated Lepidus as high priest.[4]

As part of their deal, Lepidus then left Rome, hurrying off to Nearer Spain, a province whose governorship he continued to hold under Caesar's decree. Importantly, as far as Lepidus's ally Antony was concerned, once there Lepidus would take command of the four legions based in Nearer Spain, with which the pair could counter Albinus's three legions in Cisalpine Gaul.

Antony, at the height of his powers now, and with his various schemes falling into place, was in no mood for interference from a teenager whom Caesar had seen fit to make his chief heir. Antony greeted Octavian with brusque familiarity. He "despised" Caesar's young heir, considering him "a stripling" and "inexperienced in business," and it showed in the haughty way he treated the handsome, fine-boned youth.[5] After each man had made the customary inquiries about the other's health, Octavian politely but promptly went to the point of his visit and asked Antony to be so good as to hand over his inheritance from Caesar.

Antony was taken aback by the youth's forthrightness. His annoyance soon gave way to amusement and disdain. According to Appian, Antony patronizingly referred to Octavian as "my lad," claimed that Caesar's estate was nowhere near as large as Octavian imagined, and declared that he did not have the money himself.[6] After a brief and ineffective interview, Octavian was dismissed by Antony and escorted back to the street.

As the gates banged shut behind him, Octavian "was furious."[7] But he would not be put off. As had been the case when his great-uncle had crossed the Rubicon River in January 49 B.C. to launch war against his own country, the die had been cast, and the young man would gamble everything on winning.

# XXVII

# APRIL 14, 44 B.C.

## THE AEDILE'S REFUSAL

The eight-day Ludi Ceriales, a festival celebrating Ceres, goddess of the harvest, was in full swing. Many of the festivities were taking place in the countryside, but on the last day, April 19, there would be "games" at the circus at Rome to culminate the festival.

Young Octavian, determined to celebrate his great-uncle's legacy and to promote his own position, knew that in the months leading up to Caesar's death the Senate had promulgated a particular decree—among the many ingratiating decrees it made to honor Caesar at that time—that at all festival games in the future the Dictator's throne of gold and ivory should be prominently displayed in the official box of the director of the games, to represent Caesar's presence when he was away from Rome. No provision for Caesar's throne had been made for these Ludi Ceriales games, but now that Octavian was at Rome he set his mind on having the measure adopted at all games from then on.

The next games would be on May 12, for the Ludi Martiales festival. The official responsible for organizing those games and acting as their director was an aedile named Critonius. So Octavian informed Critonius that he wished to have Caesar's throne displayed at the Ludi Martiales games and asked him to make provision for it. The aedile Critonius clearly sympathized with the Liberators and their view of Caesar, for he flatly refused Octavian, declaring that he "would not tolerate honor being paid to Caesar at his expense."[1]

Octavian would not accept this response from Critonius and promptly "brought him before Antony as consul," at Antony's house, asking him to rule that the aedile must adhere to the Senate decree. Antony, who was preparing to leave Rome within the next few days, impatiently advised Octavian that he would place the matter before the Senate and let them decide whether the decree in question was still valid.[2]

Octavian knew that the Senate was unlikely to meet again until late May or June, after a month occupied almost entirely by holy days, and that would be too late for a decision about displaying Caesar's throne at the games of May 12. Besides, Octavian believed that the decree must still be in force, for, on March 17, had not the Senate resolved that all Caesar's past acts remained valid? According to Appian, Antony's response thoroughly irritated Octavian.

"Refer it," Octavian countered, "but I shall display the throne so long as the decree is in force."[3]

Antony was incensed, and forbade Octavian to do any such thing.[4] Again Octavian went away humiliated by Mark Antony.

# XXVIII

# APRIL 22, 44 B.C.

## OCTAVIAN SEEKS CICERO'S SUPPORT

A ntony left Rome in the middle of the month, leading a large party of retired soldiers, apparently from the 8th Legion and possibly also the 7th, who had been living at Rome in expectation of settlement on rural land. With the veterans marching in good order behind a standard, Antony headed south to Casilinum in Campania, where a new military colony had been laid out by military surveyors who had been mapping colonies like this one in Italy and southern Gaul for the past two years.[1]

Antony was to spend two weeks in Casilinum, personally plowing the sacred furrow that defined the new colony's limits.[2] Some of the land allotted to veterans following Caesar's death was public land, but contrary to the initiative that Brutus had proposed on March 17—that all existing farmowners who were dispossessed of their land for the settlement of ex-soldiers should receive fair compensation—under Antony's settlement program some existing farmers dispossessed of their land for soldier settlement would not receive any compensation.

With Antony out of town and the Senate in recess, Octavian decided to use the break to cement the friendship of the most eloquent and arguably most influential voice in the Senate: Cicero. Accompanied by his mother and stepfather and a number of friends, Octavian also left Rome and traveled down to the Bay of Naples to pay Cicero a friendly visit at his Puteoli villa.

"Octavius is here with me," Cicero noted in a letter to his friend Atticus, written on the evening of the twenty-second. Cicero observed that Octavian was "most respectful and friendly" toward him. He said that Octavian's friends were calling the young man Caesar, as his adoption in Caesar's will provided. "But Philippus [Octavian's stepfather] does not, so neither do I."[3]

At this point, Cicero was suspicious of Octavian's motives, and doubted that the youth would support a return of the Republic and its democratic institutions. "My judgment is that he cannot be a good citizen. There are too many around him. They threaten death to our friends [the Liberators] and call the present state of things intolerable. What do you think they will say when the boy comes to Rome, where our Liberators cannot go safe? They have won eternal glory, and happiness too in the consciousness of what they did"—murdering Caesar. "But for us," Cicero lamented, "if I am not mistaken there is only humiliation ahead."[4]

Cicero's pessimism stemmed from the latest news of Antony's recent activities at Rome. "The things I hear from Rome! And the things I see here!" A decree had been posted all over the capital by Antony, under Caesar's seal, announcing that all Sicilians were now Roman citizens according to a law passed some time previously by the Comitia. Yet Cicero had no recollection of any such law being passed by the Comitia while Caesar was alive. Cicero's information was that Antony had received a massive bribe from Sicily to promulgate this invented law.[5]

Another Antonian decree had restored Galatian territories confiscated from King Deiotarus by Caesar when Deiotarus had supported Pompey during the Civil War. Cicero believed that Antony's wife, Fulvia, had been behind that; again, a large sum of money would have changed hands. "There are any number of such things" being done by Antony, Cicero complained. But no one had either the incontestable evidence or the courage to accuse Antony of forging Caesar's decrees.[6]

"I fear the Ides of March have brought us nothing except joy and a satisfaction for our hatred and grief," Cicero wrote glumly to his friend. That hatred had been of Caesar; the grief that Cicero referred to had been caused by Caesar. "So, I long to be away."[7]

# XXIX

# MAY 11, 44 B.C.

## I DON'T TRUST HIM A YARD

With the Senate adjourned through the first half of May until after the Ludi Martiales and the Lemuria, holy days when the ghosts of the dead were said to roam, the dispirited Cicero had not returned to Rome, but continued to reside at his Puteoli villa. There he received a constant stream of letters and visitors apprising him of the changing political situation at Rome and their opinions of that situation. Many of these men were leading players in the drama, from both sides, among them Dolabella; he was Cicero's former son-in-law, having married Cicero's daughter Tullia, who had died in childbirth. Another of Cicero's informants was Hirtius, the consul-designate. And of course Brutus and Cassius were in almost daily contact.

Cicero had that morning received a letter from Cassius, who, together with Brutus, was still at nearby Antium. Cicero had just sent Cassius's courier away carrying mail when a visitor arrived. This was Lucius Cornelius Balbus. A native of Gades, modern Cadiz, in Spain, Balbus had for many years been Caesar's financial agent and close personal adviser.

Balbus's loyalty to Caesar had never wavered. Determined to salvage Caesar's reputation in the wake of his murder, and to counter the picture of a tyrant painted by the Liberators, Balbus had recently asked consul-elect Hirtius to put together Caesar's memoirs covering the Civil War, for prompt publication. Caesar's account had ended at the defeat of Pompey at the Pharsalus battle; Hirtius, who had served on Caesar's staff throughout the Civil War, would attach accounts by other hands to Caesar's own chapters to complete the memoirs. Hirtius himself is likely to have written the chapters covering Caesar's war in Egypt, during which time Caesar began his liaison with Cleopatra.

Cicero considered Balbus particularly cagey, but the visitor was nonetheless willing to open up and tell him all he knew about Mark Antony's movements and plans. At this point Antony was still absent from Rome; after close to two weeks in Campania settling legion veterans, he had moved on to the Samnium district. Balbus told Cicero, "He is going the rounds of the veterans to get them to stand by Caesar's measures and take an oath to that effect, instructing them all to keep their arms ready and have them inspected monthly by the *ilviri* [colonial magistrates]." Balbus also complained to Cicero of being personally unpopular in some circles, as a former friend of Caesar. "The whole tenor of his talk argued friendship for Antony," Cicero wrote to his friend Atticus. "In short, I don't trust him a yard."[1]

After Balbus left, Cicero wrote his daily letter to Atticus. In it he again blamed Brutus and Cassius for not killing Antony on the Ides of March while they had the chance. "That affair was handled with the courage of men and the policy of children. Anyone could see that an heir to the throne was left behind"—Antony being that heir. In Cicero's view, armed conflict between Antony and his political opponents was only a matter of time. "There is no doubt in my mind that we are moving toward war," he told Atticus.[2]

That war, if it came, would be waged among the several different factions that had emerged in Roman politics in the short time since Caesar's death. There was the group that had murdered Caesar, the Liberators; they had in the main retired to the country for safety's sake and were playing no active part in affairs at Rome. There were the Caesarians, Caesar loyalists led by Antony, Lepidus, Dolabella, Hirtius, and Pansa. Between these two groupings stood what may be called the centrists, a grouping Cicero was calling the *optimates*, or "the best men," in mimicry of the conservative faction that had dominated the Senate once Sulla had come to power forty years earlier. And on the fringe, with a handful of supporters, there was young Octavian, who was attached to no party but at odds with Antony and on friendly terms with Cicero. Too young to hold any political office, all Octavian had in his favor was Caesar's name and inheritance; few apart from Octavian himself considered him a serious political player.

Despite his pessimism, or perhaps because of it, Cicero planned to try to win Hirtius the consul-elect from Antony's party and over to the side of the centrists, for Hirtius had friends among both the Liberators and the centrists. Hirtius also was vacationing on the Bay of Naples while the Senate was in adjournment, and Cicero was planning to dine with him the following evening. Everything that Cicero was hearing told him that the Caesarians were intent on retaining power by force. "That lot are afraid of peace, every man of them!" Cicero wrote to Atticus.[3] The Caesarians were significantly outnumbered by the Liberators and centrists, and in a peaceful state they would be voted out of power. War was looking increasingly like the Caesarians' only recourse.

Even though outnumbered, the Caesarians had the upper hand for the moment, with Antony and Dolabella in power as consuls until year's end. Hirtius and Pansa would take over the consular powers on January 1. But if Hirtius could be drawn away from Antony's party, the war party, then a peaceful new year might be guaranteed. "Anything is better than soldiering," said Cicero.[4]

# XXX

# MAY 18, 44 B.C.

## UNDERMINING ANTONY

Cicero must have received a favorable hearing from Hirtius, for, confident of strong backing, Cicero had decided to return to Rome to pursue the fight against Antony in the Senate once it resumed sitting. One of the tactics he would employ would be encouragement of young Octavian's bid to undermine Antony's support among those who remained faithful to the memory of Caesar. To Cicero's mind, if Antony could be made powerless, democracy could be preserved. There was hope yet for the Republic.

Cicero departed his Puteoli villa on May 17 and went first to Cumae to attend a funeral. He had a farm at Cumae, but he continued on to Sinuessa, where he had another, and spent the night there. He was carrying a copy of the speech that Brutus had delivered in Rome following Caesar's murder, for Brutus had asked him to polish it before it was published.

As Cicero wrote to Atticus on the morning of May 18, he considered Brutus's original speech elegant but lacking in the rhetorical "thunderbolts" that were called for on such an occasion. Cicero had rewritten the speech. "Given his chosen style and his judgment of what is the best style of oratory," Cicero wrote, "our good Brutus has in this speech attained it with perfect elegance. But I have aimed at something different, whether rightly or wrongly."[1]

Cicero continued on his way to Rome.

# XXXI

# MAY 31, 44 B.C.

## REFORMING THE PRAETORIAN COHORTS

To raise money, Octavian had been selling Caesar's property, as well as his own property inherited from his father, Gaius Octavius, and even the property of his mother and stepfather, for whatever price he could get. His cousins Pedius and Pinarius also gave him their one-third share of the inheritance from Caesar's estate. Much of the money raised by Octavian in this way he gave to the officials of Rome's voting tribes, for distribution among male citizens at Rome according to the terms of Caesar's will, which provided for a largesse of three hundred sesterces to every citizen at Rome.

Octavian's apparent generosity was rightly perceived by Mark Antony as a strategy to win public favor at the expense of Antony's popularity. Antony had just returned to Rome after spending four to five weeks visiting the veteran colonies in central Italy. He had not returned alone. The Senate had given him approval to raise a military force to maintain law and order at Rome, and during his travels he had enrolled as many as six thousand former legionaries, creating a number of cohorts, each a thousand men strong. Antony called them the Praetorian Cohorts. After the foundation of the Republic in 509 B.C., the praetors of Rome had raised cohorts to police Rome, and these had later come under the control of the consuls. The Praetorian Cohorts, erroneously called by later historians the Praetorian Guard, had fallen into abeyance by early in the first century B.C., but Antony, as a consul, was technically within his rights to reestablish them.

Appian, who put the number of six thousand on Antony's Praetorians, claimed all were former centurions, but that number would represent the centurions from one hundred legions, an impossible number when Caesar's army had, at its height, numbered little more than forty legions. Nonetheless, these were all experienced, hardened soldiers. Whatever the number of men involved, the Senate considered it too many. When authorizing Antony to raise this force, the Senate had made the mistake of failing to put a limit on the number of men he could recruit. Senators now called on Antony to reduce his force, which he was now using as his personal bodyguard. He undertook to do so—but when the security situation at Rome permitted.

Given renewed confidence by the Praetorian Cohorts at his back, Antony encouraged opposition to Octavian, and when some landholders brought suit against Octavian for selling land that had been seized by Caesar after they had been exiled or fled the country, putting the title in dispute, both Antony and Dolabella found in favor of the complainants and against Octavian, even though in doing so they also were finding against the acts of Caesar.

Every day, Octavian would walk through the city "accompanied by a crowd like a bodyguard," and like a modern politician he would solicit public support in the street. He urged people to overlook the "disgraceful treatment" he was receiving at the hands of the consuls but instead "to defend Caesar, their commander and benefactor, against the dishonor being inflicted by Antony."[1]

At every opportunity, Octavian would climb up on temple steps or the plinth of a statue to address the public. Typically, in one of his speeches, the eighteen-year-old said, at the top of his voice, "Don't be angry with Caesar on my account, Antony. Do not insult the man who has turned out to be your benefactor." He said that Antony could heap as much indignity on him, Octavian, as he liked, but he should stop plundering Caesar's property. "In my poverty," Octavian said dramatically, "I shall be content with my father's [Caesar's] glory, if it lasts, and the legacy to the people, if you let it be paid."[2]

Octavian was able to stoke so much feeling against Antony that the military tribunes commanding the new Praetorian Cohorts asked Antony to soften his attitude toward Octavian. These young tribunes, all members of the Equestrian Order, reminded Antony that they, like him, had loyally served under Caesar, and they did not think it right that Antony should treat Caesar's heir and adopted son so shabbily. They asked him to "moderate his arrogance," both for their sakes and his. Antony, although he complained that Octavian was "most painfully conceited despite being so young, and showed no deference to his elders," feigned a change of heart, and agreed to moderate his behavior if Octavian did the same.[3]

Armed with this concession, and with the last of Antony's Praetorian recruits due to report to him at Rome on June 1, the officers brokered a meeting between the pair. With the Praetorian officers guaranteeing his safety, Octavian came to Antony's mansion in the Carinae. After each criticized the other in front of the officers, they buried the hatchet, shook hands, and "accepted each other as friends."[4] It was a reconciliation with the capacity to totally reshape Roman politics.

# XXXII

# JUNE 2, 44 B.C.

## ANTONY OUTSMARTS THE SENATE

Antony was determined to wrest control of the province of Cisalpine Gaul, and its three crack legions, from Decimus Brutus Albinus. Antony knew that he did not command sufficient support in the Senate to have Albinus's province reassigned to him, but now that he had made an ally of young Octavian, he decided to sideline the Senate and use Octavian's popularity with the plebeians to push a law through the Comitia that achieved his purpose. Cicero and his fellow centrists, who planned to block Antony's measure in the Senate, half-expected him to attempt to circumvent them using this tactic, but were confident that the tribunes of the plebs would veto any law that Antony put before the Comitia.

On the evening of June 1, Antony discreetly sent out summonses to all the voters of the Assembly, and before dawn on June 2, with the voting place roped off by Antony's Praetorians to prevent members of the Senate from getting to them, the voters assembled. Standing by the rope as they arrived was Octavian, who urged the plebeians and Equestrians to support the measure, for he was just as anxious as Antony to deprive Albinus of his province and his legions. Octavian also felt that his support would put new ally Antony in his debt.

Antony, meanwhile, had bribed the tribunes of the plebs, who did not intercede their veto. The law depriving Albinus of Cisalpine Gaul was passed by the Comitia. The Senate would not endorse this new law, and Albinus would take no notice of it, in defiance of Antony. Despite this, Antony felt that in the Comitia's law he had a legal pretext for removing Albinus by force. But Albinus's experienced legionaries stationed in Cisalpine Gaul outnumbered Antony's Praetorians by at least three to one. Antony needed more troops, and quickly.

Back in April, Antony's fellow consul Dolabella had railroaded a law through the Comitia that took the governorship of Syria from Liberator-supporter Staius Murcus and gave it to himself, even though Murcus was already on his way to take up the appointment. Dolabella managed to gain Senate endorsement for that law by convincing a majority of senators that, as governor of Syria, he would take up where Caesar had left off and invade Parthia with the legions that Caesar had assembled for that very operation. Dolabella was so personally unpopular among senators of all persuasions that many would have voted in favor of his appointment just to remove him from Rome, perhaps even hoping that it would result in his death at the hands of the Parthians.

At the same time, Antony had won Senate approval to take up the governorship of Macedonia. His opponents would have been happy to vote for a measure that removed such a threatening figure from Rome. Besides, Dolabella's appointment had the rider that he would command all the legions assigned by Caesar to the Parthian campaign, no matter where they were camped. This took the six legions in Macedonia out of Antony's control. Antony had further lulled the Senate into a false sense of security by proposing a resolution that the post of Dictator be permanently declared illegal, with the penalty of death for anyone who proposed to appoint a Dictator and for any man who accepted the post. To optimists, this had sounded as if Antony was turning over a new leaf and that democracy might have a chance of surviving after all.

Antony went further. At the prompting of Marcus Lepidus, who was heading to Spain, and in emulation of the proposal originally put by Cassius, Antony recommended that Pompey the Great's son Sextus, still fighting a guerrilla war against Caesar's general Pollio in western Spain, be recalled to Rome, paid two hundred million sesterces in restitution for the property of his father seized by Caesar during the Civil War, and given command of Rome's navy in the western Mediterranean.[1] Young Sextus, like his late father, was seen as the embodiment of republicanism, and Antony's proposal seemed to signal reconciliation among all sides, cementing divisions created by the Civil War. Many senators almost fell over themselves in their eagerness to support this resolution.

Antony's proposals regarding the dictatorship and Sextus Pompeius had been ringingly endorsed, with speaker after speaker in the Senate praising Antony to the skies. Yet anyone who had read Decimus Brutus Albinus's mind, or his correspondence, would have known that Albinus and other leading Liberators were counting on Bassus in Syria and Sextus in Spain as potential allies. With Dolabella and Antony countering Bassus and embracing Sextus, both Bassus and Sextus were potentially removed from the equation, leaving the Liberators with nowhere now to turn for military support.

Now, six weeks later, after a rumor swept Rome that the Getae, having heard of Julius Caesar's death, had invaded Macedonia, Antony asked the Senate to give him command of the legions in Macedonia, the province it had allocated to him, so he could direct a campaign against the Getae and throw them out of Macedonia. The Senate had in the meantime sent a commission to Macedonia to investigate the truth of the Getae rumor. But after Dolabella—whom the Senate thought to be Antony's enemy—agreed to assign command of five of the six legions in Macedonia to Antony, retaining just one for himself, the Senate approved Antony's proposal before the commission of inquiry returned from Macedonia to report its findings.

When the commissioners did return, they reported that although the people of the province were afraid that the Getae might attack Macedonia once the legions left, there was no sign of the Getae in Macedonia at this time. But Antony now had his legions, five of them. And it is likely that the rumor of a Getae invasion had been planted by him. If not planted by Antony, it was certainly craftily exploited by him. Now Antony had the muscle he needed.

# XXXIII

# JUNE 7, 44 B.C.

## NO PLAN, NO THOUGHT, NO METHOD

By June 6, Cicero had left Rome. Spending the night at villas along his route, by late morning on June 7 he was nearing Antium, on the western coast of Italy.

At a June 5 sitting of the Senate, Mark Antony had made another surprise move. Although failing to receive Senate endorsement for his law that would deprive Albinus of the governorship of Cisalpine Gaul, Antony had put a fresh motion before the House that seemed to many on the Senate benches to be both reasonable and conciliatory. Antony proposed that Liberator leader Brutus should be made governor of Crete, and his colleague Cassius governor of Sicily, for the following year. A provincial governor was immune from prosecution while in office, so these appointments offered protection for Brutus and Cassius against a prosecution for the murder of Caesar should Antony somehow be able to reverse the Senate and Comitia resolutions that gave all the assassins amnesty from prosecution.

These gubernatorial appointments were readily approved by the Senate, which also endorsed a resolution by the Liberators' friends that Brutus and Cassius be appointed corn commissioners in the province of Asia, in modern Turkey, until they took up their provincial governorships.[1] The grain commission appointments, which came into immediate effect, would allow the pair to leave Italy at once, without restriction, with staff, at State expense, and also be immune from prosecution.

Cicero must have known that these appointments suited Antony's plans. They would remove Brutus and Cassius from Italy, getting them out from under Antony's feet. Notably, no legions were stationed in either Crete or Sicily, meaning that neither Brutus nor Cassius would have access to military forces with which they could challenge Antony. But at least the appointments, especially those of corn commissioners, would give Brutus and Cassius the excuse and the opportunity to find safety abroad.

Cicero was anxious to learn what Brutus and Cassius would do once they learned of these appointments, for he considered his future to be bound up with theirs. He himself was contemplating leaving Italy. He had learned en route to Antium that his loyal former son-in-law Dolabella had appointed him to join his consular staff when he went to the East to take up the governorship of Syria. If Cicero accepted the appointment, it also would give him the freedom to travel without restriction.[2]

Determined to ignore the fact that Brutus had been at odds with him of late, Cicero headed for Antium. Cicero had recently been writing and speaking in praise of Octavian, and Brutus was not well pleased by that. Brutus was not as trusting of Octavian as was Cicero, nor did he see him as a naive youth who could be easily manipulated, as Cicero seemed to think him to be. Brutus, who was awake to Octavian's ambitions, had written angry letters to Cicero, telling him that in siding with Octavian against Antony to avoid a civil war, Cicero ran the risk of facilitating "a dishonorable and infamous peace," and that in aiding Octavian to subvert Antony he would only replace one tyrant with another.[3]

Cicero arrived at Antium a little before noon. Brutus came to the door to greet him and was clearly pleased to see him, with the bitterness of his recent letters forgotten. Tidings of the June 2 law and the June 5 appointments had preceded Cicero— Brutus's close friend Marcus Favonius also was at the Antium villa, and it seems that he had galloped all the way from Rome with the news.[4]

Brutus escorted Cicero into a room where all the houseguests were gathered. Favonius was here, as were Brutus's pale wife, Porcia, and Cassius's wife, Brutus's sister Tertullia. Brutus's mother, Servilia, also was present; she had been staying not far away at a villa outside Neapolis, modern-day Naples. Cicero thought it highly incongruous that Servilia, who was Caesar's former lover and still remained intensely loyal to his memory, was staying at the house of Pontius Aquila, the tribune of the plebs who had been one of Caesar's most fervent assassins. Aquila was at this time serving on the gubernatorial staff of Albinus in Cisalpine Gaul.

"What do you think I ought to do?" Brutus asked Cicero in front of the others, who all listened intently to the conversation.[5]

"I gave the advice I had prepared on the way," Cicero was to write to his regular correspondent Atticus. "Accept the Asiatic corn commission," he told Brutus. "Your safety is all that concerns us now; it is the bulwark of the Republic itself."

Cicero was elaborating on this theme when Cassius walked in. For Cassius's benefit, Cicero repeated his advice to Brutus, that the pair take up their appointments abroad and live to fight another day.[6]

Cassius, "looking most valorous," in Cicero's opinion, "the picture of a warrior," declared that "he had no intention of going to Sicily." "Should I have taken an insult as though it had been a favor?" Cassius added. The appointment as governor of Sicily had been good enough for Porcia's revered father, Cato the Younger, to accept just prior to the Civil War, but Cassius, an experienced military commander, was not interested in governing an "unarmed province," especially not in these dangerous times.

"What do you mean to do then?" Cicero inquired.

"I will go to Greece," said Cassius firmly.

Cicero turned to Cassius's colleague. "What about you, Brutus?"

"To Rome, if you agree," Brutus answered.

"But I don't agree at all!" Cicero came back, horrified by the thought. "You won't be safe there."

"Well, suppose I could be safe. Would you approve?"

"Of course. And what's more, I would be against your leaving for a province either now or after your praetorship [which ended on December 31]. But I cannot advise you to risk your life in Rome."[7]

Brutus seemed to have some vague plan in mind for providing protection for himself at the capital, but if he did, he refrained from sharing it with Cicero. Both men knew that there were high expectations among the populace at Rome that Brutus would appear at the Circus Maximus in July to take credit for organizing the Ludi Apollinares, the seven-day festival that ran between July 7 and 13 each year. Sacred to the god Apollo, these games were intended to appease the god and avoid great national disasters.

It fell to the urban praetor to organize this festival, whose last day featured spectacles and chariot races at the circus. And despite the fact that he had absented himself from Rome, Brutus was determined to fulfill his duties in respect to the Ludi Apollinares, as great credit fell to the man who staged these games—and paid for them from his own pocket. According to Plutarch, the people of Rome "longed for the return of Brutus, whose presence they expected and hoped for at the games and spectacles which he, as praetor, was to exhibit."[8] If Brutus could safely be present to receive the crowd's accolades, this would provide him with a springboard to the leadership of efforts against Antony, and regain the momentum for the democracy movement.

For these upcoming games, Brutus had already organized, at his own expense, large numbers of wild beasts to be used in the hunting spectacles in the circus. He had sent word to Rome that to give the crowds the maximum entertainment, none of these wild beats was to be spared for later shows. He had also recently traveled to Neapolis to secure a large number of excellent Neopolitan players for the stage performances that would occupy the first six days of the festival. And he had written to friends urging them to secure a rising star among Italy's actors named Canutius for the festival.[9]

Cicero could not accept that Brutus would be safe at Rome while Antony commanded a large Praetorian bodyguard of experienced soldiers, and told him so. A great deal of talk followed among Cicero, Brutus, and Cassius. Both the Liberators, but Cassius especially, complained bitterly about opportunities that had been let slip. Albinus in particular came in for severe criticism.[10] Had Albinus marched south from Cisalpine Gaul with his three legions soon after arriving there, while Antony was away from Rome in April–May and before he had recruited his Praetorian Cohorts, Albinus could have occupied Rome with his troops and restored republican control. Instead, Albinus had remained in Cisalpine Gaul, surrounding himself with his troops, apparently intent on protecting his own neck. This was much to the displeasure of Cassius and Brutus, for "they placed most confidence in" Albinus, who had come to represent the Liberators' last hope of military intervention.[11]

After Dolabella had put Bassus's power in doubt now that the Senate had approved Dolabella's Syrian appointment, and with Sextus Pompeius expected to agree to cease hostilities and accept two hundred million sesterces and command of the Roman navy in the western Mediterranean, Albinus's legions were all that stood between Antony and total power. And yet, as Cassius and Brutus complained, instead of marching on Rome, Albinus had marched his troops into the Alps, away from Italy, and launched a campaign against fractious Alpine tribes. Now that Antony had surrounded himself with his Praetorian Cohorts and was likely to bring five legions to Italy from Macedonia, he would soon achieve military domination of his political opponents.

"To that I said it was no use crying over spilled milk," Cicero wrote to his friend Atticus. "But I agreed all the same." Cicero went on to put his own views to Brutus and Cassius on what should have been done. He confessed that his ideas were not original—he was only giving voice to "what everyone is saying all the time," although he did not voice his opinion that Antony also should have been murdered. He told Brutus and Cassius that they "should have summoned the Senate, girded the popular enthusiasm to action with greater vigor, and assumed the leadership of the entire Republic."[12]

"Well, upon my word!" exclaimed a female voice behind Cicero. He turned to see Brutus's mother, Servilia, sitting with a scowl on her face. "I never heard the like!" she added.[13]

"I held my tongue" after that, Cicero was to tell Atticus. Out of respect for Servilia, and for her affection for Caesar, Cicero did not again broach the subject of the Dictator's death or of anything connected with it in front of her. The past was left behind, as the topic of conversation returned to the future. Cicero wrote, "It looked to me as though Cassius would go" to Greece, as he had at first announced. "Brutus was soon persuaded to drop his empty talk about wanting to be in Rome." Brutus reluctantly accepted that the July games would have to be held in his absence, although under his name. "It looked to me as though he wanted to go to Asia direct from Antium," Cicero confided to Atticus.[14]

The conversation continued over dinner, but nothing changed, and Cicero was deeply depressed by the whole affair. He had come to Antium feeling obliged to see Brutus out of affection for him and a sense of duty. "Nothing in my visit gave me any satisfaction except the consciousness of having made it," he revealed in the glum letter he wrote to Atticus that night. "I found the ship going to pieces, or rather its scattered fragments. No plan, no thought, no method."[15]

To Cicero, it beggared belief that neither Brutus nor Cassius, otherwise highly intelligent men, had properly thought through measures to cover the aftermath of Caesar's assassination, that they had not made provision for a takeover of power until elections restored the Republic and its democratic institutions. After all, Rome's most senior officials on the Ides of March, including Antony as consul and Dolabella as consul-designate, had been appointed by Caesar, who had himself seized power in a military coup.

Neither Antony nor Dolabella had been elected. Constitutionally, neither man was entitled to wield any authority at this moment. But who was going to tell that to Antony, or his Praetorians? Velleius Paterculus, whose parents lived through this era, was to say, "The state languished, oppressed by the tyranny of Antony. Everyone felt resentment and indignation, but no one had the power to resist."[16]

From Antium, the disheartened Cicero wrote to Atticus, "I am now all the more determined to fly from here, and as soon as I possibly can." His last words were ominous: "I have a feeling that the sands of time are running out."[17]

# XXXIV

# JULY 13, 44 B.C.

## THE LAST DAY OF BRUTUS'S GAMES

Early in July, the month that now bore Julius Caesar's family name, the Ludi Apollinares, the week-long festival at Rome organized and paid for by Brutus, had gone off without a hitch. They were "most magnificent and costly," according to Plutarch.[1] "They were indeed magnificent," Appian concurred.[2] But Brutus was not there to see how well his money was spent, or to receive public credit for his munificence. To make matters worse, in Brutus's absence Mark Antony had assigned his brother Gaius the job of carrying out Brutus's duties as city praetor, so even though Brutus had paid for and organized the shows, it was Antony's brother who sat in the director's box and took the credit for these magnificent Ludi Apollinares games.[3]

Knowing this, the absent Brutus, in an attempt to turn the affair to his political advantage, had paid for a large group of spectators to be recruited who, when the games were at their height, began to loudly demand the return of Brutus and Cassius to Rome, trying to whip the entire crowd into joining their demand. But an even larger mob suddenly appeared, crowding into the circus and preventing the games from continuing until Brutus's people shut up. With the majority of spectators only interested in enjoying a free day at the games, "the demand faded away."[4] Brutus's tactic failed.

This latter band of demonstrators also had been paid to play their disruptive role, but not by Mark Antony, the man who could have been expected to have been behind their appearance. Their employer was actually young Octavian, who had either gotten wind of the plans for this pro-Liberator demonstration or had made preparations for prompt action should such an event occur.[5] As Brutus had previously warned Cicero, Octavian was not someone to be underestimated.

Following the Ludi Apollinares, Mark Antony dispatched his brother Gaius to Macedonia with a copy of the decree that gave him command of five of the six legions encamped there. Gaius Antonius also carried his elder brother's orders for those legions and many auxiliary cavalry *alae*, or wings, stationed with them to make their way to Italy by the fastest means possible.[6]

This army of thirty thousand legionaries and thousands of cavalry was instructed by Antony to base itself at the port city of Brundisium, in the south of Italy. Officially, Antony said that he was bringing the army to Brundisium "to have it available against emergencies." Antony's enemies would have immediately perceived his intent as that of using this army against Albinus in Cisalpine Gaul. Antony himself made it clear that he was not just grandstanding by bringing this army across the Adriatic. "Jove willing," he told his Praetorian tribunes, "we shall use it as needs dictate."[7]

# XXXV

# JULY 20, 44 B.C.

## THE LIBERATORS' MANIFESTO

**A**fter all the hopes they had placed in events at the Ludi Apollinares festival turning the public mood their way, Brutus and Cassius "were thwarted by Octavian" and decided to leave Italy for the East, where they would aim to build their resources to enable them to take on Antony and Octavian on equal terms.

In anticipation of the need for a speedy getaway should events at Rome go badly during the festival, the pair had transferred their families, themselves, and a number of friends along the coast from Antium, through Lucania, to the small port village of Elea, today's Velia.[1] Brutus took a villa in the town and made preparations to find vessels that would carry them to Greece. There at Elea they awaited news from Rome, deciding that only the men would sail for Greece if it was necessary to flee the country. The women would be sent back to their houses at the capital, where, Brutus and Cassius knew, their remaining friends, relatives, and sympathizers would ensure their safety.

Brutus's highly emotional wife, Porcia, had been striving to keep a stiff upper lip all through the last few traumatic months, but the thought of having to soon part from her beloved Brutus, a possibility that was becoming all the more likely with each passing day, made her grief-stricken, although she did her best to conceal it. On a wall in the villa at Elea there was a painting based on an event from Homer's *Odyssey*. It showed the Trojan warrior Hector parting from his wife,

Andromache, and their infant child as he set off to fight the Greeks (the Romans always strongly identified with the Trojans). Hector had never returned. When Porcia saw this sad painting, the resemblance it bore to her own situation caused her to burst into tears.[2]

This painting had such a magnetic effect on Porcia that she was drawn to it several times a day; and each time she looked at it, she wept. She was able to keep these weepy sessions to herself until, inevitably, Brutus walked in on her, accompanied by Bibulus, Porcia's son from her previous marriage, and Brutus's friend the elderly Acilius. As Brutus comforted his wife, Acilius quoted several lines from Homer in which Andromache had told Hector that he was not just a husband to her but was her father, mother, and brother, too. Brutus replied that he would not respond as Hector had in the *Odyssey*—Hector had told his wife not to think about him but to tend to her loom and manage her maids.[3]

Porcia, Brutus told Acilius, was made of tougher stuff than that. "For, though the natural weakness of her body hinders her from doing what only the strength of men can perform, yet she has a mind as valiant and as active for the good of her country as the best of us."[4]

Within days of the end of the Ludi Apollinares festival, word reached Elea of what had transpired during the festival and immediately after. The Liberators' worst fears had been realized. Calls for the return of Brutus and Cassius had been smothered. Antony still controlled Rome as if he were a monarch. And Octavian, until recently seen by Cicero as a means of bringing down Antony, was proving to be a formidable opponent to all sides, at the head of a faction of his own.

The latest news included the fact that young Octavian was planning to host the Ludi Victoriae Caesaris festival between July 20 and 30. This festival had been inaugurated by Julius Caesar in 46 B.C. in honor of Venus, his patron deity, and in celebration of his military victories. These *ludi* had been celebrated in 45 B.C. in Caesar's absence in Spain, but now that he was dead there was a reluctance among Rome's officials to stage the games in 44 B.C.

There was strong feeling among many Romans that Caesar's games, like several of the five Triumphs he had celebrated, were an affront to the Roman people. Traditionally, Triumphs were granted by the Senate for victories by Rome's generals over foreign enemies. Yet Caesar's victory in Africa had been primarily against Roman citizens—Caesar claimed that Triumph referred to his victory over King Juba of Numidia, who had sided with the republican forces in that conflict. Caesar's last Triumph, celebrated for his victory in Spain, also was for primarily killing Roman citizens. His games only reminded Romans of those insults, and there were many at Rome watching those Triumphs and those games who had lost relatives and friends in the battles they celebrated. They had never forgiven Caesar for that.

Most people just wanted to let Caesar's games pass into history, rather than continue to rub salt into old wounds, and friends of the Liberators made it known that they would take a dim view of anyone who attempted to stage them again. But Caesar's heir had no intention of letting slip this opportunity to perpetuate his adoptive father's memory. "Finding that the officials who should have celebrated Caesar's victory with public games did not dare to carry out their commission," said Suetonius, "he undertook the task himself."[5]

Octavian, who seemed to have access to an unlimited supply of funds, would pay for the Ludi Victoriae Caesaris from his own purse. Being a mere Equestrian, Octavian had commissioned Caesar's old friend Gaius Matius to superintend the festival. Matius, who was no friend of Mark Antony's, would be condemned by the Liberators and their supporters for this act.

After the event, Matius would write to Cicero, who had remained his friend through the thick and thin of the Civil War, "I managed the Ludi Victoriae Caesaris given by the young Caesar. That was a matter of private obligation, which has nothing to do with the Constitution of the Republic. Anyway, it was a duty which I was bound to perform, as a tribute to the memory and eminence of a very dear friend even after his death, and one which I could not refuse when a young man of such brilliant promise and so completely worthy of his namesake claimed it of me."[6]

Word also reached Elea that Antony intended calling a meeting of the Senate on August 1, following Caesar's games. So Brutus and Cassius sat down and composed a letter addressed to all the former consuls and former praetors of Rome. This letter, which was to become known as their manifesto, put the case for their murder of Julius Caesar and their wish for the return of constitutional republican government, and "declared that for the sake of enduring harmony in the Republic they were even ready to live in perpetual exile, that they would furnish no grounds for civil war, and that the consciousness of the service they had rendered by their act was ample reward." Velleius Paterculus was to observe that the pair had initially written their manifesto because they were genuinely "in real fear of armed violence at the hands of Antony," but also "with the objective of increasing Antony's unpopularity."[7]

The letter was copied numerous times by the pair's secretaries, then carried away to Rome by courier. Brutus and Cassius, hoping that their manifesto would give most of the members of the Senate the courage to pass a resolution endorsing their actions and summoning them back to Rome, then awaited tidings of the outcome of the upcoming sitting.

# XXXVI

# JULY 28, 44 B.C.

## CICERO'S DEPARTURE

As young Octavian was presiding over his great-uncle's games at Rome, a bright-tailed comet was seen streaking across the northern sky about an hour before sunset, for seven days in succession. "This was held to be Caesar's soul elevated to heaven," said Suetonius.[1] Having been considered a god on Earth during his lifetime, many interpreted the comet as a sign that Caesar had joined the gods in the heavens.[2]

With the Ludi Victoriae Caesaris stoking nostalgic feelings about Caesar among the populace, and with both Octavian and Antony claiming they intended punishing his murderers, despite that pair's own duel for the affections of the Roman people, Cicero had put into motion his plan to emulate Brutus and Cassius and leave Italy. Athens in Greece was to be his destination. He knew that Brutus and Cassius also would be making for Athens. And his son Marcus was at the Greek capital, studying.

To reach the East at this time of year, when the Tyrrhenian Sea off the western coast of Italy was prone to northerly gales, the well-heeled Roman would normally travel overland down to Brundisium, then Italy's principal port, on the southeastern tip of the boot of Italy, and sail from there. But that route passed through or near many military colonies, and Antony's legions were at Brundisium. By this time the ex-soldiers living in the colonies were being stirred up by both Antony and Octavian. Being closely associated with the Liberators, and having failed to hide his enmity for Antony, Cicero decided from the outset that he should make his way by sea, for safety's sake.

His Tyrrhenian Sea journey, in small boats, had taken him, always within sight of the coast, to Pompeii and Elea, then Vibo, and now to Regium, on Italy's southwestern shore, where he landed on July 28. Typically for him, Cicero had occupied his time on these voyages by writing a book inspired by Aristotle's *Topics*.

Three days before, at Vibo, Cicero had written to Atticus, who would be his eyes and ears at Rome, asking him to handle his business affairs in Italy while he was away.

In this letter, he pondered, "What am I running away from? Danger? At present, unless I am mistaken, there is none." He had plans to return, or so he told Atticus. "You say that my going abroad is enthusiastically approved, but on the understanding that I return before the Kalends of January"—January 1, when the new consuls, Hirtius and Pansa, were due to take office—"which I shall certainly make every effort to do. I would rather be frightened at home than secure in your Athens."[3]

Before long, Cicero would resume his journey, on August 6 taking passage for Greece on a cargo ship sailing from Leucopetra, modern-day Tarentine, a port on the heel of Italy.

# XXXVII

# AUGUST 16, 44 B.C.

## LIKE HECTOR THE HERO

S trong winds had driven Cicero's ship back to Leucopetra. There, staying at the house of a friend while he waited for the weather to improve, he met a group of Rhegium businessmen who had just come down from Rome. They informed him that "Antony had made an astonishing change, and was doing all things and managing all public affairs at the will of the Senate."[1]

Antony gave the appearance of only busying himself with official business. In particular, he made arrangements for a new statue of Caesar to be set up on the Rostra. At the same time, his brother Lucius, as a tribune of the plebs, had a law passed, the *lex Antonia agrarian*, for the finalization of the business of allotting land to Caesar's ex-soldiers. This law provided for a seven-man commission, headed by Antony and including Lucius, to administer the settlement program. All this seemed to be aimed at countering Octavian's claims that Antony was neglecting Caesar's memory.

The men from Rhegium also told Cicero that they had heard whisperings at Rome that were not particularly complimentary to him. Cicero's intention to depart from Italy was no secret, and some people had suggested that in doing so he was deserting his country. There was even one rumor that Cicero was going to Greece merely to be a spectator at the upcoming Olympic Games at Olympia. Thinking both suggestions equally monstrous, and heartened by the news indicating that Antony had been tamed, Cicero decided to hurry back to Rome to take a leadership role in the Senate and "bring things to a happy settlement."[2]

Cicero worked his way back around the western coast of Italy, retracing his earlier route, and on August 16 arrived at Elea. Three miles from the town, at the mouth of the Heles River, several merchant ships sat waiting for tide and wind to carry them out to sea. Brutus and his stepson Bibulus, as well as Cassius and a number of their friends and servants, were aboard those ships, having only recently made tearful farewells from their womenfolk as they set off for Greece. When word was conveyed to the ships that Cicero had returned to Italy and was in the town, Brutus and his party put back to shore.

Brutus was overjoyed to see Cicero and to learn that he intended going back to Rome and once again taking his front-bench seat in the Senate with the other "consulars." Brutus and Cassius also had heard that Antony had seemed to moderate his ways. But they did not trust him, and suspected that he still harbored monarchic ambitions. He had certainly not softened his antagonistic attitude toward Brutus and Cassius; in word and deed, Antony had actively increased the rift between them.

On August 4, Brutus and Cassius had written to Antony, "Consider again and again what you are undertaking, and what support you have for it. And be sure to remember, not how long was Caesar's life, but how short his reign." This was not so much a threat, for they were in no position to threaten anyone, but a bald reminder that history does not treat tyrants kindly. "We attach less value to your friendship than to our lives," the pair had added in conclusion.[3]

Escape abroad had come to seem their only recourse. Now, wishing Cicero every success at Rome, and promising to maintain regular contact from the East, Brutus and Cassius again put to sea. Like Hector the Trojan hero, they would never see their wives again.

# XXXVIII

# AUGUST 30, 44 B.C.

## CICERO RETURNS TO ROME

News of his coming preceded him, and now, as Cicero reached the city outskirts, he was met by a massive crowd. Such were "the compliments and civilities which were paid to him at the gates and at his entry into the city," said Plutarch, "it took up almost a full day."[1]

Antony could not help but be aware of Cicero's return. That night, runners did the rounds of senators' doors announcing that the consul Antony was calling a sitting of the Senate for first thing next day. He also wrote personally to the newly arrived Cicero, summoning him to the sitting. At dawn, Antony convened this latest meeting of the Senate. But pretending ill health following his journey back to Rome, Cicero failed to put in an appearance. Antony, greatly affronted that Cicero had ignored his summons, sent Praetorian soldiers to Cicero's Palatine Hill residence to escort him to the sitting.

Cicero refused to leave his bed. According to Plutarch, he had received reliable warning on his way back to Rome that Antony had "some design against him," and, despite his earlier expectations and the tumultuous welcome from the general public, he was now in fear for his life.[2] Antony even instructed the soldiers to burn down Cicero's residence if he refused to accompany them to the Senate. But friends of Cicero in the House interceded with Antony on his behalf, and paid sureties to him so that he would not harm Cicero. From this time forward, Cicero and Antony never spoke directly to one another again. Whenever they passed each other, be it in the Senate or in the street, neither uttered a word to the other.

That evening, Octavian visited Cicero, bringing with him his step-father, Philippus, and his brother-in-law Gaius Claudius Marcellus, who had been a consul six years before and who had married one of Octavian's sisters, an Octavia. By this time, Philippus had dispensed with his earlier opposition to his stepson's political ambitions, and he and Marcellus now joined Octavian in proposing to Cicero that they all work together to deprive Antony of power. With Octavian addressing Cicero respectfully as "Father," he promised to use his wealth and arms to protect the orator if Cicero used his "eloquence and political influence with the Senate and the people" to promote Octavian's interests.[3]

The arms that Octavian referred to were those carried by ex-soldiers of Caesar who had settled in Italy. Over the past few months, Octavian had sent messengers among these soldier settlers, promising them large financial rewards if they supported him, and in return he had received pledges of loyalty from thousands of military veterans.

This proposal well suited Cicero. With Brutus and Cassius heading abroad and currently powerless to take on Antony, Cicero was confident of being able to manipulate this inexperienced youth. While protected by Octavian he could use his oratorical skills to attack Antony and make himself the most powerful player in Roman politics. Or so he thought. Cicero struck a deal, and became Octavian's political partner. Cicero would waste no time in launching his campaign, on September 2 delivering the first of a series of public orations against Antony. Over the next six months, he would make a total of fourteen such speeches, calling them his *Philippics*, in imitation of famous addresses made by Greek scholar Demosthenes against King Philip II of Macedonia in times past.

The combatants prepared to do battle—Antony, his brothers, and Dolabella in one corner; Octavian, supported by Cicero, in the other; and the Senate in the middle, with neither leader as yet commanding overwhelming public sympathy. Much of that sympathy was reserved for the Liberators, and for Brutus in particular. But all that anyone at Rome knew of them now was that Brutus and Cassius had retired from the fight and were somewhere abroad.

# XXXIX

# SEPTEMBER 15, 44 B.C.

## THE LIBERATORS REACH GREECE

**B**rutus and Cassius had safely reached Greece. Brutus was received by the Athenians with great enthusiasm, the city fathers presenting him with various local honors. He took up residence at Athens. Plutarch, himself a Greek, wrote that Brutus "lived there with a private friend." Brutus became "so engaged in philosophical pursuits that he seemed to have laid aside all thoughts of public business, and to be wholly at leisure for study," mixing with noted philosophers such as Cratippus the Peripatetic.

But, Plutarch noted, Brutus made a point of winning over "all the young Romans that were then students at Athens. Of this number was Cicero's son, whom he [Brutus] everywhere highly extols and says that whether sleeping or waking he could not choose but admire a young man of so great a spirit and such a hater of tyranny."[1] Cicero's boy Marcus in fact now became one of Brutus's staunchest followers.

Brutus's funds had been sadly depleted by the costs of the games in July, and he would have sent Porcia back to Rome with what little remained of his ready cash. His intent was to raise money in the East for a campaign against Antony, and soon he would have to find a way to lay his hands on a large amount. Without money, and plenty of it, Brutus and Cassius had no chance of raising or equipping troops to contend with Mark Antony or anyone else.

While Brutus gave the impression that his only interest now was philosophy, his freedman servant Herostratus traveled on to Macedonia, and to the military units camped in the province, with instructions from his master "to secure the commanders there to his side."[2]

# XL

# SEPTEMBER 23, 44 B.C.

## OCTAVIAN'S NINETEENTH BIRTHDAY

To many in the Roman Senate, it hardly seemed credible that this boy Octavian, who this day turned just nineteen years of age, could rein in Mark Antony's bid for supreme power. Yet the boy had presided over the Ludi Victoriae Caesaris at the end of July and honored his dead great-uncle despite Antony's antipathy. Again Octavian had sought permission to display Caesar's golden throne, that time at Caesar's games, and again Antony, as consul, had refused to give his permission. Undaunted, Octavian had presided at the games, and had received the accolades of the crowd. The renewed feud with Octavian actually won Antony friends in the Senate. Not a few senators disliked and distrusted Octavian, thinking him but a boy with too much money to throw around and with jumped-up ideas about his station in life just because he was Caesar's heir.

Octavian, meanwhile, now buttressed by Cicero's vocal support, had begun to promote a bid by a friend of his, Flaminius, to be elected to the vacant position of tribune of the plebeians—the vacancy caused by the murder of the unfortunate Helvius Cinna by the mob back on March 20. As the day set down for the election approached, the word around Rome was that Octavian actually wanted the post for himself, and many people said out loud that they intended casting their vote for him. This was contrary to the law; not only was Octavian much too young to run for election to any office, he also was a member of the patrician upper class, Rome's traditional aristocracy, whose members were barred from running for election as tribunes of the plebeians.

Many senators were made uneasy by the rumor, not wishing to see this young upstart gain such a powerful position; under the republican constitution, tribunes of the plebeians not only had the power to put legislation before the Comitia, they also represented the common people in the Senate, where any one of them could veto a resolution.

But Mark Antony was even more unsettled by this rumor about Octavian's intention to run for election, and he issued a consular decree that "if Octavian attempted anything illegal he would use the full power of his authority against him." Antony's edict only incensed many voters, and there was a swell of support for the election of Octavian as tribune in defiance of Antony's order. In the end, to put a lid on the affair, Antony used his authority as consul to cancel the election.[1]

This battle of wits between Antony and Octavian continued to trouble the officers of Antony's Praetorian bodyguard. Again the military tribunes asked for a meeting with Antony, and again they expressed their unhappiness at the conflict between their commander and the late Dictator's adopted son. After all, the tribunes said, surely both Octavian and Antony had the same object, that of avenging the murder of Caesar.

In response, Antony declared that he had never lost sight of the goal of making Caesar's murderers pay. "We shall avenge him, deploying all our powers of body and determination to do so," he assured his officers. Antony also claimed that he was playacting with the Senate until he could get what he really wanted: vengeance for Caesar.[2]

By the end of the meeting, the Praetorian tribunes were convinced that Antony possessed "genuine hostility to the murderers and a desire to outwit the Senate." Just the same, they wanted to see a united front against Caesar's assassins and their supporters, and won agreement from Antony that he would again reconcile with young Octavian.[3]

Not content with just a promise, the Praetorian officers promptly brokered a meeting between Antony and Octavian in the sacred environs of the Capitol. There, in front of the military tribunes and Octavian's friends, the two men shook hands and agreed to again act in alliance against Caesar's murderers.[4]

It would later be reported that the night after Antony and Octavian came to their new accommodation on the Capitoline Mount, Antony had an unlucky dream in which his right arm was struck by lightning.[5]

# XLI

# SEPTEMBER 28, 44 B.C.

## THE PLOT TO ASSASSINATE ANTONY

J ust days after Octavian and Antony had renewed their alliance on the sacred soil of the Capitol, word flew around Rome that a murder plot had been discovered. Octavian had paid to have Mark Antony assassinated, or so the story went. Most people believed the story. Cicero believed it; he even heard that Antony "had caught the executioners in his own house."[1] Octavian's later biographer Suetonius also believed reports of the plot, writing that "Octavian actually engaged assassins to murder Antony."[2]

The report of the murder plot did not reflect well on Octavian. The people of Rome could understand that he had good reason to do such a thing, but Antony's position, especially in these uncertain times since Caesar's death, made the thought of another murder of one of Rome's leaders all the more repugnant to them. "The majority," Appian was to write, "seeing the insults and losses which Octavian had suffered every day, thought the slander might be true, and considered it sacrilegious and intolerable that a plot had been laid against the life of the consul Antony."[3]

"Mad with anger," and proclaiming his innocence, Octavian hurried around Rome confronting anyone who doubted him, "and kept declaring that he himself was the victim of a plot by Antony to deprive him of the favor of the people" by inventing this murder plot. Finally, Octavian went to Antony's house. Standing outside the Carinae mansion's open double doors, and with a crowd gathering in the street behind him, Octavian called on the gods to bear witness to his innocence, swearing all manner of oaths, and, shouting now, challenging Antony to bring a case against him in court.[4]

When no one appeared in the doorway to Antony's house, Octavian called, "I agree to be judged by your friends." He then tried to make his way inside, but Antony's hall porters barred his passage. Again he called out, abusing Antony, and becoming angry with the servants who would not let him pass, claiming they were preventing him from being called to account. Rebuffed, Octavian turned to the watching crowd. "Witness that if anything happens to me, my death will be due to Antony's treachery," he called.[5]

No proof would come to light that the murder plot existed, but Antony soon after assigned much of his Praetorian bodyguard to "his friends," which would have included his brothers, "on the grounds that they [the Praetorians] had been accomplices in a plot of Octavian's against him."[6] Some cynics believed this to be part of a new campaign by Antony to blacken Octavian's name. But the tribunes of Antony's Praetorian cohorts had twice recently shown their dissatisfaction and impatience with Antony's treatment of Octavian, making it quite possible that there may have been a willingness among some Praetorians to be rid of Antony. That Antony had lost confidence in his entire bodyguard would within days become quite evident.

# XLII

# OCTOBER 9, 44 B.C.

## A DREADFUL STATE OF AFFAIRS

One of the tribunes of the plebeians, Cannutius, had called Antony before a public meeting in the Forum on October 2. An undisguised opponent of Antony and a supporter of Octavian, Cannutius took Antony to task for his actions as consul since the death of Caesar. According to Cicero, Antony "came off in sore disgrace" as a result of Cannutius's speech, but not before he made a bitter defense. Standing on the Rostra where he had only recently dedicated his new statue of Caesar, which bore the inscription "To Father and Benefactor," Antony raged against Brutus, Cassius, and their fellow conspirators.[1]

"He spoke of the country's saviors [the Liberators] in terms that applied to traitors," Cicero was to complain in an October letter to Cassius, who was now somewhere in the East—Cicero knew not where—having parted from Brutus at Athens. Cicero was at this point feeling betrayed by Octavian as a result of the alliance the young man had made with Antony at the Capitol, and had renewed his hopes that the Liberators would emerge as the champions of liberty.[2]

Cicero wrote to Cassius that Antony had gone on to declare unequivocally that everything that Cassius and Brutus did and that Cannutius the tribune was now doing were on Cicero's advice. "The lunatic declares that I was the ringleader in that noble achievement of yours"—Caesar's murder. "Would to heaven that I had been! He would not be giving us any trouble now."[3]

The union between Antony and Octavian had taken the political ground from beneath Cicero's feet. "What a dreadful state of affairs!" Cicero lamented to Cassius. "We who could never tolerate a master [Caesar] are slave to our fellow slave [Antony]. Yet, while my wishes are stronger than my hopes, hope still remains in your fortitude. But where are your forces?"[4]

Where indeed? On the other hand, Mark Antony's forces were by this time at Brundisium. By September, four of the five legions that Antony had ordered from Macedonia had marched to the Adriatic, boarded a fleet of ships, and crossed to Italy. They had remained quartered at the port city awaiting Antony's orders. The fifth of these legions was still on its way. Now, on October 9, Antony and his staff set out from Rome for Brundisium to join the legions. According to Cassius Dio, Antony also took his wife, Fulvia, with him.[5]

Tellingly, Antony's Praetorian cohorts also departed the scene at this point. Some, Antony appears to have taken south with him. But once Antony left town, some of his Praetorians—apparently men he had given over to his friends after the discovery of the plot to murder him—simply went home to their farms.

And while Antony departed from Rome for southern Italy, his fellow consul Dolabella made his way to the East, encouraged by Antony to take up his appointment as governor of the province of Syria and ensure that neither Brutus nor Cassius nor Octavian nor anyone sympathetic to any of them gained control of the legions in the province. Also in Antony's party heading south to Brundisium went his brother Gaius, with orders from Antony to continue on to Greece and take charge there. The indications are that Gaius took the majority of his brother's Praetorians with him—at least four cohorts.

As both consuls were now absent from Rome, there was no one to convene or preside over the Senate. With the House apparently emasculated by the consuls' absence, and with numerous public holidays on the calendar in October and November, many senators drifted away from the capital to country homes. Cicero, for one, set off for his seaside villa at Puteoli.

As soon as Octavian learned that Antony had left Rome for the south to link up with the waiting troops, he himself left the city, taking with him his friends and a long wagon train laden with trunks full of cash. His destination was the Campania region, not far south of Rome, home to military colonies recently established for Caesar's veterans, where his agents had already secured many pledges of support from recently retired legionaries.

War had been predicted by Cicero. His prediction seemed close to being realized. Now, in despair, and feeling powerless, Cicero wrote to Cassius, "What can be done to counter force without force?"[6]

# XLIII

# OCTOBER 18, 44 B.C.

## ANTONY JOINS HIS LEGIONS

In the port city of Brundisium, Mark Antony stood on a tribunal overlooking his assembled troops. Before him spread the neat formations of four legions. On arrival in Brundisium, Antony had learned that there was much criticism of him in the ranks "for failing to follow up the murder of Caesar." When he mounted the steps to the tribunal, it was without the usual accompaniment of applause that Roman generals expected from their legionaries at the commencement of such assemblies.[1]

Now, "angry at their silence," Antony looked around the thousands of stern faces. He then proceeded to give the troops a tongue-lashing, accusing them of not being grateful for transferring them away from a war with the Parthians. He also had heard that agents from Octavian had been mixing in the ranks while these legions had been encamped at Brundisium, trying to undermine their loyalty to Antony, and he berated his legionaries for failing to arrest such men. He would discover these agents himself, he declared.[2]

Antony then announced that he would lead his legions to the rich province of Cisalpine Gaul, and to each man present he would pay four hundred sesterces. This generated laughter from the ranks, for Octavian's agents had promised Antony's men five times as much. This reaction only made Antony angrier. But individual men began to answer him back. Some, disgusted by his "meanness," simply walked away, leaving the assembly.[3]

"You will learn to obey orders!" Antony stormed. He summoned the six military tribunes of each of the four legions and instructed them to give him lists of the names of the troublemakers in their units. The officers, with some reluctance, consulted the records of each unit, and provided the list required by Antony. Antony then had the legions reassemble, and ordered the named men to draw lots. One in ten drew a short straw, and was arrested.[4]

In the Roman military, legionaries could be disciplined by having one in ten of their number executed; this was called "decimation." Julius Caesar had decimated several of his best legions when they became mutinous during the Civil War, notably after those units had refused to obey Antony's orders on one occasion. Antony now chose a percentage of the one in ten named troublemakers, and put them to death for their disobedience. The condemned men, who included centurions, were executed in front of Antony and his wife.[5] Traditionally, legionaries condemned to decimation were bludgeoned to death by their own comrades—the nine in ten who had escaped capital punishment. Antony's intention was to bring the remainder of his troops back into line, but this decimation only resulted in making many of his surviving legionaries more resentful.[6]

Ignoring the simmering discontent in some units, Antony selected one thousand soldiers from all four legions, men "who had the best physique and character," and formed them into a single new Praetorian cohort.[7] This Praetorian unit, which was to become known as the Brundisium Cohort—because of where it was formed—would loyally serve as Antony's bodyguard for the rest of his career. As for the Praetorians whom Antony had led while in Rome, most appear to have now accompanied his brother Gaius on his mission to Macedonia.

Antony called another assembly.[8] From the tribunal, he declared to his troops that he had been forced to execute a few of their number for the sake of military discipline, but could have punished many more had he chosen to do so. "You know quite well that I am neither mean nor cruel. Let us forget our ill will." But he did not increase the amount of the bounty he offered them in an attempt to match Octavian. That would have seemed as though he was giving in to the complaints of his men.[9]

He then ordered them to prepare for a campaign north of the Po River, in Cisalpine Gaul. At the same time, he dismissed the six military tribunes of each legion, apparently considering them untrustworthy, and appointed replacements from among young gentlemen of Equestrian rank who supported him. The four legions received their new officers and begrudgingly accepted Antony's four-hundred-sesterce bounty as they prepared their equipment and gathered provisions for a march up into Cisalpine Gaul. They all knew that Antony was going on the offensive against Decimus Brutus Albinus, to forcibly wrest Cisalpine Gaul from his control.

In Cisalpine Gaul, once Albinus learned that four legions had landed at Brundisium from Macedonia on Antony's orders, he quickly put two and two together and realized that Antony was serious about challenging him for control of his province. Without seeking or receiving Senate approval to do so, as he was required to do by law, Albinus promptly instructed his deputies to draft six thousand military recruits in Cisalpine Gaul and form them into a new legion, to bring his army up to a total of four legions to match Antony's force.

# XLIV

# NOVEMBER 4, 44 B.C.

## OCTAVIAN RECRUITS AN ARMY

A t Rome, the population was launching into one of the most popular festivals of the year. Stretching back hundreds of years, the Ludi Plebeian, or "people's games," ran from November 4 to 17. With various festivities, including a street parade by the members of the Equestrian Order, the fourteen-day festival would culminate in three days of chariot racing, a sure way to divert the public mind from worries of war.

Cicero always avoided the metropolitan hustle and bustle of the holidays. Now, at his Puteoli villa on the coast, he was in a quandary. He had just received two letters from Octavian in one day, with both urgently proposing a meeting in Rome. Octavian, Cicero knew, had been in Campania for weeks recruiting retired legion veterans to his cause, basing himself at Capua.[1]

Octavian had spent much time, and money, in veteran colonies such as Calatia and Casilinum, receiving an ecstatic reception from veterans settled at Cales and Teanum on the Via Latina before moving on into the Samnium region, winning the loyalty of thousands of former soldiers of the 7th and 8th legions—apparently including men recruited here by Antony to serve in his Praetorian cohorts only months before who had since gone home again.[2]

"Now he wants me to return to Rome," Cicero wrote to his friend Atticus at the capital. "He says he wants to work through the Senate.

I replied that the Senate could not meet before the Kalends [first] of January."[3] Under Roman law, when both consuls were absent from Rome the city praetor was authorized to convene sittings of the Senate. But Brutus was the current city praetor, and, of course, like the consuls Antony and Dolabella, he was away from Rome. With little likelihood that either Antony or Dolabella would soon return, Cicero gave the excuse that it was unlikely that the Senate would again be convened until the new consuls, Hirtius and Pansa, came into office on January 1, and for that reason he had no plans to return to Rome before then.

In fact, Cicero was stalling. He had not been impressed by Octavian's sudden, if brief, renewed alliance with Antony, and was not altogether certain how to deal with the young man. "He presses, and I play for time. I don't trust his age, and I don't know what he's after." Cicero's quandary was that he feared to go back to Rome yet dreaded not being there should something major occur without him being on the spot to counter it, or embrace it. "I'm nervous of Antony's power and don't want to leave the coast," he told Atticus. "But I'm afraid of some star performance during my absence."[4]

Cicero told Atticus that he had also just heard from a mutual friend, Marcus Terrentius Varro, arguably then Rome's greatest living scholar. Varro, although put in charge of Rome's library by Caesar, was an unrepentant republican who had commanded Pompey's legions in western Spain during the Civil War before surrendering to Caesar. Varro, now age seventy-two, had written to tell Cicero that he did not think much of Octavian's plan to recruit veterans with whom to counter Antony's legions. Like so many of the older senators, Varro was letting Octavian's youth get in the way of his judgment of the young man's ability.[5]

Cicero had once felt the same way, but not any longer. "I take a different view. He has a strong force at his back and can have Brutus [Albinus]"—as an ally. "And he's going to work quite openly, forming cohorts at Capua and paying out bounties. War is evidently coming any minute now."[6] But on which side would the fearful Cicero find himself?

# XLV

# NOVEMBER 18, 44 B.C.

## THE ROAD TO WAR

**M**arching up the highway from Campania to Rome came Octavian and his friends, leading an army of ten thousand men. All were ex-soldiers recruited from military colonies with the payment of bonuses of two thousand sesterces a man, and marching behind a single standard. Arriving on the Field of Mars outside the capital, the column made camp.[1]

Inside the city, there was considerable apprehension. Word had been received that Antony also was marching north, with his four legions. One rumor had even put him as close as Capua on the night of November 9, but that had proven to be false. But there was no doubt that Antony was approaching the capital. And here was Octavian on the city's doorstep with an army of experienced troops, although not a well-organized or well-equipped army, it would transpire. Some Romans feared Antony and supported Octavian; others felt just the opposite. There were even those who felt that since Octavian and Antony had sworn an alliance on the Capitol's sacred soil, their enmity since was a sham and they would soon link up and jointly seize power.[2]

Cannutius, the tribune of the plebs who had shown himself to be an unabashed enemy of Antony, went out of the city to meet Octavian on the Field of Mars and discover his plans. When Cannutius returned, he called a meeting of the Comitia, where he announced that he was convinced that Octavian was openly hostile to Antony. If the people feared an unconstitutional seizure of power, said Cannutius, they had better throw their support behind Octavian, "because they had no other military force at the present moment" with which to defend Rome from Antony.[3]

Cannutius then brought Octavian into the city to address the people at the 440-year-old Temple of Castor and Pollux, which stood in the Forum directly opposite the spot where Caesar's body had been cremated in March and where a temple would later be built to Caesar.[4] Octavian entered Rome with a strong bodyguard from his freshly recruited army of veterans. These troops, armed with sheathed swords, in contravention of the law that banned all weapons inside the city, surrounded the Temple of Castor and Pollux.

From the top of the temple steps, Cannutius addressed the large crowd that soon gathered, and with a speech that attacked Antony. When it came Octavian's turn to speak, he reminded the crowd of Caesar's cruel murder and his funeral almost on this very spot. Then he, too, attacked Antony, reminding his listeners of the humiliations he had suffered at the hands of Antony since his return from Apollonia.[5] And many leading men in the crowd cursed Antony out loud.[6] This, said Octavian, was why he had assembled this force that was now encamped on the Field of Mars, to protect himself and to serve his country. And with these men, he said, he was ready to face Antony and, if necessary, fight him.[7]

As the crowd dissolved, abuzz with conversation, Octavian was approached by representatives of his soldiery; the crowd may have been impressed with the young man's speech, but the veterans were not. The ex-soldiers' delegates told Octavian that they and their comrades had accepted his bounty and signed to serve him because he had led them to believe that he planned to take revenge on Caesar's murderers. Some even believed that Octavian intended reconciling with Antony. But now Octavian had announced that he was prepared to do battle with Antony, which was quite contrary to what he had led them to believe, and they wanted no part of it. Like them, Antony had served Caesar, and he had commanded their legions during the Civil War. He was now a consul. Many of these men were simply not prepared to raise a sword against him.[8]

A number of Octavian's troops now asked permission to go home, some ostensibly to fully equip themselves with their own weapons and then return. To save face, Octavian called an assembly on the Field of Mars and announced that those of the veterans who wished to leave could do so, some to collect arms and return, others to remain at home if they so chose. Before these men took their leave of him, he gave out another gift of money, hoping to buy their continued loyalty, and promised to reward them even more richly in the future and to employ them more as friends of Caesar than as soldiers.[9]

Overnight, as these men tramped away, back to their homes to the south, Octavian's army on the Field of Mars dwindled from ten thousand men to no more than three thousand. Realizing that his force would now be outnumbered ten to one by Antony's men in any confrontation, and that he had to find more recruits, Octavian also departed. After filling wagons with more cash, he led his much-reduced force away, toward the Etruria region. Over the coming weeks he would visit military colonies throughout central, eastern, and northeastern Italy in quest of more men from among the retired soldiers there.[10]

Octavian's progress would take him as far north as Ravenna, on the Adriatic coast. All along his route he would hand out cash and urge veterans to arm themselves and meet him at the town of Arretium in the northeast, which he made his assembly point.[11] Strategically placed on the Via Cassia military highway, Arretium, which also was home to retired soldiers, was not far from Cisalpine Gaul. From there, Octavian could, in theory, link up with Albinus and his four legions, to combine forces against Antony. Meanwhile, a number of the veterans who returned to their farms after leaving Octavian at Rome soon had second thoughts, and set off to join him in the north.[12]

# XLVI

# NOVEMBER 27–30, 44 B.C.

## ANTONY'S LEGIONS REBEL

The rumors at Rome that Antony was heading for the capital with a large body of troops soon proved to be accurate. In the fourth week of November, within days of Octavian's departure for the northeast, Antony arrived at the Field of Mars with upward of seven thousand men, and made camp.

Earlier in the month, Antony had set off from Brundisium with his new Praetorian cohort and the Alaudae Legion, a unit whose men, apparently, had been the least troublesome of his legionaries in the port city—perhaps because they were natives of Transalpine Gaul, not Italians, like most of Antony's other legionaries.[1] Antony had headed northwest along the Appian Way, but he had ordered the three remaining legions to march north from Brundisium via the coast road to Ariminium, today's Rimini, on the Adriatic. Ariminium was just south of the Rubicon River, which served as the border between Italy and Cisalpine Gaul. Antony's intent—to threaten Albinus in Cisalpine Gaul—was clear.

Antony entered Rome with his armed Praetorians and went directly to his home in the Carinae. His bodyguard surrounded the house and stood guard in successive three-hour watches, treating the mansion as a military camp and refusing to admit anyone who did not know a daily password.[2]

On November 23, Antony called a meeting of the Senate for the next day. But then stunning news had arrived. The Legio Martia, or Martia Legion, marching up the coast road to Ariminium from Brundisium on Antony's orders, had, on reaching the town of Alba Fucens in the Picenum region of eastern Italy, revolted against its senior officers and, to a man, had vowed loyalty to Octavian. The origins of the Martia Legion seem to have gone back to the Marsi, the Italian tribe that inhabited the Picenum region and made Corfinium their capital, and it is possible that on reaching their home territory, the men of the Martia Legion were influenced by the locals to revolt against Antony. Antony immediately sent subordinates to verify this report about the Martians, and postponed the Senate sitting until he knew more.

On the afternoon of November 28, senators were notified that there would be an emergency meeting of the Senate that evening. When the members of the House arrived after dark—a highly unusual time for the Senate to meet—Antony called the meeting to order, then quickly dealt with seemingly minor pieces of business. Once this business had been resolved, Antony terminated the sitting, hurriedly took his leave, went directly to the city gate, passed through it, and joined the troops on the Field of Mars.[3] In his wake, some members of the House were left bemused; others, confused.

When senators awoke the next morning, it was to find that Antony had departed for Alba Fucens. Now, too, the senators learned why Antony had made such a rushed departure. Not only was it true that the Martia Legion had revolted against Antony, it also was now revealed that just as Antony was about to go into the Senate meeting, he had received a dispatch informing him that the 4th Legion, marching up the road several days behind the Martia, also had rebelled against Antony and gone over to Octavian once it reached Alba Fucens.

Antony was marching rapidly east to Alba Fucens, intent on regaining the loyalty of the two legions, which had set up camp in the town. In Rome there was both astonishment and anger at this turn of events. Widespread astonishment was registered because half of Antony's troops had deserted him. The anger came from many senators who were indignant that the revolting legionaries had declared their loyalty to young Octavian, who was merely a private citizen and had no official authority, and not to the Senate of Rome, under whose authority Rome's legions were raised, paid, and discharged.

When Antony arrived outside Alba Fucens, he found the town gates closed against him and its walls lined with the rebellious men of the two legions. When he attempted to approach the walls, the troops sent a rain of javelins in his direction, and Antony was forced to hurriedly withdraw out of range. "Deeply disturbed," Antony returned to Rome, from where, to secure their loyalty, he sent two thousand sesterces to every man still serving him, including the legionaries of the Alaudae and those of the other legions from Macedonia, the latter still on the road to Ariminium accompanied by the auxiliary cavalry.[4]

When Cicero found out about the defection of the two legions, he was overjoyed. In December he would write to Albinus in Cisalpine Gaul crowing that the men of the Martia and the 4th had "branded their consul a public enemy and rallied to the defense of the Republic."[5] The two legions had not exactly done the former, and it remained to be seen if they would do the latter.

Again Antony departed from Rome. But this time he went dressed in military uniform and armor, and wearing his sword, signaling that he was going to war. He only marched his Praetorians and the Alaudae Legion a short distance east along the Via Tiburtina Valeria, to the summer resort town of Tibur, modern Tivoli, on the slopes of the Sabine Mountains. There he set up camp and sent recruiting officers ranging far and wide to enroll more retired soldiers. From military colonies as far away as Samnium and Apulia, thousands of retired veterans of the 5th Legion answered his call.[6]

Realizing that Antony was still on their doorstep, and with a formidable and growing force, hundreds of senators flooded out of Rome to Tibur—almost the entire Senate, according to Appian. With them came the majority of the members of the Equestrian Order and the leading plebeians. Apparently fearful that Antony would lead his troops into Rome and let them plunder the city, they had all come "to pay their respects" to him.[7]

They arrived in a mass, to find Antony swearing his existing troops, along with a large number of veterans who made up his reconstituted 5th Legion, to an oath of allegiance to him. He then called on the senators and their companions to take the same oath. So even the men who had so recently cursed Antony during the public meeting convened by Cannutius and Octavian outside the Temple of Castor and Pollux now publicly took an oath, administered by Antony, "that they would never cease to give him their goodwill and loyalty."[8]

Antony then set off for Ariminium with his Praetorian cohort, the Alaudae Legion, and the new, understrength 5th Legion, to join the other legion from Brundisium that had remained loyal to him. There, too, he would be joined by the last of the five legions from Macedonia, which had finally landed at Brundisium.[9] By the middle of December, despite having lost two legions to Octavian, Antony would be in a position to threaten Albinus's four legions in Cisalpine Gaul with a force of equal size.

# XLVII

# EARLY DECEMBER 44 B.C.

## THE RISE OF THE LIBERATORS

W hile the focus at Rome had been on Antony, Octavian, and Albinus, in the Roman East Brutus and Cassius had not been idle. Sympathy and support they had aplenty. The one thing they lacked was money. As Octavian and Antony were proving in the West, it took money, and enormous amounts of it, to secure and equip troops. In the late days of autumn, word had reached Brutus at Athens that a friend of his, Marcus Apuleius, who had served as quaestor of Asia until recently handing over to the quaestor of the province's new governor, Marcus Trebonius, was coasting around the Aegean toward Greece from Asia with a convoy of warships and cargo vessels laden with treasure he intended to deliver to the Treasury at Rome.[1] This money was the result of official Roman tax-gathering in eastern provinces for the year, which traditionally took place in the summer.

Brutus hurried to Carystus, a small port on the eastern coast of Greece, in time to meet Apuleius and his treasure fleet after they had put in there. And Brutus persuaded Apuleius to hand over the ships and their contents to him rather than continue on to Italy with them. What's more, Apuleius joined Brutus's staff, becoming one of his chief recruiting officers. All the quaestors of the provinces of the Roman East would subsequently endorse this handover of tax monies to Brutus, much to the disgust of later Roman official Velleius Paterculus.[2] According to

Plutarch, this financial coup netted Brutus as much as two hundred million sesterces.[3] Now Brutus and Cassius could finance a war.

Cassius immediately set off for Syria, taking the lion's share of the loot with him as his war chest, for there were as many as ten legions stationed in Syria and Egypt whose loyalty would need to be bought. Brutus was left with some forty million sesterces.[4] Brutus, appointing Cicero's son Marcus and the other young Romans who had been studying at Athens his military tribunes, headed up into Thessaly and Macedonia and began building an army.

Brutus's first rank-and-file recruits emerged from towns and villages along his route. These turned out to be legionaries of Pompey the Great who had taken refuge with the locals following Pompey's defeat by Caesar at Pharsalus in Thessaly four years before. Ever since, these men had been living among the sympathetic Greeks, who retained deep affection for Pompey. When they heard that Brutus was raising an army to restore the Republic, Pompey's former soldiers "joyfully" flocked to him.[5]

Using his little fleet of ships, Brutus proceeded to intercept a flotilla of cargo vessels carrying five hundred auxiliary cavalry to join Dolabella, who had by this time arrived in Asia, and brought them under his own command. Next, putting in at the Greek port of Demetrias, Brutus seized the vast arms cache that Caesar had created there for his campaign against the Getae and Parthians, just as preparations were being made to ship those arms to Antony in Italy. Now Brutus had both money and arms.[6]

Landing in Macedonia with his growing fleet, plus funds, war matériel and the nucleus of an army, Brutus was greeted by Quintus Hortalis Hortensius, the ex-praetor who was governing Macedonia in Antony's name. Hortensius happily handed control of Macedonia and its resources over to Brutus and put himself under his command. Those resources did not extend to a large number of troops. The province had been denuded of the six legions until recently stationed there—Antony had by this time shipped five to Italy, and when Dolabella recently came through Macedonia, he had picked up the sixth of the legions and taken it with him to Asia, with intentions of confronting the province's new governor, Trebonius the Liberator.

Brutus soon gained support from another quarter. When all the kings and potentates of the region heard that Brutus had taken possession of Macedonia, they came to him and offered their services, and those of their ethnic troops. Mark Antony they disliked, Octavian they did not know. But like the ordinary peoples of the region, eastern kings and potentates held Pompey's memory in high regard, and equally, they respected Brutus's reputation as a man of integrity.

Word then reached Brutus that Antony's brother Gaius had crossed the Strait of Otranto and had landed in Epirus, on the western side of Greece. Gaius had landed with only a modest body of troops—apparently the Praetorians that his elder brother had handed over to him. Learning that Brutus had gained control in Macedonia, Gaius decided to march up the western coast of Greece to take over the three legions that the governor of the province of Illyricum, Publius Vatinius, had recently stationed at Apollonia and Dyrrhachium, today's Durres in Albania. Brutus, realizing Gaius's intent, decided to make a dash across Macedonia to beat him to Dyrrhachium, just as Pompey had beaten Caesar to Dyrrhachium four years before.

The winter snows were falling as Brutus made his forced march west with his cavalry and few infantry. His pace, and the difficult weather, saw his baggage train lag farther and farther behind, and he pressed on without provisions. As he approached Dyrrhachium, having won the race, Brutus fell ill. His servants went on ahead to the town and begged bread from the sentries. When the sentries heard that it was Marcus Brutus who needed food, they deserted their posts and came to him with bread, meat, and drink. Brutus subsequently occupied the town.[7]

After Gaius Antonius reached Apollonia, south of Durres, the town from which Octavian had set off for Italy the previous March after hearing of Caesar's murder, Brutus advanced south, forcing Gaius to retreat. In the process, three of Gaius's infantry cohorts were "cut to pieces" by Brutus's cavalry. Brutus was not yet fully recovered from his illness, so he gave the command of his forces to young Marcus Cicero, "whose conduct he made use of often and with much success."[8]

Marcus fought a pitched battle with Gaius's mauled force, and Gaius was cut off in marshland with his bodyguard. Brutus came riding up just as young Cicero's troops were clamoring for the kill, but Brutus talked Gaius's men into surrendering themselves and their commander. In this way, Mark Antony's brother Gaius became Brutus's prisoner, while Gaius's troops were welcomed into Brutus's army.

This was an ironic near-repetition of events during the Civil War. In 49 B.C., Gaius Antonius had attempted an amphibious landing in Illyricum for Caesar, but his flotilla had been intercepted on the Adriatic by a republican battle fleet, and all seventy-five hundred of Gaius's

Caesarian legionaries had defected to Pompey. Apparently Gaius had given his parole to Pompey that he would not play any further part in the war, which he did not, and was allowed to return to Rome. And here, five years later, he was again taken prisoner by the other side after the surrender of his troops and in much the same area as before. This time Gaius was not released. But Brutus did not put him in irons; instead he showed his high-ranking prisoner "all marks of honor and esteem."[9]

# XLVIII

# SECOND HALF
# OF DECEMBER 44 B.C.

## ANTONY MAKES HIS MOVE

Cicero had returned to Rome on December 9. At this point neither he nor the rest of Rome had yet to learn of Brutus's successes in the East. As for Cassius, there had been no word of him or his activities since he left Italy.

Cicero was banking on Albinus in Cisalpine Gaul defeating Antony by force of arms. For the moment, Antony's army was camped just south of the border between Italy and Cisalpine Gaul, with Antony, in his capacity as consul, sending Albinus demands to hand over the province to him in compliance with the law passed by the Comitia that gave Cisalpine Gaul to him.

Albinus was ignoring these demands. To begin with, he had led his legions up into the foothills of the Alps, in today's Piedmont and Savoy, and sent them against warlike local tribes who had yet to submit to Roman authority. Albinus had feared that the loyalty of his troops might be purchased by Antony or Octavian, and, running out of funds himself after borrowing heavily from friends and relatives, his mountain campaign was all about giving his legionaries as much opportunity as possible to fill their purses. His men had stormed into the mountains with enthusiasm and had captured numerous villages and laid waste to great tracts of farmland as crops and animals were snaffled up. Albinus had even written to Cicero asking him to seek a Triumph from the Senate for him when it next sat, as a reward for this plundering expedition.

As far as Cicero was concerned, if this stalemate was to be broken, Albinus must launch offensive action against Antony. But legally Albinus could not lead his troops across his province's border without Senate permission. Even if the Senate were convened for the purpose, there were a number of senators, including all but one of the former consuls—"the consulars," Cicero called them—who did not favor authorizing Albinus to go to war with a sitting consul.

Anxious to spur Albinus into action, Cicero hosted a meeting at his house on Rome's Palatine Hill. His guests were several of Albinus's friends and relatives, including his cousin Servius Sulpicius Rufus, who had been a consul in 51 B.C. By the time this meeting ended, two of the attendees were on their way to Cisalpine Gaul to pass on Cicero's sentiments to Albinus.

To make sure that Albinus was left in no doubt about his views, Cicero dashed off a letter to him and sent it north by courier. "The main point which I want you to grasp and carefully bear in mind," Cicero wrote to Albinus, "is that in preserving the liberty and welfare of the Roman people you must not wait to be authorized by a Senate which is still enslaved. For, in doing so, you would be condemning your own act"—the assassination of Caesar. "You know that it was not by public authority that you liberated the Republic, and that makes the achievement all the more magnificent and glorious."[1]

Cicero goaded Albinus by reminding him that "the young man, or rather boy" Octavian had not waited for anyone's approval before he took on Antony. Cicero was by this time calling Octavian "Caesar," despite his earlier reluctance to do so. Nor, he said, had the Martia Legion or 4th Legion sought anyone's approval but their own before they deserted Antony. "When its formal sanction is held back by intimidation, the *wishes* of the Senate should be considered the equivalent of official sanction. Lastly, you have twice chosen which side you are on, first on the Ides of March, and again recently when you enlisted new forces." Albinus must not wait for orders, Cicero urged, but give them, and take action against Antony.[2]

Cicero also found a way to give Albinus moral support. In emergencies, the tribunes of the plebs could convene a sitting of the Senate without the presence of the consuls. Cicero was able to convince several of the tribunes to call just such an emergency meeting on December 20.

Knowing that he did not have enough votes to censure Antony, Cicero proposed a resolution in which the Senate upheld all existing gubernatorial appointments. In this roundabout way, Albinus received an endorsement from the House, while Antony, and his ambition to unseat Albinus, received a rebuke.

In Cisalpine Gaul, once he received Cicero's advice, Albinus ordered his force of four legions and his gladiator bodyguard to prepare to march out of the mountains and head toward Italy.

Octavian had hurried to Alba Fucens to take command of the Marta Legion and 4th Legion, the units that had defected to him from Antony, combining them with a legion of veterans he had by this time put together on his latest recruiting drive in the east and north. Combined, these units made up a formidable little army of some eighteen thousand men. Octavian had written to the Senate at Rome to offer his army in the service of the Republic, and had received a reply that the House would vote on what Octavian and his troops should do as soon as the new consuls came into office and convened a sitting.[3]

Centurions of his legions offered Octavian five lictors and fasces if he were to proclaim himself a propraetor. Octavian thanked them, but said that he could accept such an honor only if it were conferred by the Senate. Legally, he was much too young for such an appointment. The soldiers were determined to see him made a praetor and were preparing to send a delegation to Rome to urge the appointment on the Senate, but Octavian prevented them from going. The Senate would be more likely to make such an appointment "if they see your eagerness and my reluctance," he sagely observed.[4]

The men were unhappy at this until Octavian let them into his thoughts. He told them that he believed the Senate was leaning his way, not because it wished him well but because he opposed Antony, and the Senate had no troops of its own until such time as the Liberators managed to raise an army. In the meantime, the Senate would use him, and he would use it. "If we snatch the magistracy, they will accuse us of high-handedness or violence," he confided to his officers. "But if we show deference, perhaps they will freely bestow it through fear that I will take it for myself."[5]

Octavian then went to watch the men of the two existing legions going through their training drills. Facing each other, the men of the

Martia and 4th "unstintingly did all they had to do in a real battle except kill." Octavian was so pleased with their enthusiasm that he presented every man with another two thousand sesterces from his seemingly bottomless cash box, and promised them that should it come to war and they were victorious, each of his troops would receive another five thousand sesterces.[6]

As soon as Mark Antony heard that Albinus's troops were on the move, he acted to seize the initiative. As winter was descending on northern Italy, Antony led his legions into Cisalpine Gaul, claiming to be acting under the authority of the law of the Comitia.

The two armies marched toward each other. Albinus came down the Via Aemilia. Arriving at the city of Mutina, today's Modena, he ordered his army to fortify the city and prepare to sustain a lengthy siege. Cattle were killed and salted and other provisions gathered as the local farmers flooded into the city for protection. The gates were closed, and Albinus waited. He did not have to wait long. Antony arrived with his army, and surrounded the city with entrenchments. The siege of Mutina had begun, and the Roman people were once again embroiled in civil war.

# XLIX

# JANUARY 1–4, 43 B.C.

## DEBATING ANTONY'S FATE

O n New Year's Day, the new consuls Hirtius and Pansa took
office. From this day forward, neither Antony nor Dolabella
held consular power. A Senate sitting that would run for three
days was inaugurated at the Temple of Jupiter on the Capitol, with the
new consuls making sacrifices to the principal god of Rome.

With the scene set for dramatic change, Cicero took the Senate
floor, delivering the latest of his *Philippics*, the fifth, which took the form
of a broad condemnation of Antony and a plea for government of the
people by the people. And in return for putting Albinus under siege at
Mutina, Cicero proposed that the Senate declare Antony an enemy
of the state, just as Caesar had been declared an enemy of the state by
the Senate after he crossed the Rubicon from Cisalpine Gaul to invade
Italy in January 49 B.C. Once declared an enemy of the state, a Roman
citizen was liable to be killed on sight.

Piso, Caesar's father-in-law, who was looking after Antony's business interests in his absence, sprang to a spirited defense of Antony in
the House, a defense that was supported by a number of other speakers. Not only did they defend Antony against specific charges laid by
Cicero, these senators also expressed the view that Antony should be
given a hearing in person, "because it was not their custom to condemn
a man unheard." The debate continued, without any resolution, until
nightfall, when the sitting was adjourned until the following day.[1]

When the sitting resumed the next morning, Cicero again force-fully put the case for declaring Antony an enemy of the state, and others countered his argument as best they could, until finally a vote was called for. But before a vote on the resolution could be taken, one of the tribunes of the plebs, Salvius, imposed his veto, and the House rose without a resolution. Cicero and others reviled Salvius inside the Senate and outside it, and inflamed a crowd in the Forum so much that Salvius remained in the Temple of Jupiter for the time being to prevent his being physically attacked.[2]

At sunup on January 3, the Senate again came to order, and a variety of motions were proposed, debated, and voted on. In lieu of condemna-tion of Antony, a resolution was passed commending Albinus for refusing to give up Gaul to Antony. Many in the Senate were anxious to ensure that Octavian did not again ally himself with Antony, but at the same time the Senate wanted to make Octavian its servant, not vice versa. So a fresh resolution called on Octavian to share command with the new consuls, Hirtius and Pansa, of the legions he had at Alba Fucens.[3]

Specifically, Octavian was instructed to hand over command of the Marta and 4th legions to the consul Hirtius, on the basis that they were legions that had originally been raised on the Senate's authority. Octavian would be permitted to retain command of the legion of vet-erans and a legion of raw recruits that he himself was raising. In return, it was agreed that the Senate would pay the five-thousand-sesterce vic-tory bonus that Octavian had promised all his troops.[4]

A motion by Octavian's stepfather, Philippus, for the erection of a gilded statue of Octavian was swiftly approved. Another resolution passed to grant Octavian a seat in the Senate, with the rank of ex-consul, against all precedent. On the motion of Albinus's cousin Servius Sulpicius, it also was agreed that Octavian be permitted to run for election as a consul in ten years' time, which would still be thirteen years ahead of the legal age for a consulship. The House then adjourned until the following day.[5]

It was widely believed that the resolution declaring Antony a pub-lic enemy would again be put up for debate the next day, and during the night the houses of the leading senators of Rome were visited by Antony's mother, Julia, and his proactive wife, Fulvia, who brought with them Antony's son Antyllus, who was perhaps four years old by this time. Antony's womenfolk pleaded with the senators on his behalf.

The next morning, as the members of the Senate made their way to the Temple of Jupiter Capitolinus just before dawn, they found Julia and

Fulvia at the temple doors, clad in mourning black. The women threw themselves wailing and lamenting at the senators' feet as they entered the chamber, begging them not to declare Antony a public enemy. This performance visibly influenced some members of the House, who were reminded of "this sudden change of fortune." Antony, the man who three days earlier had been the most powerful in the land, entrusted with the legal power over life and death, was now reduced to begging for his own life via his wife and mother. The debate about Mark Antony resumed, and a perturbed Cicero again called for Antony's condemnation. And again Piso spoke in his defense.[6]

In the end, against Cicero's wishes, a compromise resolution was agreed on by a majority of members. Under the olive branch of peace, a Senate delegation of three ex-consuls would go to Antony outside Mutina to inform him that the Senate had not approved of his acquisition of Cisalpine Gaul. The delegation also was to enter Mutina and thank Albinus and his troops for their loyalty before reporting back to the House with Antony's response.[7]

It was a mild resolution, and its mildness ensured its safe passage. But friends of the Liberators had the House agree to nominate Cicero to draft the letter that would be carried by the Senate's delegates to Antony. With a supposed eye to fairness, those delegates were to be Piso, as Antony's man; Philippus, as Octavian's man; and Albinus's cousin Sulpicius. Of course, Cicero used the opportunity to write a sealed letter that, in the names of the Senate and consuls, demanded that Antony lift the siege of Mutina and stop plundering Gaul and raising troops; to relinquish Gaul to Albinus and withdraw south of the Rubicon River into Italy, but remaining no closer to Rome than two hundred miles; and to submit all his activities of the judgment of the Senate.[8]

After the Senate rose, Antony's friends in the House congratulated themselves on preventing Antony from being declared an enemy of the state, and the Senate delegation made a hurried departure for Cisalpine Gaul. Later that same day, Cicero addressed a public meeting in the city at which, in his sixth *Philippic*, he revealed the contents of the demand being delivered to Antony. It was a demand that Cicero could not have expected Antony to agree to. In fact, he revealed in his speech that he had absolutely no confidence in the success of the delegation's mission, and argued passionately that the only way to resolve this matter was with immediate military action to lift Antony's siege of Mutina—by Octavian's legions.

L

# LATE DECEMBER 44 B.C.– EARLY JANUARY 43 B.C.

## THE FIRST ASSASSIN TO FALL

T oward the end of spring, tubby, self-confident, twenty-six-year-old Dolabella, Caesar's former favorite who had been assigned the province of Syria by the Senate, had traveled east overland, picking up the legion left for him in Macedonia via his deal with Antony. He had entered Asia at the beginning of winter.

The province of Asia was governed now by Gaius Trebonius, one of the leading Liberators. Even though they had been on the same side while Caesar was alive, Trebonius and Dolabella loathed each other. When Dolabella attempted to enter the towns of Pergamum and Smyrna to gain supplies in late December, he had found the gates barred to him, on Trebonius's orders. Trebonius, who was himself inside Smyrna, the provincial capital, had condescended to permit Dolabella, who then still had some days to run in office as consul, to purchase provisions outside the town walls.

Dolabella exploded with rage at this insult and had his legion attack Smyrna's walls with missiles. To stop this, late in the day Trebonius sent a message to say that he would give Dolabella permission to enter the town of Ephesus, some distance away. Dolabella immediately led his legion down the road in the direction of Ephesus as the sun was setting. Trebonius, who apparently had raised a legion locally to police the province, sent several of his cohorts to shadow Dolabella. After they had followed Dolabella for some distance, the majority of these troops returned to Smyrna, leaving a handful of scouts to continue following Dolabella's column.

In the darkness, Trebonius's inexperienced scouts stumbled into an ambush laid by Dolabella; all were captured without a fight. Dolabella disarmed these men before having them executed on the spot. He then led his legion on a silent return to Smyrna in the night. Arriving in the early hours of the morning, they found the town's gates closed, but no sentries on the walls. Dolabella selected an assault party from the men of his legion, who quickly set up scaling ladders. Without a sound, these legionaries mounted the walls and flooded into the town undetected. Trebonius was in his bed when a group of Dolabella's legionaries burst into his bedchamber. They dragged him from his bed and to his feet.

"Take me to Dolabella," Trebonius demanded, showing no fear. "I am quite willing to go with you."[1]

One of the centurions leading the group sneered in reply, "Go where you like, but leave your head behind. Our orders are to bring not you, but your head."[2]

There in his bedchamber, Trebonius was pressed to his knees on the cold tile floor. Without another word, the centurion swung his sword and cleaved Trebonius's head from his shoulders. At daybreak, Dolabella entered Smyrna. On being presented with Trebonius's severed head, he ordered it displayed on the governor's tribunal in the town, from where Trebonius had only recently been issuing life-and-death rulings as chief magistrate of the province.

Dolabella permitted the men of the legion, and the camp followers who thronged into the city in their wake, to do what they wanted with Trebonius's remains. His body was "treated in various degrading ways," while his head was removed from the tribunal and thrown "like a ball from one to another across the town paving" amid much laughter until inevitably it fell to the flagstones.[3]

Using his authority as consul, Dolabella added Trebonius's legion to his own, then left Smyrna and continued the march toward Syria with his expanded army. Once the troops had gone, the locals collected Trebonius's remains and sent them back to Rome to enable his family to conduct a funeral. "This was how Trebonius, the first of the murderers [of Caesar], was punished," Appian was to write with satisfaction.[4]

# LI

# FEBRUARY 4, 43 B.C.

## STATE OF EMERGENCY

The Senate's delegation to Mark Antony had arrived back at Rome on February 2. It returned one man short. Albinus's cousin Servius Sulpicius had died en route, apparently from a heart attack. Cicero would miss him greatly, having considered him a tower of strength among consulars who were otherwise almost entirely without energy or principle.

Not surprisingly, Antony had dismissed Cicero's ultimatum out of hand, haranguing the delegates with "a long invective against the Senate and Cicero." Antony had declared to the delegates, "I swear to you that these developments will put an end to our unloved amnesty."[1]

In a letter that the delegates brought back to the Senate, Antony said that he would pursue Albinus for failing to give up Cisalpine Gaul and, as an example to all who had participated in Caesar's murder, he would seek vengeance for Caesar by taking Albinus's life, and Albinus's life alone, considering him representative of a now "tainted" House dominated by Cicero.[2]

On the morning of February 3, the consul Pansa convened a sitting of the Senate to hear from the delegates. After considering Antony's letter, the House again debated declaring Antony an enemy of the state, as Cicero continued to demand. But there were enough senators against the idea, notably all but one of the consulars, that again no such resolution could be agreed to. The exception among the ex-consuls was

Julius Caesar's cousin Lucius Caesar, who was firmly with Cicero and against Antony.

The best that Cicero could obtain from the House was a resolution declaring a state of emergency. This at least gave the Senate the power to instruct Hirtius and Octavian to prepare to take action in support of Albinus with their legions—which had already crossed into Cisalpine Gaul—and for the consul Pansa to prepare new recruits who had been enlisted and assembled to Rome to march north as soon as the winter weather improved.

Cicero now wrote a letter to Cassius in the East, to bring him up to date with the latest happenings. He still had not heard a word from Cassius since he left Italy, but rumors reaching Rome suggested that Cassius was "in Syria at the head of a force." Cicero hoped that to be the case, and that Cassius was finding as much success as Brutus—news that Brutus had taken control of Macedonia and Illyricum and made Antony's brother Gaius a prisoner was by this time circulating on an excited tide at Rome. "Our friend Marcus Brutus has won extraordinary distinction," Cicero wrote to him. "His achievements have been so substantial and so unexpected that, welcome as they are in themselves, they are magnified by their rapid succession."[3]

"If you possess all that we think you do," Cicero wrote to Cassius, "the props that support the Republic are strong. From the west coast of Greece all the way to Egypt we shall find support in governments and armies led by citizens of the greatest loyalty." Yet the most immediate problem was resolving the situation at Mutina, where Antony continued to besiege Albinus. "If, as we hope, he succeeds in breaking out of Mutina," said Cicero, "it appears that the war will be over."[4]

Cicero felt confident that the senatorial forces now in Cisalpine Gaul and Italy could now deal with Antony. "Our friend Hirtius is at Claterna, Caesar [Octavian] at Forum Cornelium, each with a trustworthy army." Octavian had consented to the Senate demand that he give it the Martia and 4th legions, now commanded by Hirtius. "At Rome, Pansa has collected a large force, raised by an Italian levy."[5]

Despite all this, the lack of news from Cassius meant that there were fear and uncertainty in Cicero's mind, which would only be exacerbated by the news that Dolabella had killed Trebonius at Smyrna and was marching for Syria, news that by March would reach Rome with Trebonius's remains. Cicero's hopes hung on Cassius achieving all that the Liberators' friends hoped he was achieving. In concluding his letter to Cassius, Cicero prayed that Cassius's valor would shine forth, "from wherever you are in the East."[6]

# LII

# APRIL 14–26, 43 B.C.

## THE MUTINA BATTLES

E ight miles southeast of Mutina, on April 14, a hectic and bloody battle took place between Antony's forces and senatorial forces sent to relieve Albinus's army, which had been besieged inside Mutina for the past four months.

On April 15, Servius Sulpicius Galba, one of the Senate's generals and one of Caesar's assassins, sat down in his headquarters tent and dashed off a quick note to Cicero at Rome to tell him about the battle the previous day. Hirtius was encamped near Mutina with two legions. Pansa and Octavian were coming up to reinforce him with four legions of new recruits, and Hirtius had sent Galba a hundred miles south to hurry them up.

On the night of April 13–14, Pansa, Octavian, and Galba were only a dozen miles from Mutina when they were met in the night by the Martia Legion and two senatorial Praetorian cohorts formed by Hirtius that Hirtius had sent to strengthen their otherwise raw army on the road. The next day, as the combined senatorial army marched up the Aemilian Way to join Hirtius at his camp, Mark Antony withdrew from his entrenchments around Mutina with two of his four legions, together with two Praetorian cohorts and thousands of cavalry. Antony's intent was to prevent the senatorial reinforcements linking up with Hirtius.

Keeping his infantry at the village of Forum Gallorum, modern-day Castelfranco, Antony sent his cavalry scouting ahead. "When Antony's cavalry came into sight there was no holding the Martian Legion and the Praetorian cohorts," Galba proudly wrote. Pansa had no choice but to follow with two legions of recruits, and this drew Antony out of the village with all his infantry. The Battle of Forum Gallorum was fought on the highway, between marshes on one side of the road and woodland on the other. "Both sides fought as fiercely as men could fight," said Galba. On Galba's right, the Martians threw back Antony's 35th Legion. But Pansa's left wing gave way. The senatorial army was forced to retreat to its marching camp back down the road, which Octavian held with two legions.[1]

Late in the day, having achieved his objective, Antony marched away, back toward his lines at Mutina. His troops were singing a victory song when suddenly Hirtius arrived on the scene with his two remaining legions and charged. Antony's infantry were routed. It was the middle of the evening by the time Antony and his cavalry could escape, courtesy of the darkness and the marshland. Hirtius's troops captured both eagle standards of Antony's legions, the 2nd and the 35th, and sixty subunit standards. "It is a victory!" wrote the exhausted Galba, who had been in the thick of the early fighting.[2]

Five days later, after news reached Rome of the Battle of Forum Gallorum, which cost thousands of lives, the Senate finally declared Antony an enemy of the state. That same day, after the combined senatorial armies advanced on Mutina, Albinus made his expected breakout, fighting his way through Antony's encirclement. Antony, vastly outnumbered, was forced in a bitter running battle to retreat to the north, with his army in tatters.

This was a senatorial victory, but the price was heavy. The consul Hirtius was killed in the fighting on April 21, as was Albinus's deputy Pontius Aquila, another of Caesar's assassins. The remaining consul, Pansa, was seriously wounded. Although expected to recover, Pansa died several days later. Pansa's quaestor, Manlius Torquatus, suspected the attending physician, Glycon, of poisoning Pansa, and arrested him. It would be rumored that Octavian, who visited Pansa on his deathbed, had paid the physician to administer poison to the wounded consul, for Octavian could sorely use a vacant consulship.

Albinus pursued Antony north with his legions and Pansa's units. But while Antony had been rebuffed, with the death of the two consuls the Republic had suddenly and unexpectedly become a rudderless ship.

# LIII

# MAY 7, 43 B.C.

## CASSIUS OVERRUNS SYRIA

When Cassius arrived in Syria after parting from Brutus in Greece, he had landed with a considerable amount of cash and high hopes, but little else. He found that the pro-Liberator senator Lucius Staius Murcus had arrived in the province several months earlier to claim the gubernatorial appointment given to him by Caesar. Combining with Marcius Crispus, the governor of Bithynia, Murcus had laid siege to Caecilius Bassus, the former Pompeian officer who had taken control of Syria, at the garrison city of Apamea.

In a remarkable piece of statesmanship, Cassius was able to convince Murcus and Crispus to cease hostilities against Apamea and to hand their legions over to him. The legion under Bassus in Apamea subsequently deserted to Cassius. Overnight, Cassius found himself with two good generals, eight legions, and control of Syria. News of Cassius's success, combined with the fact that Brutus now controlled Macedonia and Illyricum, would encourage Cicero to put a resolution before the Senate at Rome that, by the end of April, was approved, officially giving Cassius the government of Syria and confirming Brutus's command in the provinces he controlled.

Meanwhile, Dolabella, after executing Trebonius in Asia, had sent one of his officers, Aulus Alienus, to Egypt, to bring the four legions stationed there to join him in Syria. Alienus had subsequently marched into Syria with these legions, but once again Cassius proved enormously persuasive; Alienus joined the Liberators and put his legions under Cassius's command.

On May 7, Cassius wrote to Cicero at Rome, bringing him up to date with his startling progress in Syria. As Cassius was finishing this letter, he received word that Dolabella had arrived in Cilicia, a Roman province northwest of Syria, with two legions, intent on taking control of Syria. At this point, neither Dolabella nor Cassius knew that the governor-ship of Syria had only a few weeks before been taken from Dolabella and given to Cassius by the Senate. Neither did young Dolabella yet know that Alienus had handed the four legions from Egypt over to Cassius, or that Cassius now commanded a massive army of twelve legions—more than seventy thousand soldiers—versus his two legions.

# LIV

# MAY 30, 43 B.C.

## LEPIDUS'S BETRAYAL

Contrary to the belief of Cicero and others, Mark Antony's force was far from spent, and the new civil war was far from over. Antony had escaped over the Alps into Transalpine Gaul. His men had resorted to drinking muddy water from roadside puddles and stripping bark from alpine trees to feed their animals, but Antony, his cavalry, the reasonably intact 5th Legion, and remnants of several others had reached the green fields of Provence. At this point Antony apparently combined the remnants of the 5th Legion and the Alaudae Legion to create the 5th Alaudae Legion. On his way west, Antony had opened up slave barracks at every town and pressed the freed inmates into service as his soldiers. And at Vada, between the Apennines and the Alps, he had been joined by his friend the praetor Publius Ventidius, who had recruited three legions in Italy on Antony's behalf then boldly marched them across the mountains to join him.

Marcus Lepidus, as governor of Nearer Spain and Narbon Gaul, had brought his five legions to the Var River border between Narbon Gaul and Transalpine Gaul, all the while writing to Cicero that he would faithfully serve the Senate and take action against enemy of the state Antony. On March 16, Assinius Pollio had written to Cicero to say that he was marching his two legions from Farther Spain to Gaul to also serve the Senate against Antony, assuring Cicero that he thoroughly despised Antony.[1] Cicero felt confident that both Lepidus and Pollio could be relied on.

Albinus, pursuing Antony over the Alps with his victorious legions, trusted neither "that shifty creature Lepidus," as he described him, nor Pollio. "Lepidus will never act honestly," Albinus wrote to Cicero. Besides, Albinus had heard that before Antony crossed the Alps he had assured his surviving men that he had "an agreement" with Lepidus.[2]

This was not surprising; Antony and Lepidus had been in league immediately after Caesar's murder, and nothing had occurred since to damage that alliance. Pollio had been a dedicated Caesarian for years past, and Albinus wrote to Cicero that he saw through what he perceived to be Pollio's pretense of support for the Senate.[3]

Lucius Munatius Plancus, governor of Transalpine Gaul, had been ordered by the Senate to prevent Antony's escape. His five legions, which were "trim for war," in his own opinion, were closing in on Antony's force, which his scouts told him was twenty miles away at the Argenteus River, today's Argens.[4] Antony was camped opposite Lepidus's legions, which had lately moved into Transalpine Gaul. For days, Plancus negotiated with Lepidus's deputy, Laterensis, an earnest, trustworthy man who assured Plancus, to whom he was related, that Lepidus would remain faithful to the Senate and would demand Antony's surrender.

In contradiction of those assurances, on May 29 Lepidus joined forces with Antony. The following day, Lepidus issued a proclamation claiming that his entire army had mutinied and compelled him to join Antony. Few Romans believed this claim, especially when it became known that Antony had given nominal command of their combined legions to Lepidus. Lepidus's deputy Laterensis was so disgusted by his chief's duplicity that he took his own life. Lepidus also would be declared an enemy of the state by the Senate, on June 30. Meanwhile, Antony's and Lepidus's combined army now advanced on Plancus, forcing him to retreat.

Suddenly the balance of power had swung back Antony's way. Soon it would swing even farther his way. As Albinus had feared, Pollio and his two legions also would join Antony once they arrived from Spain. Then Pollio would convince Plancus to go over to Antony. And in a major reversal of fortune, Albinus's own army would mutiny and change sides, with some of his legions going to Antony, others to Octavian.

Albinus would be forced to flee into the mountains with just ten men, intending to make for the East to join Brutus and Cassius. Albinus would be captured by Gallic bandits, whose chief, Camelus, would send envoys to Antony asking what he should do with Albinus. In reply, Antony would send troops to Camelus's village. Albinus, one of Caesar's chief assassins, would lose his head to Antony's execution squad there in the Alps. "Thus he met his just deserts and paid the penalty of his treason to Gaius Caesar," wrote Velleius seventy-three years later.[5]

Within a few months, Antony was backed by more than twenty legions, and the only remaining hope of Cicero and the Senate for success in the West lay with young Octavian. Antony and Octavian now had just one thing in common: a pledge to punish Caesar's assassins. But could the Senate trust Octavian?

# LV

# AUGUST 19, 43 B.C.

## OCTAVIAN CHARGES CAESAR'S MURDERERS

O
ctavian was just nineteen years of age, but he had the old men of Rome quaking. Antony, Lepidus, and their multitudinous legions stood poised to invade Italy. The Senate had shipped two of Caesar's old legions from the province of Africa and dug them in, together with a legion of recruits, around Rome's outskirts. But it was Octavian's now eight legions that would make the difference. For weeks the Senate had been sending envoys to Octavian, and Octavian's legions had been sending centurions to Rome demanding a vacant consulship for their teenage commander, but the Senate had refused that demand. So Octavian marched on the capital. And when he arrived, the three senatorial legions defending the city defected to him; their humiliated commander committed suicide. Rome was defenseless, and at Octavian's mercy.

Octavian, now commanding eleven legions, entered the city with a large bodyguard. He was greeted by the leading men of Rome "with every sign of friendliness and spineless readiness to serve" him. Cicero was the last to come to him, reminding Octavian that he had recently proposed to the Senate that Octavian and he be allowed to run for the consulship as colleagues. Octavian would have the consulship, but not with Cicero at his side. He had the consular election immediately brought on, with his cousin Quintus Pedius and himself as the sole candidates, despite Octavian's youth. The Senate made no complaint.[1]

On August 19, Octavian and Pedius were elected consuls of Rome. Octavian's first act was to immediately have his adoption by Caesar validated by a law of the Comitia. He promptly had another law passed making the murder of Julius Caesar a crime and canceling the previous Senate- and Comitia-endorsed amnesty for the assassins. Murder charges were laid at once, not only against Brutus, Cassius, and those who had struck the blows on the Ides of March, but also against sympathizers who had not even been in Rome on the day of the murder. Apparently on Octavian's orders, Cicero was not one of those charged.

The cases against the accused were combined, and all were heard on the same day. All were found guilty, most in their absence. A single juror voted to acquit, and his name was duly noted by Octavian. Under a law introduced by Pedius, all the convicted men were sentenced to banishment from Italy and loss of all their property.[2]

But if lovers of democracy thought they now had a powerful champion, they were in for a rude surprise.

# LVI

# EARLY NOVEMBER 43 B.C.

## THE TRIUMVIRATE AND
## THE PROSCRIPTION

There was a low island in the middle of the Lavinius River, not far from Mutina in Cisalpine Gaul. On a spring morning, ten legions drew up on the riverbanks facing each other. Five legions belonged to Octavian, five to Antony and Lepidus. Octavian advanced to a bridge to the island with three hundred men. Antony and Lepidus did likewise at a second bridge. Lepidus then crossed to the island alone, and when satisfied that it was secure, he waved his cloak and was joined by Antony and Octavian. The trio sat down together, "with Octavian in the center presiding, because of his office" as consul.[1]

For three days the leaders conferred, from dawn till dusk on the first two days. Mirroring the alliance among Caesar, Pompey, and Crassus that had ended a decade earlier, these three formed the Board of Three for the Ordering of State; this became known as the Triumvirate, and the three leaders as the Triumvirs. They agreed that their alliance would last five years, with each man wielding consular power. They distributed the provinces among themselves—Antony received Gaul, except for Narbon Gaul, which Lepidus retained along with Spain; Octavian took Africa, Sicily, and Sardinia. They agreed that in the new year, Lepidus would take charge at Rome with three legions, while Antony and Octavian went to the East with their combined armies to take on Brutus and Cassius.[2]

Finally, the trio agreed to draw up a list of two hundred opponents, proscribing them for summary execution. According to Appian, that list would grow to three hundred senators and fifteen hundred Equestrians. Lepidus put his own brother, Paulus, at the top of his list. Octavian named a number of men, including the juror who voted to acquit Caesar's murderers. And Antony was quick to nominate his uncle, Lucius Caesar. But the first name on Antony's list was that of Cicero. Octavian resisted approving Cicero's execution, and for two days held out to save him, "but on the third day yielded," with Antony making it clear that the fate of their alliance hung on Cicero's demise.[3] The names of Cicero and many of his relatives and friends were added to the execution list.

Legionaries and Praetorians were soon marching into Italy bearing copies of the death list, knowing that the Triumvirs would pay twenty-five thousand sesterces for the head of each proscribed man. Within ten days of the Triumvirs agreeing on their pact, the executions began.

# LVII

# DECEMBER 7, 43 B.C.

## KILLING CICERO

**M**arcus Cicero and his brother Quintus were at a villa at Tuscullum when news of the proscriptions reached them. The shock to Cicero must have been immense. From the East, the latest news of the Liberators was all good. In Syria, Cassius had defeated Dolabella, whose own bodyguard had decapitated him after his defeat. Cassius had taken the island of Rhodes by storm when it resisted him, and had done the same to cities in Syria, and in Judea, where "he reduced four cities into a state of slavery" after the Jewish authorities had refused to pay taxes he levied.[1] Cassius and Brutus now controlled the Roman East in the name of the Republic. Yet here, in Italy, the enemies of the Republic were running riot.

The first proscribed man to die was Salvius, tribune of the plebs. Although he had initially prevented the Senate from naming Antony an enemy of the state, Salvius had later sided with Cicero against Antony. Salvius was dining with friends when legionaries stormed in. As the horrified dinner guests were made to watch, a centurion grabbed Salvius's hair, pulled him full-length across the dining table, and hacked off his head.

Cicero's younger brother Quintus had served Caesar as a faithful but inept army commander during the Gallic War, but his blood connection with his elder brother was enough to now put a price on his head. Once they learned of the death list, the brothers immediately set off in their litters for Astura, on the coast, planning to acquire a boat and sail to Macedonia to join Brutus. Halfway there, Quintus decided to return home to secure his valuables. The pair embraced; then Marcus continued on while Quintus turned back. On reaching his home, one of Quintus's servants informed on him. Caught by searching troops, Quintus was beheaded on the spot, together with his young son.

Marcus Cicero reached Astura and set sail, but when the boat put into shore because of bad weather he decided to return to Rome, telling himself that Octavian, whom he had supported so strongly, would save him. A dozen miles into this journey he changed his mind; from Macedonia, Brutus had repeatedly written to warn him not to trust Octavian, and now Cicero's doubts prevailed. He returned to the coast and took a boat to Capitae. From there he set off down the coast in a litter, accompanied by a large band of retainers. But an execution squad led by a military tribune, Gaius Popillius Laenas, was in the vicinity, and, tipped off by a former slave of Cicero's brother, the soldiers set off in pursuit of Cicero's party.

The troops intercepted Cicero's litter as it emerged from a shady walk near the sea. Cicero ordered his bearers to set his litter down. He recognized the tribune, having some years before successfully defended Laenas in court when he was accused of his father's murder. The tribune may have hesitated, but a centurion named Herennius did not, pulling Cicero's head toward the edge of the litter and raising his sword. "It took three blows and some sawing through" to sever the famous man's head. Cicero's hands also were chopped off—the hands that had written the *Philippics* in condemnation of Antony.[2] Eleven months earlier, Cicero had said, "If I am called on to lay down my life, I think I shall have accounted for myself not without glory."[3]

"When Cicero was beheaded, the voice of the people was severed," Velleius was to lament.[4] The tribune Laenas conveyed Cicero's head and hands to Antony, who displayed them on the Rostra at Rome for the world to see. Antony was so pleased with Cicero's death that he multiplied the reward money received by Laenas ten times, to 250,000 sesterces. Only Brutus and Cassius, controlling the East, remained to carry the republican standard.

# LVIII

# OCTOBER 1–21, 42 B.C.

## THE BATTLES OF PHILIPPI

By the spring of 42 B.C., Cassius had joined his army with that of Brutus in Macedonia. With twenty legions they encamped at Philippi, today's Filippoi, stretching entrenchments between their hilltop camps, which straddled the Agnatian Way, and all the way to their supply base of Neapolis, modern Kavala, eight miles away on the coast.

In the summer, Antony and Octavian landed in Greece with their army. With Octavian ill, Antony advanced into Macedonia with nineteen legions, and in mid-September built two camps facing the Liberators' Philippi positions. Octavian, too weak to walk, arrived ten days later, in time for his twentieth birthday. Antony built entrenchments toward the Liberators' lines. Then, one day at the beginning of October, with the armies of both sides lined up on the plain in battle order, Antony led nine legions in an unexpected assault on the defenses below Cassius's camp.

The 4th Legion, which had fought against Antony at Mutina, now fought for him, on his left wing. It was soon overwhelmed by Brutus's right wing. Two of Brutus's legions broke through and took Octavian's camp. Octavian escaped with his life, having just previously left the camp. Antony, meanwhile, led a breakthrough on his right wing that took Cassius's camp, forcing Cassius to flee to a hilltop. From the hill, Cassius could see nothing of the hectic battle below because it was obscured by a huge dust cloud raised by the feet of the 250,000 infantry and cavalry involved in the largest battle to that time between Roman armies. Seeing his camp taken, Cassius thought the battle lost. At Cassius's command, his armor bearer Pindarus killed him.

In fact, the battle ended in a stalemate. Once the dust had literally cleared, Antony had taken Cassius's camp and Brutus had Octavian's camp. The Triumvirs had lost 16,000 men; the Liberators, 8,000. That same day, a convoy bringing 2,000 Praetorians and 2 legions, including the Martia, to Greece as reinforcements for the Triumvirs was intercepted on the Adriatic by Statius Murcus with 130 Liberator warships and was almost entirely destroyed. Of the two sides, that of the Liberators had fared the better on both land and sea. But Cassius was by far the better of the republican generals, and his loss was sorely felt by Brutus and his subordinates.

For close to three weeks both sides now faced off, with Brutus prepared to wait it out until the Triumvirs' growing supply problems weakened them. But his officers urged him to attack, warning him that his confident troops might mutiny if he did not lead them against the enemy. Brutus gave in to his officers, and on October 21 led his legions out to do battle a second time. Octavian and Antony accepted the challenge and also drew up their legions.

Both sides charged simultaneously. The troops on Octavian's wing eventually drove the opposing line back until it gave way. While Octavian's troops surrounded Brutus's camp, Antony chased Brutus and several legions to the mountains. There, Brutus and fourteen thousand surviving Liberator troops were surrounded.

After Brutus's legionaries refused to execute his plan for a breakout, calling instead for surrender terms from Antony, Brutus said to his friends, "I am no use to my country any longer if this is the attitude even these men take." He ordered Strato of Epirus to kill him, and as Brutus looked the other way, Strato reluctantly plunged a sword into Brutus's side, near the left nipple, piercing his heart.[1]

So died the leader of the conspiracy to kill Julius Caesar. He and Cassius were men of "unchallenged virtue," according to Appian,[2] although Plutarch did not believe Cassius to be Brutus's equal "in proved virtue and honor."[3] In the summation of Velleius, "Cassius was the much better general, as Brutus was the better man. Of the two, I would rather have Brutus as a friend, but would stand more in fear of Cassius as an enemy." Brutus, he said, had "kept his soul free from corruption until this day"—the Ides of March—when "the rashness of a single act" robbed him of his virtue.[4] Mark Antony had Brutus's body reverently cremated and his remains sent to his mother, Servilia.

A number of Caesar's assassins fought at Philippi alongside Brutus and Cassius. Labeo also committed suicide following the defeat, as did Quintillius Varus, father of the general of the same name who would famously lose three legions to the Germans in the Teutoburg Forest in A.D. 9. Other assassins, and leading supporters of the Liberators including Marcus Favonius, were taken prisoner. Most were immediately executed by Antony and Octavian, among them Quintus Hortensius; months before, after hearing of Cicero's decapitation, Hortensius had executed Antony's brother Gaius in reprisal.

Some Liberator supporters escaped and survived, including Cicero's son Marcus, who, years later, was made a consul by Augustus. Of the men who had physically taken part in the assassination of Caesar, the last to die was another Cassius, Gaius Cassius Parmensis.[5]

In the summer of 43 B.C., not long after Brutus fled Italy, his unhappy wife, Porcia, unable to bear separation from the husband she loved, had painfully committed suicide at Rome by swallowing hot coals. Junia Tertullia, Brutus's sister and Cassius's wife, lived at Rome for many more years, passing away in her eighties or nineties in A.D. 22. The emperor Tiberius permitted a funeral oration for her in the Forum and other honors, including a funeral procession in which the busts of twenty illustrious Romans were carried before the dead woman. But the busts of her famous husband and brother were banned. And for this very reason, said Tacitus, that day "Cassius and Brutus outshone them all, from the very fact that their likenesses were not to be seen."[6]

The end of the Liberators spelled the end of the Republic. Octavian, Antony, and Lepidus jointly ruled the Roman Empire until 36 B.C., when Lepidus made a miscalculated grab for power. The legions deserted Lepidus, and Octavian exiled him to a remote Italian village for the rest of his days, permitting him to retain his post of pontiff maximus until he died in 13 or 12 B.C.

Octavian and Antony fell out several years later, after Antony allied himself with Cleopatra and deserted Octavian's sister Octavia, whom he had married to cement their alliance. They went to war in 31 B.C., with Octavian emerging victorious at the Battle of Actium. After Antony and Cleopatra committed suicide in 30 B.C., Octavian ruled as Rome's first emperor for the next forty-three years. Like Caesar,

Octavian would be offered many honors by a compliant Senate after he became sole ruler, but unlike Caesar he wisely declined most of them. Most notably, he accepted the title of Augustus, or "revered," rather than that of "king"; took the veto powers of the tribunes of the plebs for himself; and asserted the right to personally appoint all consuls.

Octavian's rule and the end to hopes of restoring the Republic were inevitable. Julius Caesar had been grooming Octavian to be his successor, and it is not unlikely that had Caesar not been murdered in 44 B.C., Octavian would still have succeeded him, only some years later.

# LIX

# JUDGING THE ASSASSINS AND THE VICTIM

**W**as Caesar's murder justified? Was he a despot, as Brutus, Cassius, Cicero, and others claimed?

Suetonius, Caesar's first-century biographer, said that while Caesar did much that was creditable, numerous were his words and deeds that "justify the conclusion that he deserved assassination."[1] "It has also been suggested," Suetonius noted, referring to writers of his day, "that constant exercise of power gave Caesar a love of it, and that after weighing the strength of his opponents against his own, he took this chance of fulfilling his youthful dreams by making a bid for the monarchy."[2]

Plutarch, Greek historian of the late first century and early second century, from whom we know most about Julius Caesar, Mark Antony, and Cleopatra, and who was Shakespeare's key source, was in no doubt that Brutus and Cassius were liberators of democracy and that both Caesar and Antony were despots. "Antony, who enslaved the Roman people, just liberated from the rule of Caesar, followed a cruel and tyrannical object."[3]

Appian, another Greek historian, while considering Caesar's assassination a crime, saw the murder conspiracy arising out of the title of king, and its clumsy handling by Caesar and his supporters. "On reflection," Appian wrote, "I am of the opinion that the plot did originate over this additional title." Yet Caesar, in Appian's view, was monarch of the Romans already, by another name. "The difference it made was only of a word, since in reality the dictator is exactly like a king."[4]

Seneca, famed, flawed, but oft-quoted first-century Roman philosopher, was in no doubt that none of the members of the so-called First Triumvirate—Caesar, Pompey, or Marcus Crassus—could justifiably be considered a friend of freedom.[5]

Support for the Liberators lived on among the Roman people for hundreds of years after their deaths. Pliny the Younger noted that in the second century, during the reign of the emperor Trajan, the senator Titinius Capito set up the busts of Brutus, Cassius, and Caesar's other great adversary, Cato the Younger, in his home. There, he paid respect to them, "not being able to do so elsewhere," with the emperors frowning on any outward commemoration of the heroes of republicanism.[6]

Cassius Dio, writing three hundred years after Caesar's death, expressed the view that Caesar had acted badly when he celebrated his final Triumph, in 45 B.C., following his victories in Spain: "He showed no moderation, but was filled with arrogance, as if immortal."[7] Did Caesar come to think of himself immortal? Certainly he was famously considered lucky in his lifetime; he knew it, and he exploited it.[8]

Was his reported epilepsy a symptom of a form of mental illness that eventually led him to believe he was immortal, and untouchable? And was that why he dispensed with bodyguards? Caesar's known symptoms, including epileptic fits and other seizures, heightened sexuality, and an inability to sleep deeply, together with a belief that he could ward off his seizures by staying off his feet and by keeping himself constantly busy, indicate that he may have suffered from a form of mania connected with bipolar disease and schizophrenia. That mania would have made him a workaholic, charismatic, and self-confident to the point of ultimately feeling indestructible.

Mental illness also could have given Caesar a belief that he knew best and that rules and laws did not apply to him. Even Caesar's closest friends knew that what he did to gain power was questionable. Gaius Matius wrote to Cicero seven months after the assassination, "I am well aware of the criticisms which people have leveled at me since the death of Caesar. They make it to my discredit that I am sorely grieved by the death of a very intimate friend and resent the fall of one I loved. For they declare that patriotism must come before friendship, as if they have already proved that his death had been to the benefit of the State." Matius then made an interesting observation. "I was not a follower of Caesar in our civil dissensions but of a friend whom I did not abandon, however much I was offended by his actions. Nor did I approve of the Civil War, or even of the cause of the quarrel."[9]

Like Matius, other friends of Caesar had not approved of his waging war on his own country and seizing power by force. Yet some, like Matius, had continued to serve him despite his bloody military coup. Matius's excuse was that he considered Caesar "a great man to whom I was intimately bound."[10]

Gaius Asinius Pollio, who crossed the Rubicon at Caesar's side and served under him faithfully until his death, also would claim that he did not approve of the Civil War. He said that he chose a side on which he had the least enemies, as an act of self-preservation, and was "forced along a path far from pleasing to myself" by Caesar.[11] In both these cases, the unspoken plea, the Caesar's henchman plea, seems to have been one of "I know what Caesar did wasn't right, but it was right for me at the time."

Half a century after Caesar's assassination, in August A.D. 14, his ultimate successor, Octavian, who became the emperor Augustus, also died, but from natural causes. As the day for Augustus's funeral approached, his successor, Tiberius, issued a proclamation warning the Roman populace "not to indulge in that tumultuous enthusiasm which had distracted the funeral of the Divine Julius [Caesar]."[12]

As leading Roman historian Tacitus, himself a closet republican, made it clear, half a century after Caesar's murder the opinion of the people of Rome was split between those who thought his assassination justified and the assassins heroes, and those who reviled both the act and its perpetrators. Tacitus wrote, "On the day of the funeral [of Augustus], soldiers stood round as a guard, amid much ridicule from those who had either themselves witnessed or who had heard from their parents of the famous day when slavery [of Roman citizens] was still something fresh, and freedom had been resought in vain, when the slaying of Caesar, the Dictator, seemed to some the vilest, to others, the most glorious of deeds."[13]

There can be no escaping the fact that by any definition Caesar was a tyrant: he gained power via a bloody premeditated coup; employed brutal force; suppressed democracy; and, brooking no opposition, ruled through fear. Furthermore, he may have been a tyrant suffering from brain disease who had come to think of himself as immortal. However, at a distance of more than two thousand years, and without an accurate medical diagnosis, we can only speculate on the state of his mental health.

Yet, despite the fact that he was a tyrant and the possibility that he might have been mentally ill, what did the murder of Caesar achieve? Cicero wrote glumly to Cassius the year following the assassination, "We seem to be rid of nothing except our detestation for a vile being and indignation under tyranny, while the country lies still prostrate amid the troubles into which he plunged her."[14]

Caesar opened historical floodgates, washing away the old democratic system. Modern scholars suggest that the republican ideal for which Brutus, Cassius, and Cicero gave their lives was an illusion, that one strongman or another would always rise to power within Rome's republican system. Perhaps so. But after taking power, Sulla soon bowed to the system and retired, and Pompey was tamed by it. Only Caesar overthrew the system, and buried the ideal. And to this day many a patriot, misguided or not, still will give his or her life for an ideal.

The most striking thing about the more than sixty assassins is that in putting their lives on the line to join the conspiracy, none asked for anything; all were content simply to take the appointments that Caesar had laid out for the next five years. They merely wanted to be rid of Caesar, the man Cicero described as "odious." Only a barely concealed hate of Caesar and a driving lust for his removal can explain why the assassins were blind to what would follow his death.

The Liberators were seasoned politicians, some were hardened generals, yet none properly thought through Caesar's removal. Even if Brutus and Cassius had made more careful provision for the return to democracy, backed by the military—and it is astonishing that they thought the system would simply right itself once Caesar was removed—and even if they had murdered Antony at the same time, Caesar had shown that the legions were more powerful than the Constitution, that the man who commanded the loyalty of the legions could rule Rome.

All the evidence shows that Caesar precipitated his own violent death. Not only did he make some poorly calculated moves in the last weeks of his life, he also was a poor judge of character, trusting men who ultimately participated in his murder or who failed to warn him and allowed it to take place. Dolabella is said to have been aware of the assassination plot and done nothing to warn Caesar. It is possible that Antony likewise knew but did nothing, in hopes of himself taking power. Yet if that were the case, like Brutus and Cassius, Antony made no preparations to win the allegiance of the legions, as he must.

As Shakespeare was to write, Brutus was an honorable man. Brutus was also compassionate and well intentioned. Cassius was none of these things, and his brutal rule in the East during 43–42 B.C. suggests that had he and Brutus defeated Octavian and Antony, he may have rid himself of Brutus, taken sole power for himself, and been just as oppressive a ruler of Rome as Caesar, Antony, and Octavian.

In the end, Caesar's murder achieved nothing more than opening the door to the next tyrant, Antony, and then the next, Octavian, and imperial rule. One hundred twenty years later, when the emperor Nero considered executing all potential claimants to his throne, Seneca dissuaded him with the reminder that a ruler can never kill his successor, for the line of successors waiting outside a tyrant's door is endless.

# NOTES

### Author's Note

1. Noted British historian Sir Ronald Syme once said that if history is to be written at all, it must be written with the violent and complex reality of serious fiction. Cited by R. S. O. Tomlin in Wilkes, *Documenting the Roman Army*, "Documenting the Roman Army at Carlisle," Note 1.

### Introduction

1. Seneca, *Letters*, CIV.
2. Ibid.
3. Parenti, *The Assassination of Julius Caesar*, 9: "The Assassination."
4. Seneca, *Letters*, CVIII.
5. Suetonius, *Lives of the Caesars*, I, 76.
6. Appian, *The Civil Wars*, II, 138.

### I. January 26, 44 B.C.: Seven Weeks before the Assassination

1. Suetonius, I, 45; Cassius Dio, *Roman History*, XLIV, 49.2.
2. Suetonius, I, 45.
3. Ibid.
4. Dio, XLV, 30.
5. Suetonius, I, 79.
6. Suetonius, I, 76.
7. Plutarch, *Lives of the Noble Grecians and Romans*, Caesar, XXIV.
8. Plutarch, *Lives*, Antony, V.
9. Dio, XLIV, 9.
10. Ibid.
11. Appian, II, 108.
12. Dio, XLIV, 10.
13. Appian, II, 122.
14. Suetonius, I, 79.
15. Velleius Paterculus, *Compendium of Roman History*, II, LXVIII, 4.
16. Suetonius, I, 79.

17. Appian, II, 108.
18. Plutarch, *Caesar*, XXIV.
19. Plutarch, *Antony*, V.
20. Appian II, 109.
21. Suetonius, I, 79.

## II. February 15, 44 B.C.: The Lupercalia

1. Suetonius, I, 76.
2. Dio, XLIV, 5.
3. Plutarch, *Lives*, Caesar, XXIV.
4. Ibid.
5. Ibid.
6. Dio, XLIV, 1. Appian and Velleius say that Antony actually put the crown on Caesar's head, but other accounts contradict them, saying that Caesar avoided the crown each time Antony offered it.
7. Plutarch, *Lives*, Caesar, XXIV.
8. Appian, II, 109.
9. Plutarch, *Lives*, Antony, V.
10. Dio, XLIV, 11.
11. Velleius Paterculus, II, LVI, 4.
12. Plutarch, *Lives*, Antony, V.
13. Dio, XLIV, 11.
14. Ibid.
15. Ibid.
16. Appian, II, 110.
17. Plutarch, *Lives*, Marcus Brutus, XI.

## III. February 22, 44 B.C.: The Caristia Reconciliation

1. Plutarch, *Marcus Brutus*, V.
2. Dio, XLIV, 12. This blood connection is questioned by Dio, who wrote that the original Brutus had killed his own children and therefore had no descendants.
3. Suetonius, I, 80.
4. Suetonius, I, 76.
5. Dio, XLIV, 7.
6. Suetonius, I, 52.
7. Dio, XLIII, 27.
8. Suetonius, I, 52.
9. Dio, XLIII, 52.

10. Dio writes that Cleopatra settled in Caesar's Janiculum house in 46 B.C., but makes no reference to when she departed. Some historians believe that she had returned to Egypt by the time of Caesar's death, but there is no proof either way.
11. Dio, XLIII, 52.
12. Ibid.
13. Suetonius, I, 78–79.
14. Plutarch, *Lives*, Caesar, XXIV.
15. Ibid.
16. Dio, XLIV, 8.
17. Suetonius, I, 79.
18. Dio, XLIV, 15.
19. Appian, II, 112.
20. Plutarch, *Lives*, Marcus Brutus, III.
21. Ibid.
22. While it is known that the pair reconciled during this period, the exact date is not recorded. The nature of the Caristia holiday makes it highly likely the reconciliation took place on that day.
23. Plutarch, *Lives*, Marcus Brutus, IV.
24. Ibid.
25. Cicero, *Letters to His Friends (Ep. Ad. Fam.)*, XV, 19.
26. Seneca, *Letters*, CIV.
27. Valerius Maximus, *Memorable Deeds and Sayings*, II, 10, 8.
28. Appian, II, 113.
29. Plutarch, *Lives*, Marcus Brutus, V.
30. Ibid.
31. Ibid.
32. Ibid.
33. Plutarch, *Lives*, Cicero, XIX.
34. Plutarch, *Lives*, Marcus Brutus, V.
35. Ibid.
36. Appian, II, 113.

## IV. February 24, 44 B.C.: Pressuring Brutus

1. Appian, II, 112–113.
2. Plutarch, *Lives*, Marcus Brutus, V.
3. Ibid.
4. Ibid.

## V. March 1, 44 B.C., The Kalends of March: Dictator for Life

1. Suetonius, I, 76.
2. Suetonius, I, 80.
3. Ibid.
4. Appian, II, 107.
5. Suetonius, I, 86.
6. Plutarch, *Caesar*, XXV.
7. Suetonius, I, 46.
8. Some modern authors question whether Caesar actually slept at the Regia. Suetonius, at I, 46, is quite clear that "as pontifex maximus he used the official residence on the Sacred Way." Seven of the eight kings of Rome had lived at the Regia. Classical sources indicate that Caesar departed from the Regia as he left for the Theater of Pompey on the Ides of March, having previously not left the "house" since rising, despite having taken the auspices at the Regia before dawn. This, and the claim that Caesar had been awoken, in part, by the rattling of the spears of Mars, which were in the Regia's shrine to Mars, all point to Caesar making the Regia his home. Octavian, once he became emperor of Rome, built a palace, the Palatium, on the Palatine Hill, after which the Regia was used solely as a shrine and religious archive.
9. Suetonius, I, 13.
10. Suetonius, I, 74.
11. Cicero to Atticus, Cicero, *Letters to Atticus*, December 25–26, 50 B.C.
12. Plutarch, *Lives*, Antony, IV.
13. Ibid.
14. Ibid.
15. Ibid.
16. Julius Caesar to Cicero, reprinted by Cicero in a letter to Atticus of March 26, 49 B.C.
17. Plutarch, *Lives*, Antony, IV.
18. Ibid.
19. Ibid.
20. Suetonius, I, 71–72.
21. Plutarch, *Lives*, Antony, IV.
22. Ibid.
23. Ibid. Plutarch felt that Caesar was referring to both Brutus and Cassius, but Caesar's later reaction to Brutus suggests he never suspected him, right up to the assassination.
24. Classical sources record that the pair met to discuss the plot during this period, but do not give the precise day. The Matronalia offered

the perfect excuse for just such an extended meeting, while the outcomes of the March 1 sitting of the Senate would have made such a
meeting that evening almost mandatory.

25. Dio, XLIV, 5.
26. Ibid.

## VI. March 2, 44 B.C.: Recruiting Fellow Assassins

1. Pliny the Younger, *Letters*, XXXVI, 121.
2. Plutarch, *Lives*, Marcus Brutus, V.
3. Ibid.
4. Suetonius, I, 78.
5. Suetonius, I, 77.
6. Suetonius, I, 9.

## VII. March 7, 44 B.C.: A Visit from One of Caesar's Generals

1. Appian, II, 111.
2. Plutarch, *Lives*, Marcus Brutus, IV.
3. Ibid. The precise date of the meeting between Brutus and Albinus is
   not recorded.
4. Ibid.
5. Suetonius, I, 80.
6. Plutarch, *Lives*, Marcus Brutus, VI.
7. Julius Caesar, *Commentaries: The Civil War*, III, 20.
8. Plutarch, *Lives*, Marcus Brutus, VI.
9. Ibid.

## VIII. March 9, 44 B.C.: Porcia's Secret

1. Plutarch, *Lives*, Marcus Brutus, VI.
2. Ibid.
3. Ibid.
4. Ibid.
5. Plutarch, *Lives*, Antony, V.
6. Ibid.

## IX. March 14, 44 B.C., Afternoon: Cleopatra and the Equirria

1. Suetonius, I, 52.
2. Ibid.
3. Dio, XLIII, 27.

4. Suetonius, I, 79.
5. Plutarch, *Lives*, Antony, XI.
6. Ibid.
7. Suetonius put the number of legions in Egypt at that time at three, but all other classical sources, including Cassius Longinus, in his correspondence, say it was four.
8. Suetonius, I, 76.

## X. March 14, 44 B.C., Evening: The Best Sort of Death

1. Cicero to Atticus, December 19, 45 B.C., Cicero, *Letters to Atticus*.
2. Velleius, II, LVII, 1.
3. Appian, II, 109.
4. Velleius, II, LVII, 1.
5. Appian, II, 110.
6. Suetonius, I, 86.
7. Ibid.
8. Ibid.
9. Velleius, II, LXXX, 1.
10. Suetonius, I, 53.
11. Plutarch, *Lives*, Caesar, XX.
12. Suetonius, I, 48.
13. Plutarch, *Lives*, Caesar, XX.
14. Cicero to Atticus, December 19, 45 B.C., Cicero, *Letters to Atticus*.
15. Ibid, Cicero to Atticus, April 7, 44 B.C.
16. Cicero, *Ep. Ad. Fam.*, XII, 1.
17. Cicero to Atticus, April 22, 44 B.C., Cicero, *Letters to Atticus*.
18. Velleius, II, LIX, 4.
19. Appian, III, 9.
20. Suetonius, I, 53.
21. Plutarch, *Lives*, Caesar, XXV.

## XI. March 15, 44 B.C., The Ides of March: Caesar Awakens

1. Polybius, *The Histories*, VI, 35–37.
2. Plutarch, *Lives*, Caesar, XXV.
3. Dio, XLIV, 18.
4. Plutarch, *Lives*, Caesar, XXV.
5. Suetonius, I, 50.
6. Plutarch, *Lives*, Marcus Brutus, III.
7. Suetonius, I, 50.
8. Plutarch, *Lives*, Caesar, XXV.

## XII. March 15, 44 B.C., The Ides of March: In the Dark before Dawn

1. Suetonius, I, 80; Plutarch, *Lives*, Marcus Brutus, VII, mentions Cassius's Liberalia party on this day.
2. Appian II, 113.
3. Ibid.
4. Plutarch, *Lives*, Marcus Brutus, VII.
5. Pompey's Theater was a half-round drama theater, as distinct from the circular and oval Roman amphitheaters where gladiatorial fights and beast hunts were staged. Although Pompey's Theater no longer stands, buildings on the site trace its shape, and some walls and cellars from the original structure remain, incorporated into later buildings.
6. Seneca, XC.
7. Seneca, CVIII.
8. Dio, XLIV, 16.
9. Plutarch, *Lives*, Marcus Brutus, VII.
10. Plutarch, *Lives*, Caesar, XXV.
11. Ibid.
12. Ibid.
13. Suetonius, I, 45.
14. Suetonius, I, 82.
15. Cicero, *Ep. Ad. Fam.*, IX, 24.
16. Suetonius, I, 81.
17. Suetonius, I, 59.
18. Dio, XLIV, 18; Suetonius, I, 81.
19. Ibid.
20. Appian, II, 116.
21. Ibid.
22. Ibid.

## XIII. March 15, 44 B.C., The Ides of March: Caesar Must Suffer Caesar's Fate

1. Dio, XLIV, 16.
2. Appian, II, 115.
3. Dio, XLIV, 17.
4. Dio, XLIV, 18.
5. Plutarch, *Lives*, Caesar, XXVI.
6. Ibid.
7. Ibid.
8. Ibid.

9. Ibid.
10. Ibid.
11. Appian, II, 116.
12. Plutarch, *Lives*, Marcus Brutus, VII.
13. Ibid.
14. Ibid.
15. Ibid.
16. Appian, II, 115; Plutarch, *Lives*, Marcus Brutus, VII.
17. Plutarch, *Lives*, Marcus Brutus, VII.
18. Appian, II, 115; Plutarch, *Lives*, Marcus Brutus, VII.
19. Ibid.
20. Plutarch, *Lives*, Marcus Brutus, VII.
21. Ibid.
22. Dio, XLIV, 18.
23. Suetonius, I, 81.
24. Plutarch, *Lives*, Marcus Brutus, VII.
25. Appian, II, 118.
26. Suetonius, I, 44. Caesar's theater was never built.
27. Plutarch, *Lives*, Caesar, XXVI.
28. Appian, II, 116.
29. Ibid.
30. Ibid.
31. Ibid.
32. Dio, XLIV, 19; Plutarch, *Lives*, Marcus Brutus, VII; Appian, II, 117.
33. Plutarch, *Lives*, Marcus Brutus, VII.
34. Ibid.
35. Appian, II, 116.
36. Plutarch, *Lives*, Marcus Brutus, VII.

## XIV. March 15, 44 B.C., The Ides of March: The Crime

1. Plutarch, *Lives*, Marcus Brutus, VII.
2. Ibid.
3. Appian, II, 117.
4. Plutarch, *Lives*, Marcus Brutus, VII.
5. Appian, II, 117.
6. Suetonius, I, 82.
7. Ibid.
8. Plutarch, *Lives*, Caesar, XXVI.
9. Suetonius, I, 82.
10. Plutarch, *Lives*, Caesar, XXVI.
11. Ibid.

12. Appian, II, 117.
13. Suetonius, I, 82; Dio, XLIV, 19.
14. Appian, II, 117.
15. Plutarch, *Lives*, Marcus Brutus, VIII.
16. Plutarch, *Lives*, Caesar, XXVI.
17. Dio, XLIV, 20.
18. Appian, II, 118.
19. Ibid.
20. Appian, III, 34.
21. Plutarch, *Lives*, Antony, V.
22. Appian, II, 118.
23. Plutarch, *Lives*, Caesar, XXVI; Appian, II, 119.
24. Appian, II, 119.
25. Plutarch, *Lives*, Marcus Brutus, VIII.
26. Ibid.
27. Ibid.
28. Appian, II, 116.
29. Dio, XLIV, 52.
30. Suetonius, I, 82; Appian, II, 118.

## XV. March 15, 44 B.C.: The Gathering Storm

1. Appian, II, 118.
2. Ibid.
3. Ibid.
4. Ibid.
5. Ibid.
6. Plutarch, *Lives*, Caesar, XXVII.
7. Dio, XLIV, 22.
8. Suetonius, I, 82.
9. Plutarch, *Lives*, Caesar, XXVII.
10. Appian, II, 118.
11. Plutarch, *Lives*, Marcus Brutus, VIII.
12. Appian, II, 120.
13. Ibid.
14. Appian, II, 119.
15. Appian, II, 133.
16. Appian, II, 119. The timing of this meeting is disputed by some modern authors who believe it took place the following day. Yet Plutarch, Appian, and Dio all say that Brutus and his associates addressed a public meeting on the day of Caesar's murder. The logical course of events would have been for them to address the Roman people

as soon after the murder as possible. Brutus had, after all, originally planned to address the Senate immediately after the murder. There was no reason for them to wait until the next day, and every reason to act swiftly.

17. Cicero to Atticus, May 18, 44 B.C., Cicero, *Letters to Atticus*.
18. Plutarch, *Lives*, Marcus Brutus, VIII.
19. Ibid.
20. Appian, II, 122.
21. Appian, II, 121.
22. Ibid.
23. Plutarch, *Lives*, Marcus Brutus, VIII.
24. Dio, XLIV, 52. Dio wrote that the thunderstorm followed Caesar's murder on the Ides of March, without indicating a time. Other classical authors make no mention of the storm. If it did indeed take place, it must have been during the late afternoon lull in action.
25. Ibid.
26. Dio, XLIV, 21.

## XVI. March 16, 44 B.C.: Pleading for the Republic

1. Plutarch, *Lives*, Antony, V.
2. Appian, II, 123.
3. Appian, II, 124.
4. Ibid.
5. Ibid.
6. Appian, II, 125.

## XVII. March 17, 44 B.C.: The Jostle for Control

1. Appian, II, 126.
2. Appian, II, 127.
3. Ibid.
4. Ibid.
5. Appian, II, 128.
6. Ibid.
7. Appian, II, 122.
8. Velleius, II, LVIII, 3.
9. Appian, II, 129.
10. Appian, II, 130.
11. Ibid.
12. Ibid.
13. Appian, II, 131.

14. Ibid.
15. Appian, II, 131–132.
16. Appian, II, 132.
17. Ibid.
18. Appian, III, 34.
19. Appian, II, 133–134.
20. Ibid.
21. Appian, III, 34.
22. Appian, II, 136.
23. Appian, II, 141.
24. Ibid.

## XVIII. March 18, 44 B.C.: The Liberators Gain the Advantage

1. Cicero to Atticus, April 22, 44 B.C, Cicero, *Letters to Atticus*.
2. Dio, XLIV, 32.
3. Ibid.
4. Appian, II, 142.
5. Cicero to Atticus, December 25–26, 50 B.C., Cicero, *Letters to Atticus*.
6. Dio, XLIV, 34.
7. Dio, XLIV, 51.

## XIX. March 19, 44 B.C.: Caesar's Will

1. Suetonius, I, 83.
2. Plutarch, *Lives*, Marcus Brutus, IX.
3. Ibid.
4. Appian, II, 143.
5. Ibid.
6. Suetonius, I, 83.
7. Appian, II, 143.
8. Ibid.
9. Plutarch, *Lives*, Marcus Brutus, IX.

## XX. March 20, 44 B.C.: Caesar's Funeral

1. Suetonius, I, 84.
2. Appian, II, 143.
3. Suetonius, I, 84.
4. Appian, II, 144.

5. Appian, II, 145.
6. Appian, II, 146.
7. Plutarch, *Lives*, Antony, VI.
8. Appian claimed that a wax effigy of Caesar also was raised, showing all twenty-three stab wounds, but no other classical author confirms this.
9. Suetonius, I, 84.
10. Plutarch, *Lives*, Caesar, XXVII.
11. Suetonius, I, 85.
12. Trebonius arrived in Athens on May 22 on his way to Asia: Cicero, *Ep. Ad. Fam.*, XI, 15.
13. Dio, XLIV, 52.

## XXI. March 21, 44 B.C.: Antony Consolidates His Grip

1. Plutarch, *Lives*, Antony, VI; Appian, III, 17. The exact date of Antony's meeting with Calpurnia and demand for Caesar's valuables is not recorded. Appian said it took place "immediately after the murder." Antony would have wasted no time in taking control of Caesar's estate, and the day following the funeral, with the Liberators on the run, would seem the appropriate time.
2. Velleius, II, LX, 4.
3. Cicero, *Ep. Ad. Fam.*, XI, 1. Several dates have been attributed to this letter, including March 17, prior to Caesar's funeral. But one of Cicero's translators, Professor Shackleton Bailey, has placed it on March 22, after the funeral and after the change in public mood sponsored by Antony's funeral oration. The letter's content makes a March 22 dating the more likely.
4. Ibid.
5. Ibid.
6. Ibid.
7. Ibid.

## XXII. March 24, 44 B.C.: Enter Octavius

1. Appian, III, 9.
2. Velleius, II, LIX, 5.
3. Appian, III, 9.
4. Ibid.
5. The precise date of Octavius's departure from Apollonia for Italy is not recorded.

## XXIII. March 27, 44 B.C.: The Name of Caesar

1. Appian, III, 10. The precise date when Octavius landed back in Italy is not recorded, but it would have been March 27 or thereabouts.
2. Appian, III, 11.
3. Ibid.
4. Velleius II, LX, 2.
5. Appian, III, 11.
6. Appian, III, 12.
7. Ibid.

## XXIV. April 7, 44 B.C.: Wise Oppius

1. Cicero to Atticus, April 7, 44 B.C., Cicero, *Letters to Atticus*.
2. Ibid.
3. Ibid.

## XXV. April 10, 44 B.C.: Caesar's Heir

1. Josephus, *The Jewish Antiquities*, 14, 10, 9–10.
2. It is recorded that Octavian met with Mark Antony the day after Octavian's arrival at Rome; Antony left the city by the middle of April, meaning he would not have been in the city on April 20.
3. Velleius, II, LIX, 6.
4. Velleius, II, LX, 1.
5. Appian, III, 14.
6. Ibid.

## XXVI. April 11, 44 B.C.: Octavian Meets with Antony

1. Velleius, II, LX, 3; Appian, III, 14.
2. Velleius, II, LX, 4; Appian, III, 5 and 12; Dio, XLIV, 53.
3. Dio, XLIV, 53. There is no record of the marriage going ahead.
4. Ibid.
5. Dio, XLIV, 5.
6. Appian, III, 20.
7. Appian, III, 21.

## XXVII. April 14, 44 B.C.: The Aedile's Refusal

1. Appian, III, 28.
2. Ibid.

3. Ibid.
4. Ibid.

## XXVIII. April 22, 44 B.C.: Octavian Seeks Cicero's Support

1. Keppie, *Colonisation and Veteran Settlement in Italy*, 3, I.
2. Ibid.
3. Cicero to Atticus, April 22, 44 B.C., Cicero, *Letters to Atticus*.
4. Ibid.
5. Ibid.
6. Ibid.
7. Ibid.

## XXIX. May 11, 44 B.C.: I Don't Trust Him a Yard

1. Cicero to Atticus, c. May 11, 44 B.C., Cicero, *Letters to Atticus*.
2. Ibid.
3. Ibid.
4. Ibid.

## XXX. May 18, 44 B.C.: Undermining Antony

1. Cicero to Atticus, May 18, 44 B.C., Cicero, *Letters to Atticus*.

## XXXI. May 31, 44 B.C.: Reforming the Praetorian Cohorts

1. Appian, III, 28.
2. Ibid.
3. Appian, III, 29.
4. Appian, III, 30. The exact date of this meeting is unrecorded, but it had to take place prior to June 2.

## XXXII. June 2, 44 B.C.: Antony Outsmarts the Senate

1. Dio, XLV, 10.

## XXXIII. June 7, 44 B.C.: No Plan, No Thought, No Method

1. Appian, III, 6.
2. Cicero to Atticus, June 7, 44 B.C., Cicero, *Letters to Atticus*.
3. Plutarch, *Lives*, Marcus Brutus, XII.
4. Cicero to Atticus, June 7, 44 B.C., Cicero, *Letters to Atticus*.

5. Ibid.
6. Ibid.
7. Ibid., for the entire conversation.
8. Plutarch, *Lives*, Marcus Brutus, XII.
9. Ibid.
10. Cicero to Atticus, June 7, 44 B.C., Cicero, *Letters to Atticus*.
11. Appian, III, 6.
12. Cicero to Atticus, June 7, 44 B.C., Cicero, *Letters to Atticus*.
13. Ibid.
14. Ibid.
15. Ibid.
16. Velleius, II, LXI, 1.
17. Cicero to Atticus, June 7, 44 B.C., Cicero, *Letters to Atticus*.

## XXXIV. July 13, 44 B.C.: The Last Day of Brutus's Games

1. Plutarch, *Lives*, Marcus Brutus, X.
2. Appian, III, 24.
3. Appian, III, 23.
4. Appian, III, 24.
5. Ibid.
6. While some modern-day authors dispute Gaius Antonius's trip for lack of other evidence, Appian is quite clear that Gaius made the trip. The Macedonian legions certainly received Antony's orders and were soon on the move.
7. Appian, III, 37.

## XXXV. July 20, 44 B.C.: The Liberators' Manifesto

1. Plutarch, *Lives*, Marcus Brutus, X.
2. Ibid.
3. Ibid. Plutarch said that this episode came from a firsthand account from Brutus's stepson Bibulus, in a book written by Bibulus titled *Brutus*.
4. Ibid.
5. Suetonius, II, 10.
6. Cicero, *Ep. Ad. Fam.*, XI, 28.
7. Velleius, II, LXII, 3.

## XXXVI. July 28, 44 B.C.: Cicero's Departure

1. Suetonius, I, 88.
2. Dio, XLV, 7.

3. Cicero to Atticus, July 25, 44 B.C., Cicero, *Letters to Atticus*. Atticus was a native of Athens.

## XXXVII. August 16, 44 B.C.: Like Hector the Hero

1. Plutarch, *Lives*, Cicero, XVIII.
2. Ibid.
3. Cicero, *Ep. Ad. Fam.*, XI, 3.

## XXXVIII. August 30, 44 B.C.: Cicero Returns to Rome

1. Plutarch, *Lives*, Cicero, XVIII.
2. Ibid.
3. Ibid.

## XXXIX. September 15, 44 B.C.: The Liberators Reach Greece

1. Plutarch, *Lives*, Marcus Brutus, XI.
2. Ibid.

## XL. September 23, 44 B.C.: Octavian's Nineteenth Birthday

1. Appian, III, 31.
2. Appian, III, 38.
3. Appian, III. 39.
4. Plutarch, in *Lives*, Antony, VI, says that the murder plot that came to light in late September and ended the new alliance between the pair was just "some few days after" the meeting on the Capitol. It is likely that the Praetorian tribunes deliberately arranged the meeting for Octavian's birthday, to give the occasion special significance. The new alliance was undone by the end of September.
5. Plutarch, *Lives*, Antony, VI.

## XLI. September 28, 44 B.C.: The Plot to Assassinate Antony

1. Cicero, *Ep. Ad. Fam.*, XII, 23.
2. Suetonius, II, 9.
3. Appian, III, 39.
4. Ibid.
5. Ibid.
6. Ibid.

## XLII. October 9, 44 B.C.: A Dreadful State of Affairs

1. Cicero, *Ep. Ad. Fam.*, XII, 3.
2. Ibid.
3. Ibid.
4. Ibid.
5. Dio, XLV, 13.
6. Cicero, *Ep. Ad. Fam.*, XII, 3.

## XLIII. October 18, 44 B.C.: Antony Joins His Legions

1. Appian, III, 43.
2. Ibid.
3. Ibid.
4. Ibid.
5. Dio, XLV, 13.
6. Appian, III, 43.
7. Appian, III, 45.
8. The precise dates of these October 44 B.C. assemblies held by Antony in Brundisium are not recorded.
9. Appian, III, 44.

## XLIV. November 4, 44 B.C.: Octavian Recruits an Army

1. Cicero to Atticus, November 4, 44 B.C., Cicero, *Letters to Atticus*.
2. Keppie, *Colonisation and Veteran Settlement*, 3, I.
3. Cicero to Atticus, November 4, 44 B.C., Cicero, *Letters to Atticus*.
4. Ibid.
5. Ibid.
6. Ibid.

## XLV. November 18, 44 B.C.: The Road to War

1. Appian, III, 40.
2. Ibid.
3. Appian, III, 41.
4. The precise date of Octavian's entry into the city is not recorded, but it is likely to have been after the Ludi Plebeian ended on November 17.
5. Appian, III, 41.

6. Appian, III, 46.
7. Appian, III, 41.
8. Appian, III, 42.
9. Ibid.
10. Ibid.
11. Ibid.
12. Ibid.

## XLVI. November 27–30, 44 B.C.: Anthony's Legions Rebel

1. Some modern-day authors refer to this unit as the 5th Alaudae Legion, in error. The Alaudae Legion and the 5th Legion were in 44–43 B.C. two separate units, both under Antony's command. After the 43 B.C. Mutina battles, Antony combined the remnants of the two units to create the 5th Alaudae Legion.
2. Appian, III, 45.
3. Ibid.
4. Ibid.
5. Cicero, *Ep. Ad. Fam.*, XI, 7.
6. Keppie, *Colonisation and Veteran Settlement*, III, 1.
7. Appian, III, 46.
8. Ibid.
9. The two remaining units were the 2nd Legion and the 35th Legion.

## XLVII. Early December 44 B.C.: The Rise of the Liberators

1. Plutarch, *Lives*, Marcus Brutus, and Appian, III, 63. Plutarch called this man Antistius. But Appian identifies him as Marcus Apuleius, who was indeed a quaestor in 45–44 B.C.
2. Velleius, II, LXII, 2.
3. Plutarch, *Lives*, Marcus Brutus, XI.
4. Appian, III, 63.
5. Plutarch, *Lives*, Marcus Brutus, XI.
6. Ibid.
7. Ibid.
8. Ibid.
9. Ibid.

## XLVIII. Second Half of December 44 B.C.: Antony Makes His Move

1. Cicero, *Ep. Ad. Fam.*, XI, 7.
2. Ibid.
3. Appian, III, 47.

4. Appian, III, 48.
5. Ibid.
6. Ibid.

## XLIX. January 1–4, 43 B.C.: Debating Antony's Fate

1. Appian, III, 50. This account follows Appian's chronology, which had the Senate sitting over four days. Some historians believe it only sat over three days.
2. Appian, III, 51.
3. Ibid.
4. Ibid.
5. Cicero, *Ep. Ad Brutum*, XXIV, I, 15; Appian, III, 51.
6. Appian, III, 51.
7. Cicero, 6 *Philippic*; Appian, III, 61.
8. Ibid.

## L. Late December 44 B.C.–Early January 43 B.C.: The First Assassin to Fall

1. Appian, III, 26.
2. Ibid.
3. Ibid.
4. Ibid.

## LI. February 4, 43 B.C.: State of Emergency

1. Appian, III, 62.
2. Appian, III, 63.
3. Cicero, *Ep. Ad. Fam.*, XII, 4.
4. Ibid.
5. Ibid.
6. Ibid.

## LII. April 14–26, 43 B.C.: The Mutina Battles

1. Cicero, *Ep. Ad. Fam.*, X, 30.
2. Ibid.

## LIV. May 30, 43 B.C.: Lepidus's Betrayal

1. Cicero, *Ep. Ad. Fam.*, X, 31.
2. Ibid., XL, 9, 13.

3. Ibid., 9.
4. Ibid., 8.
5. Velleius, II, LXIV, 1–2.

## LV. August 19, 43 B.C.: Octavian Charges Caesar's Murderers

1. Appian, III, 94.
2. Velleius, II, LXIX, 6.

## LVI. Early November 43 B.C.: The Triumvirate and the Proscription

1. Appian, IV, 2.
2. Ibid., 3.
3. Plutarch, *Lives*, Cicero, XIX.

## LVII. December 7, 43 B.C.: Killing Cicero

1. Josephus, *The Jewish Antiquities*, 14, 11, and 2.
2. Appian, IV, 20.
3. Cicero, *Ep. Ad. Fam.*, IX, 24.
4. Velleius, II, LXVI, 2.

## LVIII. October 1–21, 42 B.C.: The Battles of Philippi

1. Velleius, II, LXXX, 5; Appian, IV, 131.
2. Appian, IV, 131.
3. Plutarch, *Lives*, Brutus and Dion Compared, I.
4. Velleius, II, LXII, 1.
5. Ibid., LXXXVII, 3.
6. Tacitus, *The Annals*, III, 76.

## LIX. Judging the Assassins and the Victim

1. Suetonius, I, 76.
2. Suetonius, I, 30.
3. Plutarch, *Antony and Demetrius Compared*, I.
4. Appian, II, 111.
5. Seneca, CIV.
6. Pliny the Younger, I, 17.
7. Dio, XLIII, 42.
8. Velleius, II, LI, 1.

9. Cicero, *Ep. Ad. Fam.*, XL, 28.
10. Ibid.
11. Cicero, *Ep. Ad. Fam.*, X, 31.
12. Tacitus, *Annals*, I, 8.
13. Ibid.
14. Cicero, *Ep. Ad. Fam.*, XII, 1.

# BIBLIOGRAPHY

Abbott, F. F., and A. C. Johnson. *Municipal Administration in the Roman Empire.* Princeton, N.J.: Princeton University Press, 1926.

Appian. *Roman History.* Translated by H. White. London: Loeb, 1913.

———. *Roman History: The Civil Wars.* Translated by H. White. Cambridge, Mass.: Harvard University Press, 1913.

Augustus. *Res Gestae Divi Augusti.* Translated by F. W. Shipley. Cambridge, Mass.: Harvard University Press, 1924.

Boardman, J., J. Griffin, and O. Murray. *The Oxford History of the Classical World.* Oxford, U.K.: Oxford University Press, 1986.

Bouchier, E. S. *Spain under the Roman Empire.* Oxford, U.K.: Blackwell, 1914.

Boyne, W., with H. Stuart Jones. *A Manual of Roman Coins.* Chicago: Ammon, 1968.

Brogen, J. *Roman Gaul.* London: Bell, 1953.

Buchan, J. *Augustus.* London: Hodder & Stoughton, 1937.

Caesar. *Commentaries on the Gallic and Civil Wars.* Translated by W. A. M'Devitte and W. S. Bohn. London: Bell, 1890.

Carcopino, J. *Daily Life in Ancient Rome.* London: Pelican, 1956.

Chevalier, R. *Roman Roads.* Translated by N. H. Field. London: Batsford, 1976.

Church, A. J. *Roman Life in the Days of Cicero.* London: Seeley, 1923.

Cicero. *Letters to Atticus.* Translated by O. E. Winstedt. Cambridge, Mass.: Harvard University Press, 1912.

———. *The Letters to His Friends (Including Letters to Brutus).* Translated by W. Glynn Williams. Cambridge, Mass.: Harvard University Press, 1927.

———. *Philippics.* Translated by T. Ramsey. Cambridge, U.K.: Cambridge University Press, 2003.

Cowan, R. *Roman Legionary 58 B.C.–A.D. 69.* Botley, U.K.: Osprey, 2003.

Cowell, F. R. *Cicero and the Roman Republic.* London: Penguin, 1956.

Croft, P. *Roman Mythology.* London: Octopus, 1974.

Cunliffe, B. *The Celtic World.* London: Bodley Head, 1979.

———. *Rome and Her Empire.* Maidenhead, U.K.: McGraw-Hill, 1978.

Dando-Collins, S. *Blood of the Caesars: How the Murder of Germanicus Led to the Fall of Rome.* Hoboken, N.J.: John Wiley & Sons, 2008.

————. *Caesar's Legion: The Epic Saga of Julius Caesar's Elite Tenth Legion and the Armies of Rome*. New York: John Wiley & Sons, 2002.

————. *Cleopatra's Kidnappers: How Caesar's Sixth Legion Gave Egypt to Rome and Rome to Caesar*. Hoboken, N.J.: John Wiley & Sons, 2006.

————. *Mark Antony's Heroes: How the Third Gallica Legion Saved an Apostle and Created an Emperor*. Hoboken, N.J.: John Wiley & Sons, 2007.

————. *Nero's Killing Machine: The True Story of Rome's Remarkable Fourteenth Legion*. Hoboken, N.J.: John Wiley & Sons, 2005.

Delbruck, H. *History of the Art of War*. Translated by J. Walter Renfroe Jr. Lincoln, Neb.: Bison, 1990.

Depuy, R. E., and T. N. Depuy. *The Encyclopedia of Military History: From 3500 B.C. to the Present*. London: MBS, 1970.

Dio. *Roman History*. Translated by E. Cary. Cambridge, Mass.: Harvard University Press, 1914.

Emile, T. *Roman Life under the Caesars*. New York: Putnam, 1908.

Forestier. A. *The Roman Soldier*. London: A. & C. Black, 1928.

Frank, T., ed. *An Economic Survey of Ancient Rome*. Newark, NJ: Pageant, 1959.

Frontinus, S. J. *Stratagems: The Aqueducts of Rome*. Translated by C. E. Bennet. Cambridge, Mass.: Harvard University Press, 1969.

Fuller, J. *Julius Caesar: Man, Soldier, and Tyrant*. London: Eyre & Spottiswoode, 1965.

Gardner, J. F. *Family and Familia in Roman Law and Life*. Oxford, U.K.: Oxford University Press, 1998.

Goldsworthy, A. *The Complete Roman Army*. London: Thames & Hudson, 2003.

————. *Roman Warfare*. London: Cassell, 2000.

Grant, M. *The Army of the Caesars*. Harmondsworth, U.K.: Penguin, 1974.

————. *History of Rome*. Harmondsworth, U.K.: Penguin, 1978.

————. *Julius Caesar*. Harmondsworth, U.K.: Penguin, 1969.

————. *Roman History from Coins*. New York: Barnes & Noble, 1995.

Haywood, R. M. *Ancient Greece and the Near East*. London: Vision, 1964.

————. *Ancient Rome*. London: Vision, 1967.

Home, G. C. *Roman London*. London: Eyre & Spottiswoode, 1948.

Jimenez, R. *Caesar against the Celts*. Conshohocken, Pa.: Sarpedon, 1996.

Jones, A. H. M. *Augustus*. New York: W. W. Norton, 1972.

Josephus. *The New Complete Works* (including *The Jewish Antiquities* and *The Jewish War*). Translated by W. Whiston. Originally published 1737. Reprint, Grand Rapids, Mich.: Kregel, 1999.

Keppie, L. *Colonisation and Veteran Settlement in Italy, 47–14 B.C.* London: British School at Rome, 1983.

————. *The Making of the Roman Army: From Republic to Empire*. New York: Barnes & Noble, 1984.

Laking, G. F. *A Record of European Armour and Arms through Seven Centuries*. New York: A-MS, 1934.

Leach, J. *Pompey the Great*. New York: Croom Helm, 1978.

Marsden, E. W. *Greek and Roman Artillery*. Oxford, U.K.: Oxford University Press, 1969.

Mattingly, H. *Roman Coins from the Earliest Times to the Fall of the Western Empire*. London: Methuen, 1927.

Mommsen, T. *The Provinces of the Roman Empire*. Edited by T. R. S. Broughton. Chicago: University of Chicago Press, 1968.

Parenti, M. *The Assassination of Julius Caesar*. New York, TNP, 2003.

Parker, H. D. M. *The Roman Legions*. New York: Barnes & Noble, 1958.

Petronius, Arbiter. *Satyricon*. Translated by W. C. Firebaugh. New York: Boni & Liveright, 1927.

Philo Judaeus. *The Works of Philo*. Translated by C. D. Yonge. Peabody, Mass.: Hendrickson, 1993.

Pliny the Elder. *Natural History*. Translated by H. Rackman. London: Loeb, 1938–1963.

Pliny the Younger. *Letters*. Translated by W. Melmoth. London: Loeb, 1915.

————. *The Lives of the Noble Grecians and Romans*. Translated by J. Dryden. 1683–1686. Reprint, Chicago: Encyclopaedia Britannica, 1952.

Polybius. *The Histories of Polybius*. Translated by P. Holland. 1606. Reprint, New York: LEC, 1963.

Robertson, D. S. *Greek and Roman Architecture*. Cambridge, U.K.: Cambridge University Press, 1943.

Rostovtzeff, M. I. *The Social and Economic History of the Roman Empire*. New York: Biblio & Tannen, 1957.

Schwarzkopf, H. N. *It Doesn't Take a Hero*. New York: Bantam, 1992.

Scullard, H. H. *Festivals and Ceremonies of the Roman Republic*. London: Thames & Hudson, 1981.

Seneca. *Letters from a Stoic*. Translated by R. Campbell. Harmondsworth, U.K.: Penguin, 1969.

Simkins, M. *Warriors of Rome*. London: Blandford, 1988.

Strabo. *The Geography of Strabo*. Translated by H. L. Jones. Cambridge, Mass.: Loeb, 1924.

Suetonius. *Lives of the Twelve Caesars*. Translated by P. Holland. Originally published in 1606. Reprinted, New York: New York Limited Editions Club, 1963.

Syme, R. *History in Ovid*. Oxford, U.K.: Oxford University Press, 1979.

Tacitus. *The Agricola and the Germania*. Translated by H. Mattingly. London: Penguin, 1948.

————. *Annals and Histories*. Chicago: Encyclopaedia Britannica, 1952.

Todd, M. *The Northern Barbarians, 1000 B.C.–A.D. 300*. New York: Blackwell, 1987.

Valerius Maximus. *Memorable Deeds and Sayings: One Thousand Tales from Ancient Rome*. Translated by H. J. Walker. Indianapolis, Ind.: Hackett, 2004.

Vegetius. *The Military Institutions of the Romans*. Translated by J. Clark. Harrisburg, Pa: Military Service Publishing, 1944.

Velleius Paterculus. *Compendium of Roman History*. Translated by F. W. Shipley. Cambridge, Mass.: Harvard University Press, 1924.

Vitruvius. *On Architecture*. Translated by F. Granger. Cambridge, Mass.: Harvard University Press, 1934.

Warry, J. *Warfare in the Classical World*. London: Salamander, 1989.

Watson, G. R. *The Roman Soldier*. Ithaca, N.Y.: Cornell University Press, 1969.

White, K. D. *Greek and Roman Technology*. Ithaca, N.Y.: Cornell University Press, 1983.

Wilkes, J. J., ed. *Documenting the Roman Army*. London: ICS, 2003.

Wiseman, F. J. *Roman Spain*. New York: Bell, 1956.

# INDEX